The Keeper's Recital

## DATE DUE

| | | | |
|---|---|---|---|
| MR 28 08 | | | |
| | | | |
| | | | |
| | | | |
| | | | |
| | | | |
| | | | |
| | | | |
| | | | |
| | | | |
| | | | |
| | | | |
| | | | |
| | | | |
| | | | |
| | | | |
| | | | |
| | | | |
| | | | |

DEMCO 38-296

## CRITICAL CONDITIONS: FIELD DAY ESSAYS AND MONOGRAPHS

Edited by Seamus Deane

Critical Conditions: Field Day Essays

# The Keeper's Recital

## Music and Cultural History in Ireland, 1770–1970

## Harry White

UNIVERSITY OF NOTRE DAME PRESS
*in association with*
FIELD DAY

e United States in 1998 by
of Notre Dame Press
Dame, IN 46556

And in Ireland by
Cork University Press
University College Cork, Ireland

*Library of Congress Cataloging-in-Publication Data*

White, Harry.
    The keeper's recital : music and cultural history in Ireland,
        1770–1970 / Harry White.
            p.    cm. — (Critical conditions : 6)
        Includes bibliographical references and index.
        ISBN 0-268-01232-6 (pbk.)
        1. Music—Ireland—19th century—History and criticism. 2. Music—
    Ireland—20th century—History and criticism. 3. Music and
    society—Ireland. 4. Music—Social aspects—Ireland. 5. Music—
    Political aspects—Ireland.     I. Title. II. Series.
    ML287.W5 1998
    780'.9415—dc21                                               98–16129
                                                                      CIP
                                                                      MN

For Fiachra

# CONTENTS

# PREFACE

*At the Water's Edge*

On Devenish I heard a snipe
And the keeper's recital of elegies
Under the tower. Carved monastic heads
Were crumbling like bread on water.

from *Field Work* (1979) by Seamus Heaney

Although this is the first book to survey the development of musical thought in modern Irish cultural history, *The Keeper's Recital* is not a history of music in Ireland. That would be another day's work. This study does not therefore comprise an unbroken narrative of Irish music between 1770 and 1970. Its purpose rather is to register the function of music as a dynamic agent in the history of Irish ideas during this period.

The neglect of music in that history has served as a primary stimulus to this investigation, in the belief that Ireland's verbally dominated culture has nevertheless depended on music throughout its evolution. The fact that this dependence has been scarcely recognised, still less researched, does not detract from the inherent presence of music as a vital issue in Irish cultural thought. To examine that presence and its impact on the formation of a notably polarised Irish cultural matrix is the principal objective of this study. Arising from that objective is an attempt to survey the reception of music in Irish cultural history, and with this in mind the structure of the book does adhere to a (loosely) chronological narrative. It would otherwise be impossible to recognise adequately the development of central concepts of Irish music which determined that reception history and which also conditioned the development of music itself.

The nature of this development is such that it intensively reflects those preoccupations which so narrowly determined the growth of the Irish mind in modern history. The impact of these preoccupations on music has never been disclosed. Seamus Deane remarks that the enforced intimacy between literature and politics was unique and tragic in Ireland: this book argues that the intimacy between music and politics was closer still. As a result, the emancipation of music in Ireland was overtaken by those cultural ideologies which it helped to foster.

Foremost among these ideologies were the integrity of sectarian culture, the political expression of cultural autonomy and the symbolic force of Celticism. Each of these preoccupations was radically conditioned by music in Ireland and each of them affected that music in turn. Thus the preservation of the ethnic repertory of music helped to establish the currency of a Gaelic culture which otherwise struggled against the tide of linguistic decline; the transformation of this repertory as the definitive intelligencer of romantic nationalism consolidated an understanding of Irish music which wedded it inexorably to verbal communication; finally, the status of music as a symbol of Gaelic civilisation (as in the Gaelic League) and as an image of imaginative regeneration (as in the development of Anglo-Irish literature) was of such durability and prestige that the cultivation of music itself was attenuated, if not wholly disengaged, by the end of the nineteenth century. It is the supreme irony of Irish cultural history that music should have shown itself so fertile as a conceptual intelligence even as it languished under the duress of its own polarised condition. How and why this was the case are the questions which *The Keeper's Recital* tries to answer.

Given that these questions inform the design of the book, a word about the dates 1770–1970 may prove useful. One might paraphrase Roy Foster and ask 'When does the history of music in modern Ireland begin?' The publication of Walker's *Historical Memoirs of the Irish Bards* (1786) and the Belfast Harp Festival (1792) mark important stages in the perception of an indigenous musical culture from within the folds of Ascendancy thought, but the history of musical ideas with which I am concerned does not originate with either of them. And so '1770' signifies a notional beginning, by which a fragmented series of publications and actual musical events throughout the eighteenth century attains to a single insight which acquired conventional status during the 1770s. This insight is an awareness of two cultures of music in Ireland and of the precarious condition of original composition which existed between them.

To move forward two centuries is (in this instance) to acknowledge Seán Ó Riada's attempt to resolve that crisis, an attempt which ended with his death in 1971. This boundary contains the central queries of the book, although I have strayed beyond it in the epilogue as a matter of necessity (partly to explain the sense of an ending which occurred in the aftermath of Ó Riada's decease). The essential timeframe of the book, then, might be more cumbrously (but more accurately) defined as being *between c.* 1770 and *c.* 1970.

I would like to acknowledge here those people who read earlier drafts of this book in whole or in part: Seamus Deane, Joseph Kerman and Seán Connolly provided especially helpful advice on the structure and focus of the argument which this book advances; I am grateful also to Axel Klein, Joseph Ryan, Barra Boydell and Brian Boydell for many interesting discussions on music in Ireland over the years. My debt to Joseph Ryan's outstanding dissertation on 'Nationalism and Music in Ireland' (1991) is particularly evident in the notes to chapter five. I should also like to thank Gerard Gillen and Michael Adams, both of them fellow conspirators in the development of the series *Irish Musical Studies*, and a number of anonymous readers whose (sometimes conflicting) advice on the question of revisionism in Irish historiography enabled me to think afresh about the reception of music in Irish cultural history. If I have persisted in sticking to my last despite their counsel, the responsibility is all my own. I am also grateful to various members of my graduate seminar on music and Irish cultural history over the past five years, especially John Page, who re-entered the archives at my request when time was in short supply. Sara Wilbourne has proved to be a sterling editor and publisher.

Finally, I should like to express my deepest thanks to the members of my family who bore overmuch with me while this book passed through the difficult process of reaching publication. Fiachra remained his stoic self throughout the whole business, and made the journey to Lough Erne with me not once, but twice. Those 'carved monastic heads' must know something.

Harry White

# INTRODUCTION
## Music and the Perception of Music in Ireland

It is only in the case of musical instruments that I find any commendable
diligence in the people. They seem to me to be incomparably more
skilled than any other people that I have seen. . .

They glide so subtly from one mode to another, and the grace notes
so freely sport with such abandon and bewitching charm around the
steady tone of the heavier sound, that the perfection of their art seems to
lie in their concealing it, as if 'it were better for being hidden. An art
revealed brings shame.'

Hence it happens that the very things that afford unspeakable delight to
the minds of those who have a fine perception and can penetrate carefully to the secrets of the art, bore, rather than delight, those who have
no such perception – who look without seeing, and hear without being
able to understand.[1]

If we broaden our definition of culture, as we surely must, to include the
whole mode of life of a community, we shall find, with some honourable
exceptions, that our histories do not tell us much about many things
which make up such a mode of life. And these deficiencies are equally
glaring, whether we are thinking about day-to-day details of existence, or
about patterns of belief, or about intellectual influences, both internal
and external.[2]

. . .the notion of an 'Irish mind' should be comprehended in terms of a
multiplicity of 'Irish minds'. This tension between unity and difference is
crucial.[3]

The neglect of music in the reanimation of ideas which have so transformed
our comprehension of the Irish mind within the past twenty years must rank
as an outstanding failure of Irish cultural history.[4] It is a failure not easily
explained, although it has been borne almost without demur. Although this
book is an attempt to redress that state of affairs, the condition of intellectual
neglect extends far beyond its purview. At one and the same time, it is possible to advert to a history of music in Ireland which confirms and enhances
the terms of the cultural debate itself and to a widespread indifference of

numbing magnitude. In a climate which thrives on enquiry, which consents to the superiority of ideas over the continued recitation of facts, the presence of music remains undiscovered. One looks in vain for any indication that the facts of music in Ireland have been absorbed into the continuum of cultural debate. And yet: the facts themselves, as this book argues, constantly disclose the truth and candour of John Blacking's observation that 'musical change cannot take place in a social vacuum'.[5] This may appear to be an unexceptional insight deprived of its context, but it has yet to register in any significant way on those who would otherwise so vigorously renew the terms of Irish cultural discourse. The conspicuous absence of music from this discourse impoverishes our understanding of Ireland, of music in Ireland and of Irish music in European culture.

This impoverishment is not an indication of contempt. It reflects, rather, the marginalisation of music in Ireland except as an expression of those forces which have overtaken it, namely: the language question, religious and political history and the complex culture arising therefrom. In addition to this cultural eclipse, Irish music endures in an educational void which is perhaps unparalleled in postwar Europe. Those who define the terms of Irish cultural discourse are consequently less than concerned with its manifestation in music.

This kind of explanation, however, is insufficient to the cause, which lies within the cultural history of music in Ireland itself. The disclosure of that history can help to identify Irish music as an essential conduit of intellectual and cultural formation. If the history of music in Ireland is not to be regarded as an amorphous gathering of disparate events which are remaindered in the wider context of cultural debate, then that history is in urgent need of a conceptual paradigm. The strength and intelligence of the current reassessment of Irish ideas provide one. Rather than repudiate this assessment for its neglect of music, it is more profitable to investigate it. In this respect we might usefully modify Blacking's thesis to read: 'musical change cannot take place in a *cultural* vacuum'.

By 'conceptual paradigm' I intend a model of cultural history which will permit the interpretation of music as an intelligible factor in the development of Irish ideas. More than one paradigm, of course, is available in the considerable literature which has grown around the reanimation of Irish intellectual discourse, but certain models predominate. To inspect these models here (however briefly) is to countenance their validity for the purposes of understanding the cultural significance of music in Ireland.

The critical paradigm which has dominated the reception history of Irish ideas is the dialectic between ethnic and colonial ideologies of culture, which history itself provides. This is not an invention of contemporary cultural discourse; for our purposes, it is useful to note that it extends at least to Edmund Burke and the revival of Celtic antiquities in the late eighteenth century. And prior to that development, we encounter it virtually as an *idée fixe* in writing about Ireland, from the *Topographia Hiberniae* of Giraldus Cambrensis in the twelfth century through to the literature of the Elizabethan Conquest, as in Edmund Spenser's *A View of the Present State of Ireland* (1596). As Breandán Ó Buachalla has remarked of seventeenth-century Irish poetry, 'change within continuity has been the central pattern of the Irish cultural tradition'.[6] A central feature of that continuity is the abiding presence of conflict between two versions of Irish culture. In early Irish history, that conflict is voiced as between two projections of high civilisation: the culture of (tribal) Gaelic communities and successive phases of Norman and English colonisation. What is remarkable is that notwithstanding long periods of cultural assimilation, this conflict endures and is perpetuated in modern Irish history.[7]

Within the period addressed in this book, this trope of cultural conflict constantly adorns the rhetoric of Irish political and social discourse. It is a usage notably revivified by religious denomination, by political agitation and by cultural identity. Catholic emancipation, republican insurrection, the Act of Union and the language question, for example, all invest the cultural history of Ireland in the late eighteenth and early nineteenth centuries with fresh significance, precisely in terms of this conflict. As a model of thought, it confers meaning upon the vivid disharmony of modern Ireland.

To write of cultural conflict in this way is not (necessarily) to subscribe to the 'seven hundred years of conquest' view of Irish history which has been largely disowned by modern Irish historiography. Although Roy Foster has famously remarked of Irish historians that 'we are all revisionists now', it is fair to observe in turn that not all revisionists are of the same hue. The spectrum of historical interpretation in Ireland is notably wide, and if a liberal consensus is in the ascendant, it is nonetheless apparent that *pace* revisionism, readings of Irish historiography can and do differ sharply.[8]

This is strikingly true of recent Irish cultural history.[9] But it is equally true that the notion of cultural conflict, or, more moderately, cultural polarisation, remains a constant feature of this discourse. It is as if the polemical condition of Irish art requires that this be the case: Seamus Deane's observation that 'the enforced intimacy between politics and literature was unique and tragic in Ireland' summarises this belief.[10]

That this concept of polarisation functions prominently in the current reinvigoration of Irish cultural discourse is self-evidently expressive of two cultures in Ireland during the period 1770 to 1970 (and beyond). Although this dialectic drastically simplifies the complex of religious, political and hence cultural interests which obtains in recent Irish history,[11] there can be little doubt that its appeal resides in the fact that so much of Irish literature in particular is defined by its relationship with one culture and its alienation from the other. 'Culture' in this sense can transcend linguistic barriers: the literature of romantic nationalism, for example (specifically, of the Young Ireland movement of the 1840s and 1850s), was conducted through the medium of English; but it cannot transcend political alignment. Although the proposition of a 'Catholic–Gaelic–Nationalist' synthesis in opposition to a 'Protestant–English–Colonial' reading constantly defers to the actual facts of Irish history, the ideologies of such an intensively political culture remain polarised.[12]

The Celtic revival of *c.* 1870 to *c.* 1920 illustrates this phenomenon as it is understood in contemporary Irish cultural discourse. Seamus Deane's reading of the essential spirit of that movement recovers the colonial–ethnic paradigm in this way:

> Nationalism, as preached by Yeats or by Pearse, was a crusade for decontamination. The Irish essence was to be freed of the infecting Anglicizing virus and thus restored to its primal purity and vigour. The Gaelic League pointed one way towards this restoration – the recovery of the Irish language and the displacement, partial or total, of English. Yeats and Synge looked to the emergence of a new literature in English vivified by the linguistic energies of an Irish civilisation not yet blighted by the inanities of 'parliamentary speeches and the gutter press'. The presiding opposition between a 'spiritual' Ireland and a 'mechanical' England lent itself to an immense number of subsidiary variations – sexual purity as opposed to sexual squalor, ancestral faith as opposed to rootless urban alienation, just rebellion as against imperial coercion, enduring faith as against shallow modernism, imaginative vitality as against dehydrated utilitarianism.[13]

There are two paradigms disclosed in this reading: restoration (or revival) and opposition (or polarisation). The latter secures a continuity of discourse for the Celtic revival with the literature of Ascendancy culture and of romantic nationalism in Ireland. Indeed, as Deane has argued, Yeats's own reading of history bestowed upon the Ascendancy an idealism which he associated with the folk tradition in Ireland: this idealistic (and spurious) conjunction fortified precisely that degree of difference between Yeats's own aesthetic of regeneration and the 'filthy modern tide' which he condemned.[14] Yeats found common ground with Pearse in that enterprise, and the notion of 'blood-sacrifice' which the latter espoused echoes in turn the mutation from revival to revolution which Yeats's early plays advocate.

We are entitled to recognise three forms of polarisation within the folds of the revival: the restoration of Irish language and culture in opposition to English language and culture (as exemplified by Douglas Hyde); the restoration of Celtic mythology *and* contemporary Gaelic culture in the English language (Yeats, Synge, Lady Gregory); and the progression from cultural to political self-determination in the radical politics of Pearse and the other parties to revolution in Ireland. In each of these three cases, the paradigm of polarisation is gradually overtaken by the model of revival itself: everything that is new in Irish politics and culture of the period obstinately reaches back into the past. And therein it finds the bewildering condition of two mutually inhospitable systems of language, polity and civilisation.

It is language which resolves this bewilderment. In Yeats, and especially in Synge, the energies of a ruined civilisation are respectively re-mythologised and replicated: the extreme condition of Synge's English bears musical witness to the latter. But this resolution remains partial: the rehousing of Gaelic structures and imaginings in English entailed a secondary polarisation as between the Gaelic League and those who purveyed this 'Celtic note': a whole chapter on Irish cultural history might profitably be devoted to that tension. Here, we can summarise the matter by suggesting that 'revival' for the Gaelic League entailed a severe rebuke to any form of assimilation with English (language or culture) and ultimately an insistence on political autonomy; for the Irish literary movement it meant first and last a new literature in English, whatever might be achieved by heroic imaginings along the way. The 'Irish Ireland' of the new state, which inherited from Hyde and the Gaelic League a vision at once powerfully conservative (the Catholic–Gaelic–Irish synthesis) and culturally inert, would increasingly find itself at odds with the plural vigour of Irish writing in English. The dominant assumptions of cultural nationalism after 1921 could only be contained by exclusion (and censorship). A different degree of polarisation would characterise the Gaelic–Catholic hegemony of the new Republic, in its antagonistic relations with a liberal culture that undermined the pieties of the ruling dispensation.[15]

A third paradigm has recently widened the interpretative scope of polarisation and revival as models of cultural thought in Irish literature. Richard Kearney's formulation of a 'transitional narrative' in Irish culture derives from the perception of two dominant tendencies in modern Irish writing: a revivalism which gravitates towards tradition and the past (as in Yeats) and a modernism which resolves to 'demythologise the orthodox heritage of tradition in so far as it lays constraints on the openness and plurality of experience' (as in Joyce).[16] In the case of modernism, the myths of the Irish literary revival are deprived of political intelligence: they fade in the colder dawn of Europe. Before they disappear completely, as they do in Samuel Beckett, they are integrated with the very essence of modernist fiction through *Ulysses* and *Finnegans Wake*.[17]

Richard Kearney argues that contemporary Irish literature reflects a transitional crisis between revivalism and modernism which can be located in the literary revival and its immediate aftermath. Rather than posit Joyce as an intellectual exile from the great movement of Yeats's circle, Kearney prefers to locate Joyce and Yeats along a transitional continuum which runs between the extremes of Yeats's aesthetic of high culture and Joyce's ebullient repossession of Irish history towards the creation of new myths.[18] Kearney's principal interest in establishing this continuum is to show that it obtains in contemporary Irish literature, so that he discerns in Seamus Heaney and Brian Friel, for example, writers preoccupied by the claims of the past and their impact upon the present. This preoccupation is formulated expressly in terms of that intimacy between myth and history which underpins modern Irish writing in the early decades of the twentieth century. Kearney's reading of Brian Friel's play *Translations* depends upon this notion of mediating between past and present, between languages, traditions, political perspectives and civilisations which the play so memorably enacts. *Translations* is a drama of cultural eclipse; Kearney's reading of it as a 'transitional narrative' which exemplifies the movement 'between Irish and European culture, between thinking and writing, between politics and art'[19] illustrates the usefulness of this paradigm. In conceiving of *transitional* modes of Irish writing, Kearney argues against the notion of a self-contained literature:

> Many of the major works of contemporary Irish culture may be viewed as attempts to *narrate* the problematic relationship between tradition and modernity . . . one might say that cultural narratives represent a dialogue of sorts, however conflictual, between various Irish minds and the tradition from which they derive, and which they often seek to transform or transcend.[20]

The relationship which Kearney proposes between the past and the present is not then a simple question of the presence *of* the past in contemporary literature. It is instead a mediational paradigm which functions as a model of cultural history. In Kearney's reading, the cultural history of literature in Ireland thereby attains to contemporary significance.

These paradigms of literary culture patently derive from extra-literary considerations: my argument is that they are also validated by the history of music in Ireland. In fact, the failure to comprehend music as an essential expression of Irish cultural history attenuates insights which have been so abundantly drawn from the literature (in Irish as well as in English) of the past two centuries. This is because music has not only reflected those paradigms of polarisation, revival and transition: it has also nourished and defined them. I would argue further that in respect of music, the crucial paradigm is that of cultural polarisation. It clarifies the perception of music during this period in three ways. Firstly, it identifies the function of music in Ascendancy thought as a dislocated articulation of two cultures; secondly, it explains the fundamental preoccupation with music as a resource in the development of Irish political consciousness; thirdly, it confronts the advancement of the native musical repertory as a symbol of renascent Irish civilisation.

The paradigm of cultural revival likewise provides a coherent model of understanding with regard to that central enterprise of musical preservation which endures in Irish cultural history from the collections of Edward Bunting through to the reanimation of traditional music in the film scores and ensemble arrangements of Seán Ó Riada. Throughout this book, I contend that the cult of revival – in a phrase, the preoccupation with 'folk music' – has been profoundly affected by its proximity to that wider attempt to rationalise the integrity of Irish-language culture with the implications of reinventing that culture in English.[21]

The clearest of these implications is that a dying culture was in part redeemed by the passage of one literature into the language of another. Why no such transition was available in music is a central query in this study. In essence, the difference between literary revival and musical revival in Ireland is that the latter was contained within one tradition, whereas the former moved, with startling imaginative energy, between two. This means that cultural polarisation was of even greater consequence for music than it was for literature. Although the revival of Gaelic culture conflicted ideologically with the evolution of a new Irish literature in English, it manifestly inspired and informed that literature. This is not to suggest that cultural polarisation in language thereafter disappeared: the force of Gaelic revivalism in frequently hostile opposition to the new literature in English remained a fact of Irish cultural history long after Yeats had denounced the angry reception of Synge on the stage of the Abbey Theatre (1907). But it has scarcely been recognised that if there was a language question in Irish cultural affairs, there was also a *music* question. This book tries to recover for Irish cultural history the terms in which that question was formed and the various kinds of address it made on the Irish mind.

*    *    *    *    *

The conceptual paradigms of polarisation, revival and transition discussed here underlie the structure of the ensuing chapters, insofar as each of them identifies music not simply as a discrete sequence of events but as an expression of ideas which prevail in Irish cultural history. It is fundamental to this reading that such ideas originated not in the aftermath of modern commentary, but in the period itself. Thus the uncomplicated association which I have drawn between central figures and episodes in Irish musical history and the conceptual abstractions which these embody rests on the assumption that these abstractions transcend the detailed narrative of musical development in Ireland. 'Narrative' in this literal sense is self-evidently important in any kind of historical reading, but my purpose here is to derive from this narrative patterns of extra-musical thought which relate music in Ireland to the ideologies which determined and conditioned its existence.

These ideologies are signalled in the chapter headings (more or less explicitly) throughout the book. The concept of dislocation explored in the opening chapter arises directly from the perception of Carolan and Handel in Ascendancy culture, but it endures well beyond the eighteenth century and is sharply revived in the predicaments upon which Seán Ó Riada foundered as an Irish composer in the middle decades of this century. Within the folds of Ascendancy thought, the formation of two cultures in Ireland did not rest with the unprecedented revival of interest in Irish antiquities: rather it extended to an acute appraisal of their incompatibility. This appraisal is voiced in musical terms by Joseph Cooper Walker, but there are precedents for Walker's unease, as there are for the hostile reception which his advancement of ethnic musical culture met in England. If Cooper's celebration of Carolan can be read (as it is here) as an expression of antiquarian benevolence, it can also be taken to denote a general self-consciousness with regard to native culture which contradicts the long history of 'civilians and barbarians'[22] by which that culture had hitherto been defined in colonial thought.

\* \* \* \* \*

The 'rage for Hibernian antiquities' (of which music was perceived to be a part) was not the only term of musical understanding to issue from the Ascendancy in its decline. The rage for Handel was no less intense. It, too, would survive well into the next century, but its significance was from the start contained by a belligerent intelligentsia (personified by Swift) which resisted the music of high culture as a harbinger of popery, and also by a strictly limited conception of that culture as an import of British artistry. Handel's presence in Dublin (both literally and musically) flourished because of the permanent association which the Ascendancy drew between his oratorios and public philanthropy. When that association died away, so too did the central presence of a European aesthetic in Irish musical affairs. To be sure, art music endured with some regularity (particularly in the years leading up to the Act of Union), but Dublin would thereafter remain incapable of fostering music as a *creative* intelligence, notwithstanding its appetite for light opera.

The condition of music in Ireland after the Act of Union was indisputably as plural as it was ubiquitous, but its claims on the Irish mind were specific. The newly won integrity of the ethnic tradition (established by Bunting and the Belfast Harp Festival) guaranteed the understanding of 'Irish music' as a term which exclusively denoted the native repertory. It was an understanding which affected not only the emancipation of Gaelic culture as an object of disinterested research, but also the development of hybrid art forms in the early nineteenth century. The romanticism of Thomas Moore's encounter with Irish music in particular was to prove crucial in this process. Moore's *Melodies* were to determine the reception of this music (not only in Ireland, but further afield) in three ways. They endowed the repertory with a sense of dispossession which attained to conventional status; they supplied an influential precedent for the use of Irish music as an agent of political advancement, and they confirmed a widespread tendency to regard the function of music in Ireland as an intelligencer of verbal feeling.

The fact that Irish music thus became a sounding-board for nationalist sentiment is not, of course, to be regarded as a unique development in the history of European culture at large. On the contrary, as Carl Dahlhaus remarks, 'nationalistic music invariably emerges as an expression of a politically motivated need, which tends to appear when national independence is being sought, denied or jeopardized, rather than attained or consolidated'.[23] What is unique is the absolute condition which this music enjoyed in the development of Irish cultural awareness throughout the nineteenth century.

The popular conception of Moore's achievement – attested by his reputation as a darling of the Victorian drawing-room – should not be permitted to occlude the influence which the *Melodies* exerted in the growth of a sectarian culture in Ireland. Notwithstanding Edward Bunting's dismay at Moore's blatant conjunction of music and politics, the intensely politicised circumstances of both the Bunting collections and the *Melodies* themselves can only be adequately understood against the immediate background of the United Irishmen, the Act of Union and Catholic emancipation. Each of these issues is addressed in the second chapter of this study (the last of them through the agency of Moore's own writing) in an attempt to show how intimate was the communion between political aspiration and the growth of 'Irish music' as a recognisable entity between 1792 and 1834.

The political complexion of Young Ireland was that of romantic nationalism writ large. The literature which it produced, and in particular the ballad poetry which it published with fantastic success in *The Spirit of the Nation* (1843–5), explicitly depended on music. If antiquarianism secured the ethnic repertory as a dominant projection of Irish culture, then the balladry of Young Ireland copperfastened that projection as an essentially verbal art. Young Ireland was indifferent to music as an emancipated entity: for Thomas Davis (its principal ideologue), music could only function intelligibly as an enabler of textual communication. Insofar as music stimulated political feeling (rather than the reverse), its cultivation could be enthusiastically commended. Its redundancy otherwise was painfully apparent.

Drawn so rigidly to the template of political ferment, music in Ireland could nourish every condition except its own. In order to gain some perspective on this difficult problem, I have had recourse in the third chapter of this study to a comparison between Irish and Polish nationalism. This is a choice determined by the similar political history of both countries in the first half of the nineteenth century. Without attending to the details of that comparison here, I can nevertheless suggest that the infrastructures of musical culture which obtained in Poland did not obtain in Ireland, with the result that the proximity between music and Irish politics was all the more intense. The languid condition of art music after the Act of Union scarcely impinged on this state of affairs. Of far greater consequence was the renewal of sectarian principles of Irish culture in the wake of the Famine.

The devastations of that genocidal episode cannot be reduced to an event in Irish cultural history. But the Famine did lend tragic urgency to the enterprise of cultural regeneration: the 'awful, unwonted silence' which it engendered could only be partly redeemed, at best. In its aftermath, the cult of musical preservation was strenuously reinvigorated, so that the synonymous condition (or understanding) of 'Irish music' and the ethnic repertory became immutably central to a pervasive revival of Gaelic culture.

In this book, I argue that the ethnic repertory as a symbol of that culture became so powerful in the last decades of the nineteenth century that the music itself became an object of cultural stasis. The very concept of Irish music was so firmly removed to the past that it became incapable of inherent development. Irish music was thus preserved in two senses: it was *collected* in the interests of furthering a sectarian culture and it was *safeguarded* from the intrusions of an anglicised polity.

This argument depends on the advocations of the Gaelic League and the 'Irish Ireland' philosophy which it came powerfully to evince. The consequences of that cultural philosophy were to prove especially fateful for music.

In order to situate these consequences in context, I have sought in chapter five to examine the fragmented state of art music in Ireland during the nineteenth century, so as to explain the remarkable absorption of this musical stasis in the verbally dominated culture of the Celtic revival. It is fundamental to my reading of this process that the revival is understood as two movements which overlap: a reaffirmation of the centrality of Gaelic culture which generated the political autonomy of the new state, and an appropriation of that culture by means of a new Irish literature written in English. The contradiction between these two movements has long been recognised, but the functions of (an Irish) music which mediated between them also deserves scrutiny.

It will be clear from the epilogue that I regard the principal function of music in the Celtic revival as a symbol of the literary imagination itself. There is no doubt that Yeats, whose indifference to *actual* music was complete, responded habitually to the *symbolic* status of music in this way. If Yeats and Douglas Hyde (as president of the Gaelic League) represent the polarised condition of the Celtic revival (Anglo-Irish literature as against the preservation and restoration of Gaelic civilisation), they find common ground nonetheless in this symbolic regard for music. This being the case, it is not difficult to argue that the prospect of musical development was remote, at least in terms commensurate with the imaginative energies of the revival as a whole. On one side, the revival proclaimed music as a finite resource from the past; on the other side, this symbol of a dying culture was given new life as a literary trope of immense expressive fecundity. Between these alternatives, Irish music was silent, or struggled to overcome centuries of aesthetic impoverishment.

There was, however, another revival in Irish cultural history which has been so little noticed until recently that its impact on contemporary ideas of Irish culture has been all but non-existent. This neglect does not gainsay its historical significance, especially given the wider context to which it belongs: the devotional reform of Catholic life, especially in the second half of the nineteenth century. This is the subject of chapter four.

Two factors distinguish this revival from its Celtic counterparts. One is that it was exclusively concerned with music, and the other is that it stemmed not from indigenous culture but from the musico-liturgical reforms of central Europe.

Emmet Larkin's description of devotional reform in general as a 'substitute culture' for the post-Famine Catholic population of Ireland provides another useful paradigm for this aspect of music in Irish cultural history. The phenomenon of musical reform – exemplified by the founding of the Irish Society of St Cecilia in 1878 – belongs in fact to an emphatically bourgeois communion of Irish Catholics, whose actively conservative reanimation of high renaissance church music must be regarded as a uniquely coherent (and largely apolitical) expression of religious culture in Ireland. The presence of Heinrich Bewerunge within this culture emphasises the productive relationship which the Cecilian revival enjoyed with its European forbears: it also incidentally illustrates the different *tempi* of Irish and German musical sensibilities in this enterprise, a divergence which ultimately contributed to its demise. Nevertheless, the proliferation of musical engagement which the Cecilian movement fostered in Ireland – not least through the journal of the society and the remarkable periodical debate which it stimulated – attests to a rare consonance between Irish and European musical culture. The disintegration of consensus which signalled the decline of the Cecilian societies across Europe was felt somewhat abruptly in Ireland. But the cultural significance of the movement as a whole stands here (as in chapter four) as a vital issue in the history of Catholic church music in Ireland. Its success was inherent, but it can be traced in part to the romanising zeal of Paul Cardinal Cullen, whose synodal decrees on music imparted a new rigour to public and private acts of devotion in Ireland. The nature of Cullen's ultramontanist aesthetic and the (later) consolidation of the Irish Catholic bourgeoisie are conjoined in the Cecilian reforms of the late nineteenth and early twentieth centuries.

Evidence and explanation (as in chapter five) are also strategic to the argument advanced in the sixth chapter of this study. It is here particularly that Richard Kearney's discernment of a transitional crisis proves most instructive. In describing Seán Ó Riada's predicament as a crisis of modernism, I am conscious of the recurring difficulties of music in Ireland since *c.* 1770 coming home to roost amidst the cultural torpor of the new state. The exigent nature of Ó Riada's development as a composer indeed reflects a transitional crisis which he could not overcome. What is striking about this crisis is that Ó Riada *began* as a modernist, insofar as his original compositions declared emphatically in favour of a European aesthetic. The process by which he abandoned this aesthetic in favour of the traditional repertory represented such a drastic inversion of his original achievements that composition itself became for him a vestigial activity. This process was received with such enthusiasm by the cultural matrix to which Ó Riada belonged that it effectively silenced the claim of original art music in Ireland.

I see no contradiction between this argument and the existence nevertheless of a continuum of Irish (art) music during Ó Riada's lifetime. This is because Ó Riada's model of Irish music is the only one to have been acknowledged in any meaningful way by the interlocutors of contemporary cultural discourse. Notwithstanding Seamus Heaney's exceptionally alert 'In Memoriam' (discussed in the epilogue) which sensitively discloses what might have been had Ó Riada resolved the crisis which overcame him, the sanguine acclaim which Ó Riada's model of musical thought continues to enjoy upholds the conclusions reached here.

Given that this is the case, I am thankful that my (self-imposed) brief extends no further than 1970. It is only fair to add, however, that there are hopes for motion forward. Despite the current crisis in Irish music education (apostrophised, alas, in the epigraph from Giraldus Cambrensis which heads this introduction), the plural enterprise of original Irish music has never been more determined. If this enterprise succeeds, the quandaries described in the epilogue and in the book as a whole will finally have been overcome.

*   *   *   *   *

This reading of music in Irish cultural history depends in significant measure on the recent acceleration of scholarship which has been brought to bear on music in Ireland. Without that scholarship, my own efforts to integrate music within the history of Irish ideas would have been severely diminished. Although the origins of this resurgence can be traced to Aloys Fleischmann's *Music in Ireland* (1952), it is mainly research undertaken within the past ten years which informs what follows here.[24] I have argued elsewhere that the findings of this research can and should be consolidated in a single positivistic enterprise, namely the production of an encyclopaedia of music in Ireland.[25] But scholarly positivism cannot be the sole destination of Irish musicology. The history of ideas also beckons, especially given the long absence of music, as it were, from the Irish mind.

# CAROLAN, HANDEL AND THE DISLOCATION OF MUSIC IN EIGHTEENTH-CENTURY IRELAND

> Music, however, is sometimes the subject of conversation amongst us, and is still cultivated by a few; but it is no longer a favourite topic, nor a favourite study.[1]

To offer a distinction between the achievements of the Ascendancy mind and those of the 'Hidden Ireland' has long been a commonplace of Irish history.[2] That this distinction is essential to an adequate understanding of cultural history throughout the eighteenth century in particular is also a securely established premise. The contrast between a depleted 'underground culture' which reflected the condition of the native (indigenous) population under English rule and the spectacular achievements of the Pale is one which survives in the minds of historians (cultural and otherwise) to the present day, even if this contrast has often been modified and queried.[3] If this 'Two Irelands' perspective is especially vulnerable to the revisionist understanding of political and economic history, it nonetheless remains useful and valid for the cultural historian. This is because it is a perspective which originated not in the aftermath of modern commentary but in the period itself. Within the Ascendancy mind, the sense of two cultures was formed.[4]

To examine this mental formation through the history of music in Ireland is to seek an explanation for the poor impact of that music on the history of Irish ideas from the eighteenth century onwards. For those few who wrote about music in Ireland during the eighteenth century, a gulf lay between the native Irish tradition and the essentially modified and complex aesthetic of the Anglican Ascendancy. It is not simply that the dispossessed native population pursued one kind of music endemic to its social structures and needs while the music of the London stage held sway in Dublin. It is not merely that George Frideric Handel's reference to 'that polite and generous nation' on the success of *Messiah* in Dublin designated a society remote from the majority of people living in Ireland. It is rather that the perception of the ethnic tradition was so significantly polarised. On those occasions when music makes an appearance in one of the characteristic genres of eighteenth-century discourse (memoirs, travel writing, occasional poetry, biographical essays, periodical reviews), the native tradition is usually characterised in one of two ways. It more often than not is taken to symbolise the prior existence of an ancient civilisation in direct contrast to the degraded condition of Ireland under English rule (although this contrast is rarely explicit). Alternatively, it exemplifies

13

the notion of a wild and barbarous people hankering after an improbable past.

The troubled status of music in Ireland, the political transformation of its cultural antagonisms and the consequent dislocation of musical composition in which ethnic and European resources failed to integrate collectively attest to problems which endured well beyond the eighteenth century. Within this period, the apparent paradox of unprecedented musical activity inside the Pale and a dearth of reasoned discourse on music nevertheless is partly if not wholly explained by the disquiet which the concept of two musical traditions brought in its wake. The Ascendancy tradition espoused music as an import of British and European artistry, but it notably did not cultivate central norms of European repertory. Its indifference to musical thought stemmed partly from a hostility to these norms which is best characterised in the idiosyncratically expressed attitudes of Jonathan Swift. It is indeed reasonable to suggest that the intellectual indifference to European music which largely characterised Irish letters in the period found a correlative in the abounding popularity of ballad opera and in the absence of *opera seria* in Dublin. Music as a means of social comment and as a form of splendid recreation was plainly evident in Dublin, and was at least on occasion specially written for the capital. Music as the *direct* expression of political or ecclesiastical well-being, as an elaborate, highly wrought analogue of great architecture or sculpture, was on a much less secure footing.[5] Even the regular performance of sacred-dramatic and/or choral works for charitable purposes (which was the distinctive feature of Dublin's non-theatrical public music in the eighteenth century) failed to stimulate an urban musical culture capable of intrinsic regeneration.[6]

For the most part, music lay remote from the Anglo-Irish intellect. The contrast between musical activity and musical thought brings the small number of sources of musical commentary into sharp relief. To assess their importance, it is necessary to identify those aspects of music in Ireland which shaped the perception of the ethnic tradition from within the Pale. The case against music as an aesthetic force within the Anglican Establishment (personified by Swift) is one such aspect. The proliferation of ballad opera from 1728 onwards is another. The rise of charity performances as the prime social condition of choral music and the dissemination of the native repertory in print are also vital. But two events in particular allow a general perspective on the currents of thought which draw together the complicated mosaic of musical production and performance in Ireland during the eighteenth century. The first event is Handel's visit to Dublin in 1741–2 and the second is the publication of Joseph Cooper Walker's *Historical Memoirs of the Irish Bards* in 1786. Between them, these episodes embrace and symbolise the condition of music in eighteenth-century Ireland. In the discussion which follows, both are set in cultural and social context. It is best to begin with Walker's *Irish Bards*, because the background to this publication allows us to establish a central feature of music in Ireland which was to affect both traditions (ethnic and colonial), namely, the dislocated status of the composer within the terms of Ascendancy thought.

Between the time of Swift and the publication of Walker's *Irish Bards*, music in Ireland lacks any kind of comprehensive address from within this thought. When it does receive attention, the person and work of Turlough Carolan are frequently of prominent concern.[7] Poems such as Matthew Pilkington's *The Progress of Music in Ireland. To Mira* (1725) and Laurence Whyte's *Dissertation on Italian and Irish Musick, with some Panegyrick on Carrallan our late Irish Orpheus* (1740)[8], Oliver Goldsmith's essay, 'Carolan: The Last Irish Bard' (1760) and the forty-fourth letter of Thomas Campbell's *A Philosophical Survey of the South of Ireland* (1777)[9] illustrate a degree of consensus among Ascendancy writers upon the nature of Carolan's importance, implicitly in terms of Irish music as a whole. It is not until the appearance of Walker's *Irish Bards*, however, that Carolan and the question of Irish music are discussed at length.

As an Irish harper, Carolan (1670–1738) was one of many musicians whose livelihood depended on the sporadic patronage of Catholic families. Their reduced circumstances under the Ascendancy nevertheless allowed of the cultivation of occasional music and poetry. Gráinne Yeats remarks that he was 'the last of the harpers to compose and the only one about whom much is known',[10] but he was certainly not alone in his role as peripatetic musician to the Catholic gentry.[11] Although not accounted an outstanding performer, Carolan's gifts as a poet and composer were widely recognised, and his extant music manifests not only the central influence of the ethnic tradition of which he was a part but also the impact of contemporary European elements of musical style and structure. In this respect, Carolan may well have been unique among the Irish harpers. In particular, scholars have imputed to his musical style the influence of Vivaldi, Corelli and Geminiani, the last of whom was periodically resident in Ireland during Carolan's lifetime.[12]

Such influences, together with some admittedly slender evidence to support Carolan's association with Swift on at least one notable occasion, suggest that the composer intermittently stood between the two traditions of displaced native and ruling Ascendancy.[13] Given this unique position, and given the limited reception of his music (insofar as it was printed in Dublin between 1724 and 1786), it is not difficult to understand how Carolan came to embody the definitive idea of Irish music as this idea developed through the eighteenth century.[14]

Before we examine the major formulation and counterformulation of this idea in Walker's *Irish Bards* and Charles Burney's extensive review of this publication which appeared in 1787, it is instructive to look at some earlier and slighter formulations of Carolan's position and the art he represented.

Of the poems by Pilkington and Whyte, it is Pilkington's which is the more thoughtfully cognisant of the two traditions of Irish music and the problems attendant upon these (despite the fact that Whyte's title promises a more direct apprehension of Carolan's position).

*The Progress of Music* is pastoral and allusive in tone and diction, and the poem narrates the condition of music in Ireland in terms of a country long deprived of musical expertise:

> *Hibernia* long beheld, with Sorrow fill'd,
> Her Poets and her Sons in Arts unskill'd:
> Sons! dead to Fame, nor comely to the Sight,
> Their Customs wild, their Manners unpolite;[15]

The advent of Carolan among these musical barbarians is presaged by the general gloom which Pilkington attributes to Irish music. The allusive nature of the following lines obviously confirms this attribution; the passage may also indirectly connote a sense of oppression:

> And still the Tenor of *Hibernian* Strains,
> Those pleasing Labours of enamour'd Swains,
> From his a melancholly Turn receive,
> The Airs are moving, and the Numbers grieve.[16]

Further grieving is in store. Carolan, meanwhile, is introduced into the poem as follows:

> *Musick* henceforward more Domestick grew,
> Courts the throng'd Towns, and from the Plains withdrew;
> The vagrant *Bard* his circling Visits pays,
> And charms the Villages with venal Lays.[17]

Pilkington continues in this vein for some twenty-six lines. These verses celebrate the natural range and 'soft variety' of Carolan's music. It is absolutely clear that Pilkington's rhetoric advances the impact of such music as a phenomenon derived from nature. Towns and villages are 'transported in attention'; classical allusions to the power of music in the underworld reinforce the benign effects of this 'natural music' upon society in Ireland.[18] *The Progress of Music* is lucid in its distinction between this music and the 'new Transports' introduced by the muses from 'Albion's Isle' who subsequently settle in Ireland. This music too is clearly identified and celebrated, and individual composers, including Lorenzo Bocchi and Matthew Dubourg (both comparatively recent arrivals in the Ireland of 1725), are firmly credited with the enhancement of music by means of artifice and sophisticated ornament.

A new condition of feeling, however, enters the poem at its conclusion. The consequences for the native tradition of this encroachment of high culture are plain:

> The first rude Lays are now but meanly priz'd,
> As rude, neglected, as untun'd, despis'd:
> Dead – (in Esteem too dead) the *Bards* that sung,
> The *Fife* neglected, and the *Harp* unstrung.
>
> Harsh seem the Strains which gave Delight before,
> And far excell'd, those Strains delight no more.[19]

Both the myth and actuality of cultural neglect and subsequent contempt are thus brought to bear on Pilkington's reading of music in Ireland. One tradition occludes the other, and Pilkington's recognition of this cultural eclipse appears to prompt a conclusion which tacitly argues the case for the natural priority of the now abandoned and despised ethnic mode:

> The pausing *Muse* now shuts her vent'rous
>    Wings,
> And, anxious of Success, distrustful sings;
> O! might her Lays to thy Esteem succeed,
> For whom she tun'd her artless Voice and Reed,
> Thy Smiles would swell her Heart with honest
>    Pride,
> Approv'd by thee she scorns the World beside.[20]

This is more than wishful thinking on Pilkington's part: these closing lines modestly formulate the problem of Irish music as an aesthetic preference for one tradition over the other. *The Progress of Music in Ireland* attains to cultural significance not only because of the scarcity of similar considerations of Irish music in the early eighteenth century, but more importantly because it articulates an awareness which is variously restated by writers who follow the general argument of this comparatively early source.

Laurence Whyte's *Dissertation* eulogises Carolan as a figure from the past. The poem explicitly advances the pre-eminence of Italian music over the achievements of the ethnic tradition which Carolan personifies. Nevertheless, Whyte is antagonistic towards the expressive conventions of *opera seria*, and his line of argument seeks to rationalise the 'improvements' of art music in terms of cross-fertilisation with the native repertory:

> Sweet *Bocchi* thought it worth his while,
> In doing honour to our *Isle*
> To build on *Carallan's* Foundation,
> Which he perform'd to Admiration,
> On his *Pheraca's* went to work,
> With long Divisions on *O Rowrk* [21]

This is Carolan's first appearance in the poem, which ends a mere eleven lines afterwards with this salute:

> The greatest *Genius* in his way,
> An *Orpheus* who could sing and play,
> So great a *Bard* where can we find,
> Like him, illiterate, and blind.[22]

Overtaken by a new mode of making music, the tradition which Carolan represents in the poem recedes into myth. Carolan is dead. The society from which he emerged is itself dying away. Carolan's music provides a foundation for the resources of the new tradition, but the sense of an ending is clear. Less sensitive than Pilkington in his apprehension of this ending, Whyte holds out no hope for the regeneration of the ethnic tradition except as a source of Italian ornament and fond remembrance.

Fond remembrance is also at the heart of Goldsmith's brief address on the subject of 'Carolan: The Last Irish Bard', published in *The British Magazine* in July 1760.[23] Goldsmith also writes of Carolan as an object of curious delight. He writes as an English traveller on the wonders of an oppressed people which 'being in some measure retired from intercourse with other nations, are still untinctured with foreign refinement, language or breeding'.[24] Although this characterisation somewhat contradicts the blend of Irish and Italian musical elements portrayed by Whyte in his *Dissertation*, it shows a continuity of thought with Pilkington's poem in its advocation of two cultures, one of which is virtually defunct. For Goldsmith (at least in the circumstances of this essay), 'the Irish' are a race apart from modern civilisation, preserved – however sadly – in their ancient ways. Carolan thereby becomes all the more wonderful as 'the last and the greatest' bard to come from this race. Goldsmith compares him to Pindar and Homer as Whyte compares him to Orpheus: the tone of these comparisons, as of Goldsmith's assessment in general, is sometimes amused, sometimes affectionate, but it is not satirical. And at the last, Carolan's homeric standing is employed in order to project the mythology of 'Ireland' as a nearly vanished social and cultural entity, in preference to the actuality of Ireland as Goldsmith must have known it in 1760.[25]

Thomas Campbell's *Philosophical Survey of the South of Ireland* confronts this actuality more directly, although Campbell retreats from any kind of abrupt challenge to the contemporary (political) *status quo*. His object in writing, moreover, is to promote a better understanding of Ireland by the English and to hasten a more liberal government of the country.[26]

His letter on music begins with an historical sketch in order to show that the Irish were 'in a very early period, addicted to music':

> The fact is supported by the most unexceptional evidence; a sketch of which I cannot refrain from giving you, though I must confess that I never so much as learned the gamut. I shall not therefore pretend to write as a musician, but as an antiquarian; and you will allow me to be, like some other antiquarians, very fond of what I do not understand.[27]

This distinction is not insignificant: an antiquarian understanding of Irish culture comes to prevail in the later eighteenth century over the poetic diction espoused by Pilkington and Whyte and the fairly casual *aperçus* of essayists such as Goldsmith. But the essential perceptions of these writers remain unchallenged in Campbell's account:

> The *Cognoscenti*, I think, allow that Ireland is a school of music. *Ellen-a-Roon* has always been esteemed as one of the finest melodies of any country; *Langolee* and *Kin-du-Deelas* are of the same cast. Pasquali used to play the first of these with variations; which, they say, only weakened its original force. Though nothing can be more lively than their common jig tunes, their finest airs are of a plaintive turn, and supposed to have been those set to the elegies for renowned warriors, or to the sighs of complaining lovers . . .[28]

Here the discrimination between two cultures is voiced as a distinction between the force of the original and its absorption into the musical language of a European contemporary. Campbell's aesthetic preference for Irish music of lament is also of note because the equation between the native tradition and a sense of loss amounts to a conventional feature of subsequent writing on Irish music. Campbell's description of Carolan, therefore, is imbued with this sense of loss, even as it gives due emphasis to his musical prowess by means of an anecdote also included in Goldsmith's essay.[29] The tone throughout this description is mythic:

> They talk of a wonderful master they had of late, called Carolan, who, like Homer, was blind, and, like him, went about singing and playing his rhapsodies . . . From an early disappointment in love he is said to have attuned his harp to the elegiac strain. I have hear'd one of these compositions played, and to me these sounds were as expressive of such a situation of mind as the words of a love-sick elegy . . .
>
> I have heard divers others of his tunes called *Planxties* which are in the convivial strain, and evidently calculated to inspire good humour . . .
>
> His ear was so exquisite and his memory so tenacious, that he has been known to play off, at first hearing, some of the most difficult pieces of Italian music, to the astonishment of Geminiani.[30]

As with Goldsmith, Campbell is an Irishman writing as an Englishman, and his *Philosophical Survey*, published almost forty years after Carolan's death, belongs to the genre of travel writing. Each detail of the composer is consistent with the observations made by Whyte in 1740; Campbell and Goldsmith also agree in detail. In the *Philosophical Survey*, Carolan is to the Irish what Homer was to the Greeks. Carolan's impact on the musical life of the Ascendancy is once again a matter of wonder, astonishment and antiquarian curiosity. Carolan, in short, belongs to a dead culture.

For Pilkington, Whyte, Goldsmith and Campbell, Carolan is seen as the summation of that culture. This perception also amounts to a conventional feature of writing on music in Ireland, along with a structural progression which extends from the fabled ability of the ancient Irish in general, through the special role of the peripatetic bards, to Carolan himself. This progression finds its most elaborate expression in the writing of Joseph Walker.[31]

The *Historical Memoirs of the Irish Bards*, which comprises a history of music in Ireland and nine appendices, is a major document because of its *exclusive* concern with Irish music. Walker attempts to chronicle his subject by means of learned reference, antiquarian speculation and rhetorical persuasion. Such a combination impairs the tenability of his position on several counts. We shall see below that to read Walker in terms of accurate historiography, as Charles Burney does, is to dramatise the cruel conflict of interest between the benevolent antiquarian in search of an idea and the scientific pursuit of the music historian, hostile to anything which impedes empirical information. At another level, Walker and Burney differ irreconcilably on the idea of Ireland which underwrites or undermines these memoirs, depending on whichever of the two points of view indicated at the outset of this chapter is in force.

Walker's account charts a gradual decline from 'the state of music amongst the Ancient Irish' through the depleted and depressed condition of the bards in Elizabethan Ireland to the lethargy and neglect of the present day (i.e. the mid-1780s). The first section of this account is most blatantly indebted to conjecture, anecdote and partisan enthusiasm. We also find aesthetic observations which elevate ancient Irish music, and, by association, the self-governed society which nurtured it:

> The Irish music is, in some degree, distinguished from the music of every other nation, by an insinuating sweetness, which forces its way irresistibly to the heart, and there diffuses an extatic delight, that thrills through every fibre of the frame, awakens sensibility, and agitates or tranquilises the soul. Whatever passion it may be intended to excite, it never fails to effect its purpose. It is the voice of nature, and will be heard.[32]

A footnote to this paragraph informs the reader that 'most of the modern Italian compositions only trifle with the ear; the Welsh, the Scotch and the Irish music reaches the heart.'[33]

\*   \*   \*   \*   \*

The association drawn here by Walker between Irish music and the voice of nature as against the superficial reaches of Italian music is one which we have already seen rehearsed in Pilkington. Here, this association becomes more politically explicit as Walker traces the legislation introduced by Elizabeth I to silence the bardic tradition in Ireland:

> The character of Bard, once so reverenced in Ireland, began to sink into contempt in the reign of Elizabeth. We will, in this place, transcribe Spenser's animated description of this order of men in their fallen state, in which he sets forth his reasons for recommending their extirpation.[34]

Walker then quotes extensively from Edmund Spenser's *View of the Present State of Ireland* (1596), in which Spenser characterises the bardic tradition as one in which vindictive and immoral habits of mind deprave the 'sweet wit and good invention' of Irish poetic and musical art. Such depravity becomes political when it furthers the cause of rebellion, as Walker subsequently observes:

> Phillip of Macedon was not more jealous of the eloquence of Demosthenes, than was Elizabeth of the influence which the Irish Bards had exercised over their chieftains. Her jealousy quickening into revenge, she had acts of Parliament passed against them, and even against those who entertained them.[35]

The tone of Walker's concluding chapters in the *Irish Bards* is thereafter despondent. He laments that harpers in the seventeenth century 'degenerated into itinerant musicians', while he recognises that 'The last of this Order of men . . . was Turlough O'Carolan, a fine natural Genius, who died in the year 1738,' Walker comments upon the 'deplorable' state of harp music otherwise in this period, which coincides with the 'despotic sway' of Italian music in London and, to an extent, in Dublin.[36]

It is in this gloomy context that Appendix VI of the *Irish Bards*, a life of Carolan largely based on Walker's correspondence with the son of the composer's chief patron, Charles O'Conor, must be seen. In his *Advertisement* to this appended *Life*, Walker cites an anonymous correspondent in *Magee's Weekly Packet* of 5 June 1784 in support of a public celebration of the Irish composer:

> It has been acknowledged in Europe, that music was cultivated in Ireland when melody was scarcely known in other countries; music must have been its most distinguished characteristic, when it took the harp, as the conspicuous figure in its arms . . . Carolan, though a modern minstrel, has been admired as a first-rate musical genius – an untaught phenomenon in the cultivation of harmony. Why not commemorate *Carolan* here, as well as *Handel* on the other side of the water?[37]

Thus Carolan's achievement in terms of Irish music is equated with Handel's impact on music in England. The crucial distinction between the two composers, however, lies in the dislocated status implied by Carolan's mastery of a generally defunct tradition by comparison with Handel's reanimation of a living one. The additional complexity of Carolan's position as a 'modern minstrel', insofar as he was influenced by Italianate forms (and styles), enhances the anomalous and outmoded nature of his achievement, adapted as it was to accommodate Ascendancy taste. For Walker, this anomaly is virtually self-evident; Carolan is the last of the Irish bards, but is thus recognised only in a social and ideological context inimical to the tradition which he embodies. This is perhaps why Walker relegates his life of Carolan to an appendix. As the final personification of an abstract idea of Irish culture, Carolan is indispensable to Walker's *Irish Bards* proper. As an object of antiquarian curiosity, as a musician who successfully impinged upon a tradition which was essentially foreign to this cultural idea, Carolan complicates the main line of Walker's argument. For this reason, perhaps, he is removed to a separate space. Walker's argument proposes that the advent of one culture impoverished the other. His reading of Irish culture is not reasoned as a contribution to formal philosophy, but it does depend on ideas of conflict between the natural and the artificial which relate it to Edmund Burke's formulation of the Sublime as 'an idea belonging to self-preservation'.[38] In Walker, the natural quality of Irish music as against the artificial constructions of Ascendancy taste identify an aesthetic conflict which is political at root. The *Life* of Carolan which Walker appends to the *Irish Bards* stands apart from the book as a whole in the light of this argument. It is largely free of Walker's tendentious commentary which so enlivens his historical gloss of music in Ireland. It frankly depends instead on the letters of Charles O'Conor (of Belanagare) to provide biographical and anecdotal material which modern scholarship has drawn upon as a major source of information on the composer's life and works.[39] This *Life* addresses Carolan's habits of mind, his peripatetic career, his reliance on patronage and his general character and disposition. Walker discusses the publication of his music in Dublin[40] and even cites an anonymous recommendation for a Complete Works: 'If the life of Carolan be a national acquisition, a correct edition of all his compositions will much enhance the value of it.'[41]

The final assessment of Carolan is especially reliant on O'Conor's correspondence. In a lengthy extract from 'my friend's letter', Carolan's want of formal education and his deprived condition as a Catholic in eighteenth-century Ireland expressly account for his reduced position in the light of posterity, just as they explain the limited opportunities which he enjoyed during his lifetime:

> An Addison, a Swift, and the other luminaries of the age in which they flourished, had an academical education; the first dawnings of their genius prejudiced a discerning public in their favour; they obtained the patronage of the Great; and printing-presses were at all moments ready to spread reputations so susceptible of an increase. Far different was the fate of Carolan. His first entrance into the world was marked by poverty;[42] that poverty, together with a total privation of sight, with which he was struck at an early age, precluded many opportunities of improvement; the first dawnings of his genius were scarcely attended to; nay, the prejudices against a poor harper, must be subdued and softened only by those superior powers, which, late in life, he manifested, and which broke forth with such forcible resistance. The language, too, which he made use of, was so unfashionable, that, among the Great, to speak or study it, was deemed a mark of vulgarity. – Thus was Carolan's merit, during his lifetime, confined within the narrow circle of his acquaintance; without

the enlivening prospect, or single ray of hope, that his name, after his decease, should be held in veneration.[43]

Here, too, the anomaly of Carolan's position is implicitly addressed. But these observations hinge on the central dislocation of a cultural context which presented itself as vulgar to the Ascendancy mind. The instructive comparison with Addison and Swift is an index of this dislocation. It is not only that Carolan was denied the opportunities necessary to the full exploitation of his genius; O'Conor is also at pains to emphasise that the nature of this genius was of little concern to the cultural milieu of the Protestant Interest in Ireland.

Charles Burney's review of the *Historical Memoirs of the Irish Bards* appeared anonymously in *The Monthly Review* for December 1787.[44] In general, this is a sarcastic indictment of what Burney describes as 'the present rage for antiquities in Ireland;'[45] in particular, it comprises a detailed critique of Walker's speculative and sometimes fanciful claims for Irish music. Burney attacks the pretensions which the book makes towards learned commentary, and he mocks the disparity which lies between Walker's claims for the high civilisation of ancient Irish culture and the condition of Ireland as it is normally understood:

> Can we wonder that a nation which has had 'so many men of profound erudition, unshaken integrity and splendid abilities', who, like Orpheus, softened and instructed them with harp and song, should surpass the rest of the world in social and cosmopolite virtues?[46]

Walker's reliance on dubious authorities (especially Colonel Vallancey) is a related source of indignant amusement for Burney, whose jeering savagery underscores the absurd notion of an indigenous Irish music in terms of the governing aesthetic and stylistic prescriptions which obtain in European music:

> Now, as Ireland is a rising nation, we may hope ere long to have our operas from that neighbouring Island, instead of importing poets, singers and composers from so remote a country as Italy. And this is more likely to bring about an *union* of the three kingdoms of England, Scotland and Ireland, into one *common accord*, than all the ministerial bills or parliamentary acts that ever were or can be framed.[47]

Even in anger, Burney recognises the political implications of Walker's antiquarianism. Confronted, however, with what he clearly regards as majestic simple-mindedness (in political as well as musical terms), Burney abandons sarcasm and bluntly formulates his principal objection to the *Irish Bards*:

> It is impossible for anyone, not totally ignorant of the subject of Mr Walker's book, to read in many pages of it without discovering his knowledge of music to be small and his credulity in Hibernian antiquities to be great.[48]

This attack is double-edged, because it is invested with the authority of Burney's standing as the foremost English music historian of the day and because it undermines the *raison d'être* of the book itself. A spurious antiquarian in search of Ireland is not a reliable witness to the facts as they present themselves to a rational historian. Burney ridicules Walker's misappropriation of technical detail and virtually accuses him of fabrication ('The chief part of our Author's information seems wild and conjectural. . . .'). He also quotes at length precisely that passage from Spenser's *View of the Present State of Ireland* to be found in Walker, in order to justify his own reading of the Irish bard as 'little better than that of piper to the *White Boys*, and other savage and lawless ruffians'.[49] Without any reference to the fact that this passage occurs in Walker (where it exemplifies English cruelty), Burney allows Spenser's harsh judgement to stand as his own. In music, as in social and political aspiration, the question for Burney is a crude one of civilians and barbarians, to borrow a phrase from Seamus Deane.[50]

Although Burney appears willing to excuse the *Life* of Carolan from his general condemnation of the book as a whole, he ruthlessly criticises the extrinsic and intrinsic features of the 'rude' collection of Irish melodies which closes the *Irish Bards*. Burney's own conclusion is worthy of Jonathan Swift:

> On the whole, it seems as if the Irish should abate in some of their Milesian claims to the extreme high antiquity of their civilisation, refinement, literature, sciences and arts, with which Colonel Vallancey and others are flattering them: as our late circumnavigators to the South Seas were obliged to lower their demands on our credulity, of nine feet for the size of the Patagonians; for after their giants had been visited and measured by other voyagers, they would have been very thankful to anyone who would have allowed them six feet and a half.[51]

In this way, Burney reduces Walker's book to the level of travel writing, as a kind of *Gulliver's Travels* in earnest. Burney thus calls into question the very premise of an independent mode of Irish civilisation (including music) except in terms of wishful thinking on the part of antiquarians. Such thinking has nothing to do with history, musical or otherwise. To defend Irish music in equal terms with music in England is an absurd enterprise. Burney is tolerant of Carolan because his achievement is radically distinct from the high culture of music in England and because it does not impede on that culture except as an object of passing curiosity. Carolan is not a giant, he does not usefully compare with 'Giant Handel' (Pope's description); he is scarcely a composer at all in the commonly understood parlance of European art music. But he does stand as the embodiment of an idea of Irish music which is finally acceptable to Burney. That idea is one of itinerant culture, not high patronage, of peripheral and tribal communion, not central individualism within a powerful social order, of fanciful aspiration, not historical fact. Burney, as it were, puts Irish music in its place. He excludes it as a potential means of artistic expression amenable to English and European thought.[52]

Kevin Barry has written of the Irish philosopher James Usher (1720–72) that he is remembered 'if at all' for two distinct factors: 'One is his precocious aesthetic of music and his philosophy of loss and perpetual discontent. The other is as a convert to and apologist for a persecuted Catholic Interest.'[53] If, as Barry explains, music for Usher is 'the very texture of privation and loss', by which qualities it is aligned with Usher's defence of the Catholic position, it is tempting to extend this relation of ideas to music in Ireland. Usher does not appear to address himself directly to this issue and is not in any case concerned with the native tradition in his observations on music.[54] Nevertheless, the relationship which Barry identifies between Usher's particular reading of musical language and his political and moral concerns provides us perhaps with a philosophical basis upon which to develop the meaning of music in Ireland during the eighteenth century. The notion of music as a code for privation and loss so closely approaches the social conditions in which the ethnic tradition functioned during the 1700s that, once identified, it is hard to ignore as a possible foundation of thought.

With the Belfast Harp Festival of 1792 and the work of outstanding collectors (among them Edward Bunting and George Petrie) published in the next century, the antiquarian pursuit of music in Ireland becomes more professional. With a change in political climate, the music itself comes to represent a more well-defined Irish identity in which romantic aspiration gradually yields to the more urgent formulations of nationalism. The problems posed by the dislocated status of the contemporary composer in the eighteenth century, however, remain largely unresolved. In Carolan's lifetime, and for decades afterwards, the oppressive tension of political and social dysfunction inhibits the maturation of an Irish music capable of absorbing two mutually exclusive traditions.

*   *   *   *   *

To turn from a slender body of Ascendancy commentary on the ethnic tradition to the music of the Ascendancy itself is to be confronted by a mass of detail which requires the agency of a controlling idea to bring it into cultural focus. I have already proposed that Handel's visit to Dublin in 1741–2 can provide such an idea. We can advance here the notion that the central episode of this visit, the première of *Messiah* on 13 April 1742, vividly illustrates the prime social condition under which non-theatrical music functioned in Dublin. This was the support of charity and charitable institutions. The growth of music other than as an entertaining adjunct to theatrical fare was dependent on such support and to a lesser extent on those official occasions which celebrated the fragile condition of His Majesty's State in Ireland.

The problem of sources is on a scale which rivals and often exceeds that which attends our understanding of the transmission and content of the ethnic repertory. Despite an abundance of newspaper reports and a substantial number of librettos which are also extant, there is a dearth of actual music in proportion to the scale of activity which Brian Boydell has researched for the period 1700–60.[55] From the perspective of cultural history, this absence of sources can give a lopsided impression of Ascendancy taste which has on occasion been taken over into general history.[56] This impression, enhanced by detailed records of musical personnel which document the range of performance conditions, is one of a city obsessed by the entertaining spectacle of ballad opera, in which the expressive techniques of European music are drastically reduced and simplified. The alternative preoccupation with grand musical events in support of charitable enterprises has not been as prominently represented as it should be, given its fundamental importance as an explanation of the success of *Messiah* in particular and of Handel's sacred-dramatic and/or choral music in general, both during and especially after the composer's stay in Dublin. Behind these cultural intersections between music and public life stands the influence of foreign musicians periodically resident in Dublin, alongside a certain hostility to European norms of musical expression. Both factors contribute to our grasp of Handel's relationship with the Ascendancy.

In an important paper on 'Music, Poetry and Polity in the Age of Swift', Frank Harrison rehearsed the case against music as an aesthetic force within the pale of the Protestant Interest in Dublin.[57] Harrison shows that Swift was largely indifferent to the achievement of European music at best, and at worst that he was ignorant of it. If anything, Swift regarded such music as an intolerable harbinger of popery, Italian decadence and political instability.[58] As Harrison observes, 'the fear that having music that employed instruments in a Protestant church could imply, or even promote its adherence to the Catholic faith (in spite of the complete acceptance of such music in the Lutheran church) had been a persistent part of Protestant thinking since the Elizabethan Act of Uniformity'.[59] In a country determined by religious denomination, Swift's intemperate disdain for European norms of high musical culture (which he lampooned at length in his *Cantata*) was far more than a simple matter of personal incapacity or dislike.[60] It stemmed also from religious and ideological conviction. As a consequence, the whole question of music is marginalised in Swift's writings, as it is for the most part in the writings of his intellectual contemporaries in Ireland. Swift's famous antagonism towards the participation of vicars choral from St Patrick's Cathedral (where he was dean) in the first performance of *Messiah* is matched by several other ill-disposed observations on music.[61] By comparison, his generally favourable review and 'vindication' of *The Beggar's Opera* (1728) attacks the cultivation of Italian music as a vicious pursuit 'wholly unsuitable to our Northern climate and the Genius of the people'.[62] This last remark is an aesthetic conviction which derives from a general antipathy towards Italianate music borne out in part by the climate of Ascendancy opinion in Ireland and by the success of *The Beggar's Opera* in England. To judge, moreover, by recent research, the actual condition of music in St Patrick's Cathedral under Swift bears out his own indifference (except when disciplining his choristers for wayward living), although the paucity of sources once again prohibits a conclusive judgement in this matter.[63]

The position of visiting musicians in Dublin also attests to the marginal role of European norms in Ascendancy taste. Between the appointment of Johann Sigismund Cousser as Master of the State Music in Ireland in 1707 and the death of Francesco Geminiani in Dublin in 1762, the impact of foreign musical personnel on the quality and range of performance conditions was considerable. Cousser, Matthew Dubourg, John Lampe, Thomas Arne and Geminiani himself were among scores of singers, instrumentalists and composers who intermittently settled in Dublin, sometimes for want of similar positions in London or on the Continent.[64] In the same period, works by Albinoni, Bononcini, Boyce, Carey, Corelli, Eccles, Handel, Hasse, Pasquali, Pergolesi, Daniel and Henry Purcell, Stanley, Tartini, Vinci and Vivaldi were performed, published or sold in Dublin with greater or lesser degrees of frequency.[65]

Despite this range, a striking preference for ballad opera eclipses almost all such music from 1728 onwards, with the paramount exception of Handel's works. In isolated instances, such as Thomas Arne's setting of Milton's *Comus*, other semi-theatrical pieces survived this preference, but many did not. Brian Boydell's observation that Cousser apparently produced no full-scale operas in Dublin, despite his achievements in this genre in Germany, alerts us to the selectivity of Ascendancy taste, and not only with regard to opera.[66] The two performances of Arne's first oratorio, *The Death of Abel*, a work premièred in Dublin in 1744, may be contrasted significantly with the frequent performances of his ballad operas and masques throughout his periods of residence in Dublin. We cannot even determine with exactitude the number of birthday odes which Cousser wrote for the reigning monarch between 1709 and 1726 and which Dubourg continued to write between 1734 and 1759, still less distinguish accurately between them. If the annual performances of Handel's *Acis and Galatea* almost without break from 1748 until 1760 (with performances in 1734, 1735, 1742, 1744 and 1746 preceding these) are instructive in this respect, it may be that the Cousser and Dubourg odes were far fewer than the number of documented performances suggests. Here, too, the absence of sources is astonishing and it frustrates a vital inquiry into the impact of British and European structural norms on the publicly funded music which the Ascendancy espoused. But the principal issue is clear: notwithstanding the performance of Handel's choral and sacred-dramatic music (which comprises a cultural focus of its own) the Ascendancy did not patronise a single genre which could rival the inherent musical accomplishment of *opera seria*.

It did, however, respond enthusiastically to ballad opera. 'Ballad opera', as John Greene reminds us, is a notoriously imprecise term for the full-scale ('mainpiece') and subsidiary ('afterpiece') entertainments which dominated the Dublin stage in the middle of the eighteenth century. The term 'ballad opera' also returns us to Swift. His bizarre suggestion that John Gay should write a 'Newgate pastoral among the whores and thieves there' in 1716 was realised in *The Beggar' Opera*, first given in London in January 1728 and afterwards in Dublin (at Smock Alley Theatre) in March of the same year. Swift's defence of Gay was not disinterested: in defending *The Beggar's Opera*, after all, he defended his own suggestion. We have already seen that he vindicated the piece in terms which advanced his intense dislike of Italian music; that *The Beggar's Opera* should gleefully expose the latter as an 'unnatural practice' was all to the good.[67]

The satiric clarity of *The Beggar's Opera*, its vigorous rejection of the apparatus of *opera seria* and its coherent appropriation of a lucid English text and memorable melodies (some from Italian opera, of course) gave the work an impact which was especially forceful in Dublin.[68] The host of imitations which it spawned tended to emphasise burlesque and farce at the expense of musical material, and the position of works such as *The Dragon of Wantley*, *Damon and Phillida* and *The Mock Doctor* as afterpieces to spoken plays illustrates the often subservient position of ballad opera in Dublin.[69] There is obviously a correspondence to be acknowledged here between this development and a similar degeneration of operatic repertory in London after the widespread collapse of *opera seria* as a viable form of serious musical drama. Nevertheless, the plenitude of such performances in Dublin is partly, if not preponderantly, a question of theatrical history first and of music second. To ridicule *opera seria* as Gay had done was essentially a theatrical gesture, and our understanding of the contribution of ballad opera in terms of cultural history must take account of this insight. To write of 'the Ascendancy mind and ballad opera', notwithstanding Swift's vital connections with the genesis of the latter and his central if disturbing place in our conception of the former, is to strain these terms beyond their usefulness. In fact, the popularity of ballad opera in Dublin signifies the remoteness of the Ascendancy from a direct engagement with theatrical music as a cultural force with regard to serious patronage, professional education or public advancement. The dependence of Dublin theatres, moreover, on London prototypes and on London repertory in their presentation of ballad opera signifies a more equable spread of musical entertainment which a mercantile class would expect and demand. At the last, *The Beggar's Opera* is of more relevance to Swift and the emancipation of bourgeois taste than it is to the other issues of cultural history addressed in this chapter. But the neglect of *opera seria*, the exclusive preference for texts in English and the fundamental want of direct aristocratic musical patronage are elements which were plainly reinforced by the condition of theatre music in Dublin and which thereby enlighten our understanding of the context of Handel's visit there.

This context was provided by the performance of music for charitable purposes. In this manner the Ascendancy did espouse the cause of serious music, at least indirectly. In this regard also, Dublin differed in degree from

London. The advancement of music in Dublin for the sake of charitable enterprise was motivated by a strictly local sense of Protestant determination and commercial well-being.

Brian Boydell has shown that at least eight Dublin hospitals were regularly supported by funds which were raised through the promotion of concerts either by the boards of these hospitals or by charitable societies. The hospitals included the Charitable Infirmary (afterwards Jervis Street Hospital), opened in 1728, Mercer's Hospital, founded in 1734, Dr Mosse's Lying-in Hospital, established in 1745 (afterwards known as the Rotunda Hospital), and the Hospital for Incurables on Lazer's Hill, founded in 1744. Of some eighteen charitable societies identified by Boydell, the Charitable Musical Society for the Relief of Imprisoned Debtors (1734), the Musical Academy in Crow-Street (c. 1729), the Charitable Society for the Support of the Hospital for Incurables (1744) and the Earl of Mornington's Musical Academy (c. 1757) were the most frequently concerned with public musical performances. Between them, such hospitals and societies effectively managed the greater part of the city's non-theatrical public music. This activity extended to the provision of venues for musical performance: the 'New Hall' in Fishamble Street was built in 1741 by the Charitable Musical Society, the Rotunda was built in 1767 by the board of the Lying-in Hospital, the gardens adjacent to Great Britain Street had been planned by Dr Mosse in 1749 and featured an unbroken series of concerts between April and September of that year until 1791, and so on.[70]

This association between public music and public virtue was not unique to the Ascendancy, but its realisation was on a scale unprecedented by London standards. The concept of 'charity music' is the most instructive means of explaining how the Ascendancy came to terms with music as a source of civic culture and high celebration. That 'grand music' should support the cause of the sick and the indigent was a central insight well attuned to the Ascendancy mind, beleaguered as it was by an insecure sense of its own polity. The extravagances of popery, the remote exoticisms of Italian opera did not compromise this simple but durable equation between good works and the commercial import of music and musicians to support them. The prospect of public *subscription* concerts, moreover, could and did entice musicians to give their services in subsequent performances for charity.

George Frideric Handel was a crucial figure in this transaction. The Ascendancy discovered in his music affirmations of public well-being and Christian theism which nurtured both a political and a moral sense of belonging which were eagerly countenanced. That *Messiah* was expressly written for the Dublin charities it first benefited is a fact of cultural history which can only be wholly understood in terms of Ascendancy music in Ireland. Deprived of such terms, as Winton Dean has shown, *Messiah* acquires the status of a cultural fetish which has in the past distorted our sense of the composer's actual achievement.[71] In eighteenth-century Ireland, however, the context of charity music gives the work a cultural significance of specifically Irish importance.

In order to explain this significance, it is necessary to realise the impact of Handel's visit on the repertory of choral music performed in Dublin. It is not my intention here to rehearse in detail the circumstances of the composer's Irish sojourn, given the abundance of secondary accounts which largely depend on the information recorded in Faulkner's *Dublin Journal* (and elsewhere) as the visit took place, but a brief summary of Handel's stay is obviously useful for the purposes of this discussion.[72]

Handel's arrival in Dublin on 18 November 1741 was announced in Faulkner's *Dublin Journal* for 21 November of that year. The minutes of Mercer's Hospital for the same date record that he was invited to play the organ at a concert largely comprised of his own music to be held at St Andrew's Round Church, for the support of the hospital. This concert took place on 10 December and there followed in Faulkner's *Journal* notice of a subscription series of six 'musical entertainments' to begin on Wednesday 23 December at the new music hall in Fishamble Street. Handel began the series with a performance of *L'Allegro, Il Penseroso ed Il Moderato*, which the enthusiastic report in Faulkner's *Journal* described as an oratorio.[73] This concert was repeated on 13 January 1742. On 20 January, again in the new music hall, Handel gave his masque *Acis and Galatea* along with the (Dryden) *Ode for St Cecilia's Day*. This concert was also repeated, on 27 January. The first series of Handel concerts ended with a performance of the composer's first English oratorio proper, *Esther*. It was given on 3 February and repeated on 10 February.

\*   \*   \*   \*   \*

The second subscription series began on 17 February with another Dryden setting, *Alexander's Feast*, repeated on 2 March. A repeat of *L'Allegro . . .* on 17 March replaced an advertised performance of *Imeneo* (to be given as *Hymen* in a concert version). *Hymen* was finally performed on 24 March and repeated on 31 March. Handel's second series also closed with a performance of *Esther*, on 7 April; this was announced in Faulkner's *Journal* for 3 April, which also carried a notice for a public rehearsal of *Messiah*. This had been previously advertised as a work for 'the relief of the prisoners in several gaols, and for the support of Mercer's Hospital in Stephen's Street, and of the charitable infirmary on the *Inns* Quay', i.e. not as part of the subscription series, but as a charity benefit. *Messiah* was publicly rehearsed on 9 April and performed on 13 April in the new music hall. Members of both St Patrick's Cathedral and Christ Church Cathedral choirs took part, and the Dublin press responded with extravagant acclaim.

After *Messiah*, Handel publicly rehearsed and performed *Saul* on 21 and 25 May respectively, and he finally gave a subscription performance of *Messiah* on 3 June, at the express request of his Dublin admirers. He left Dublin on 13 August with the stated intention of returning there to resume his oratorios in the year following. He departed the city with both his standing and his finances substantially enhanced.[74]

The success of the *Messiah* première in particular stimulated a response which was immediate in its enthusiastic recognition both of the work's innate genius and its initial purpose:

> The Sublime, the Grand, and the Tender, adapted to the most elevated, majestick and moving words, conspired to transport and charm the ravished Heart and Ear. It is but justice to Mr Handel, that the World should know, he generously gave the money arising from this Grand Performance, to be equally shared by the Society for relieving Prisoners, the Charitable Infirmary, and Mercer's Hospital, for which they will ever gratefully remember his Name.[75]

This report in Faulkner's *Dublin Journal*, four days after the first performance of the work, heads a considerable body of commentary which by now is well known. Laurence Whyte, Oliver Goldsmith, Alexander Pope, John Mainwaring and Charles Burney are among those of Handel's contemporaries or near-contemporaries who repeatedly emphasise the moral dimension of *Messiah* at the expense of Handel's dramatic prowess in this and in his other oratorios. From the perspective of music in Ireland, the most interesting aspect of such commentary is its appropriation of *Messiah* as an Irish event. Charles Burney's attempt to 'wipe off the national stain' caused by the suggestion that *Messiah* was coldly received in London *before* the Irish visit does not gainsay the fact that the work failed when it did come to be given there. The controversy over the very title of the piece, its sacred subject matter and the place of performance stands in sharp contrast to the sometimes fulsome praise which surrounded the work in Dublin.[76] English and Irish commentators who characterised the Dublin visit as 'Handel's banishment to Ireland' likewise identified the source of his success in philanthropic terms: Joseph Walker, for example, gives this account:

> In the year 1740, the sublime Genius of Handel roused our feelings from the lethargy into which they had fallen. Banished from London by the spirit of party, he sought protection in Dublin. Here he was kindly received, and due regard was paid to his extraordinary merit. Soon after his arrival, he performed that matchless Oratorio, The MESSIAH, for the benefit of the City Prison. This was a Masterstroke; for by means of it he conciliated the affections of the People, and established his Fame on a permanent foundation.[77]

Inaccuracies notwithstanding ('1740'), the issue here is Handel's 'Masterstroke', which neatly eclipses the two subscription series preceding the première of *Messiah*. And the use of *Messiah* and of his other oratorios to raise money, virtually as the inevitable condition of a Dublin performance after 1742, prefigures the strong moral association between Handel's music and the public good drawn by early commentators. Laurence Whyte's *Messiah* poem, Goldsmith's remarks on Handel in his essay on 'The Different Schools of Music' and above all, perhaps, Burney's tendentious comments on the composer in his

*General History* comprise an ironic counterpart to the espousal and rejection of indigenous Irish music by these writers which we have surveyed here.[78] On the moral significance of *Messiah* in Dublin, however, they were agreed. In London, *Messiah* was to fail repeatedly, until it was given the agency of a moral purpose in the benefit performances for the Foundling Hospital which began in 1750.[79]

The most compelling association between Handel and the use of charity music in Dublin can be found in the performance of his works *after* the visit. Quite apart from the annual Mercer's benefit of *Messiah* which began in 1743, we find that the majority by far of performances of *Acis and Galatea* and the oratorios from 1742 onwards were in aid of a public or private charity. Between 1745 and 1753, for example, seven performances of *Deborah* were given in Dublin, at least four of which were for the benefit of the Charitable Infirmary. *Deborah* does not appear to have been given once in London, however, between 1744 and 1754. All five performances of *Judas Maccabeus* given in Dublin between 1748 and 1753 were charity benefits. Both performances of *Joshua* in 1751 and 1752 were for the Hospital for Incurables. Handel's music during his own lifetime became virtually synonymous with public or private acts of charity in Dublin.[80] The reverse was also almost the case. The catalogues of musical performances prepared by T. J. Walsh and Brian Boydell clearly demonstrate Handel's monopoly of publicly performed sacred-dramatic and/or choral music not merely during his stay in Dublin but for several years beyond it. The performance of his *Utrecht Te Deum and Jubilate* in 1736 as a benefit for Mercer's Hospital at St Andrew's Round Church was thereafter an annual event for some twenty years. From 1736 until 1760, *Alexander's Feast*, *L'Allegro. . .*, *Esther*, *Joshua*, *Judas*, *Samson*, *Saul, Solomon* and a host of anthems, in addition to *Acis* and *Messiah*, were all given for charity in Dublin. Apart from Dubourg's birthday odes and occasional anthems by William Boyce, these works make up the repertory upon which Dublin charities and hospitals successfully depended for the purpose of raising funds. Private benefits, especially associated with *Acis*, also largely relied on Handel's music.[81]

It is instructive to note, however, that throughout this same period, not one of Handel's operas was given in Dublin, with the partial exception of the concert version of *Imeneo*. Such works lay remote from the aspirations and conditions of Ascendancy taste. The strong vein of classical humanism which pervades Handel's oratorios, by contrast, imbued their performance as charity benefits in Dublin with a special kind of meaning. This meaning was apostrophised in the reaction to *Messiah*, which sought to rationalise the 'sublime' in Handel's music in terms of charitable endeavour. Winton Dean has attributed the greatness of the work to its unique fusion of the traditions of Italian opera, English anthem and German passion, and also to the 'coincidence of Handel's personal faith and creative genius to express, more fully than in any other work of art, the Anglican religious spirit'.[82] If Dublin recognised these qualities more rapidly than did London, the circumstances of the première of

*Messiah*, as with almost all of Handel's music in Ireland, account for this perception. If the Anglo-Irish intellect contemplated and then rejected the philosophical alternatives of benevolence and hedonism as Seamus Deane has argued,[83] it apprehended, however dimly, the pragmatic relationship between Handel's music and the public good. There can be no doubt that Ascendancy Ireland exploited this relationship to the extent that Handel performances in Dublin comprise a radically distinct entity from Handel's own career in London. The composer's assiduous cultivation of subscription oratorio concerts on his return to London therefore deserves to be distinguished from the norm of charity performances in Dublin.[84]

Handel's music afforded the Ascendancy a sense of itself. If such an assertion seems untenable, the overwhelming fact of performance after charity performance is there to support it. The cumulation of these performances demands interpretation in such broad terms, given the stable association which they repeatedly propose between aesthetic expression (the expression of high culture) and moral value. This association was in turn to circumscribe the concept of 'music in Ireland' in ways which were notably inimical to the ethnic repertory.

*    *    *    *    *

Joseph Walker ends the main section of the *Historical Memoirs of the Irish Bards* in this way:

> Soon as the Hanoverian Succession was firmly established, the Gates of the Temple of Janus were closed in both Kingdoms. Parties, indeed, for a while, ran high: but the sword had returned into its scabbard. The English now pursued with ardour the cultivation of the fine Arts: the Irish crept slowly after. Both vocal and instrumental musicians were brought, at an enormous expence, from Italy to London; and the Italian music began to reign with despotic sway in that great city . . . Its influence spread so wide, that it reached these shores. Our musical state became refined and our sweet melodies and native musicians fell into disrepute . . . But alas! in proportion as our musical taste is rectified, the pleasure we derive from pure melody is lessened. This refinement may be said to remove the ear so far from the heart . . . that the essence of music (an appellation by which melody deserves to be distinguished) cannot reach it. Nor is it necessary in this age, that the ear and heart should be closely connected. For modern music is calculated only to display the brilliant execution of the performer, and to occasion a gentle titillation in the organ of hearing.
>
> . . . Music was now the rage. Italian Singers were invited over, and the fair Dames of Ireland learned to expire at an Opera . . . Concerts were the favourite amusements in the houses of the Nobility and Gentry, and Musical Societies were formed in all the great towns of the Kingdom. In a word, every knee was bowed to St Cecilia.
>
> But the Saint was not to enjoy this homage long. In the Rotunda, indeed, her Votaries sacrificed to her for a few years. But Politics, Gaming and every species of Dissipation have so blunted the finer feelings of their souls, that their warm Devotion has at length degenerated into cold Neglect. Concerts, it is true,

are held there every Summer, but they are little attended to. Music, however, is sometimes the subject of conversation amongst us, and is still cultivated by a few; but it is no longer a favourite topic, nor a favourite study.[85]

Almost always an unreliable historian, Walker is nevertheless a chronicler of psychological truth. His attempt to distinguish between two kinds of music in Ireland and his aesthetic discriminations in favour of the ethnic repertory as against the imported artifices of the Ascendancy are both part of the cultural history of music in Ireland. From Walker's point of view, the high noon of Handel performances in Dublin must be set against the subsequent decline and gloom of the 1760s and 1770s. The neglect of indigenous music entailed by this passing enthusiasm is a price which was to be paid socially as well as aesthetically, insofar as the ethnic repertory had fallen into disrepute. Walker's redress and Burney's outright rejection both confirm this state of affairs.

In his capacity as a member of the newly established (Royal) Irish Academy, Walker would presage a more scholarly concern with the ethnic tradition, to be expressed in the collection and documentation of the 'Ancient Music of Ireland' throughout the nineteenth century. This activity itself held important implications for commentators who tried to discern an individual ethos in the ethnic repertory as against the encroachment of London's musical culture on Dublin, Cork and Belfast, particularly after the Act of Union. Walker was clearly alert to this distinction.

If the Act of Union has commonly been regarded by historians as a matter of disastrous consequence for the politically reduced Ascendancy and as one of profound disappointment for those who hoped it would emancipate the Catholic majority in Ireland, its cultural impact may be regarded in related terms. The cultural outcome of this political union was to fortify the integral potential of the native repertory as an agent of nationalist aspiration (even as parts of this repertory nourished a milder form of romantic nationalism not at all incompatible with the admittedly tenuous *status quo* of politics in nineteenth-century Ireland). Prior to the Union, the Ascendancy relationship between music and philanthrophy was strained and in decay. There is some irony in this dissolution. As the provision for hospitals and infirmaries became more centrally organised under local government legislation, the function of charity music evaporated. Thus the one social condition which partly distinguished music in Dublin from London died away. The Ascendancy cultivation of Handel receded into myth and fond memory. And as it evanesced, music in Dublin became more thoroughly indebted than before to the precedent of London norms, particularly with regard to music in the theatre.[86]

The apotheosis of Handel as a monument of respectability, however serious a misrepresentation, had good grounds in Dublin.[87] From within the Ascendancy tradition, the origins of this apotheosis in social history and its subsequent evolution as a symbol of cultural history contributed to the dislocated status of the composer in Ireland. Who might follow Handel in a musical culture that was established on the principles of artistic import? Walker's query, 'Why not commemorate Carolan here as well as Handel on the other side of the water?', begs in turn this fundamental question. This process of dislocation, as we have seen, was also furthered by the perception of Carolan in the eighteenth century. Donal O'Sullivan has argued against the attribution of a 'bardic impulse' to Carolan's music in terms which flatly contradict the projection of Carolan as a poet who celebrated the Catholic gentry as 'fallen Milesians'.[88] But once again, psychological truth conflicts with the facts of the case as they have presented themselves to historians in England and Ireland. The concept of 'bardic impulse' has survived. Although this perception stimulated an interest in the ethnic tradition beyond Carolan's own music, the Carolan myth expressed an order of difficulty as to the whole question of music in Ireland. It spelt out the impossible condition of the composer insofar as that condition entailed the absorption of ethnic and colonial traditions which remained to all purposes irreconcilable. The myth of a vanished culture, with its connotations of privation and loss, began to take hold just as the materials of that culture – the music itself – began to be collected. The concept of Irish composition was therefore located precariously between the claims of antiquarianism on one side and the claims of myth on the other. This problem was to endure throughout the nineteenth century, when fresh difficulties decisively intervened.

# HISTORY AND ROMANTICISM
## Bunting, Moore and the Concept of
## Irish Music in the Nineteenth Century

> Our National Music has never been properly collected, and while the
> composers of the Continent have enriched their operas and sonatas with
> melodies borrowed from Ireland . . . we have left these treasures in a
> great degree unreclaimed and fugitive. But we are come, I hope, to a bet-
> ter period both of politics and music; and how much they are connected,
> in Ireland at least, appears too plainly in the tone of sorrow and depres-
> sion which characterises most of our early songs.[1]

> Were we to institute a literary comparison, we could say that Moore's
> *Irish Melodies* had about them all the fascination of poetry and romance,
> Bunting's collections all the sterner charms of truth and history.[2]

There is a striking communion of interest between music and politics in nineteenth-century Ireland. One fortified and stimulated the other in a way that is
of immediate significance for Irish cultural history. The understanding of Irish
music in this period became deeply imbued with resurgent nationalism as the
claims of constitutional reform were partly eclipsed by nascent (militant)
republicanism and revolutionary struggle. Over and above such claims, Irish
music began to be determined by an attempt to rationalise and subsequently
to polarise it as an outgrowth of antiquarian research on one side and as a
coherent, politically informed expression of romantic individualism on the
other.

The development of these complementary ideas is the primary concern of
this chapter. The tension between authenticity and the uses of Irish music,
between tradition and the individual talent, is one which can be firmly
located in the political climate of the Act of Union and its aftermath. The
claims of antiquarianism and of myth identified in the preceding chapter
must now be understood in terms of political and cultural reanimation, so
that the ethnic repertory of Irish music can be understood in three ways: as
an object of preservation, as a source of romantic and political expression and
as an agent of nationalist self-determination.[3]

If these imperatives have any justification, it is that they are so easily
derived from the history of music in Ireland, *c.* 1792–1834. Between the
Belfast Harp Festival and the final issue of Moore's *Irish Melodies*, this tripar-
tite perception of music was to take firm root in the Irish mind. The waning

lament of Walker's *Irish Bards* would be usurped by a more purposeful (and more complicated) account of Irish musical thought. Undoubtedly circumscribed by political history and materially influenced in particular by the events which led up to the Act of Union, the development of Irish music in this period was to exert paradigmatic influence on its cultivation and practice in Ireland throughout the nineteenth century and for long afterwards.

The antiquarian polemics of this development would constantly endure in terms of the struggle for authenticity, a quest which in itself repudiated other forms of musical growth; while the pragmatics of balladry overtook a much vaunted (but never realised) cross-fertilisation between the ethnic and the art traditions in the service of crude political propaganda. Somewhere between the cultural stasis of 'pure Gaelic melody' and the immense success of nationalist popular song, the original dialectic between antiquarianism and romanticism withered away. Only the antipathies remained. The full-blown cultural prestige of nationalism, the implicit or explicit hostility towards European art music and the reduction of the ethnic repertory to the level of 'local colour' all lie beyond the mid-1830s: but all of these originated in this period, wherein the guiding principles of cultural debate were so firmly established and entrenched.

These principles are at the heart of the matter. Seamus Deane observes that 'The enforced intimacy between literature and politics was unique and tragic in Ireland.'[4] This intimacy adumbrated an even more telling crisis in musical affairs. It is not too much to suggest that the *rapprochement* between politics and music which so notably enabled the development of the latter between 1792 and 1834 was ultimately a ruinous accommodation. The understanding which existed between the idea of 'Ireland' in the ethnic repertory and the idea of 'music' in the Irish imagination (above all in the imagination of Thomas Moore) was one determined by politics. How political thought and action could so determine musical growth and musical perception is a vital query in what follows here.

*     *     *     *     *

The Belfast Harp Festival of July 1792 is commonly regarded as the *locus classicus* for a discussion of the origins of music in nineteenth-century Ireland. The antiquarian motivation which brought it into being was not exact: the organising committee was 'solicitous to preserve from oblivion the few fragments [of the "ancient Music and Poetry of Ireland"] which have been permitted to remain'. This general ambition supposed that surviving harpers, 'those descendants of our Ancient Bards', would possess 'all that remains of the Music, Poetry and oral traditions of Ireland'.[5] Of equal importance to the committee appears to have been the underlying reason for the project itself:

> An undertaking of this kind will undoubtedly meet the approbation of men of refinement and erudition in every country. And when it is considered how intimately the spirit and character of a people are connected with their national

> Poetry and Music, it is presumed that the Irish patriot and politician will not
> deem it an object unworthy of his patronage and protection.[6]

This credo – a belief in the political and cultural resonance of ethnic poetry
and music – bespeaks a liberal, bourgeois motivation for the pursuit of musical knowledge far removed from the enlightened myth-making of the Ascendancy. But it also characterises the straightforward equation between
systematic preservation of the cultural past and political well-being in the present which doggedly attends antiquarianism in the period 1790–1810.

Such an equation suggests that a relationship existed between Irish political philosophy at the close of the eighteenth century and an apparently
insignificant cultural event. If the Harp Festival had not been part of a wider
movement of the spirit and mind, it would have taken its place as a curiosity,
an emblematic object of delight, a three-day wonder, and not much more. But
the festival was indeed otherwise: the music it brought to life was part of that
'interior history of Ireland' which Edmund Burke identified in his decisive
condemnation of the Ascendancy mind.[7] So also was the aged, preponderantly blind and impoverished gathering of itinerant harpers which assembled
in the ballroom of the Exchange Rooms in Belfast, in order to perform 'some
of the most ancient airs now nearly obsolete'.[8]

They performed in competition. 'Liberal premiums were distributed
amongst them, according to their respective merits.'[9] An advance notice of the
festival published in *The Belfast News-Letter* also gave details of the nature and
purpose of the meeting:

> In order to revive obsolete airs, it is an instruction to the judges on this occa-
> sion, not to be solely governed in their decisions by the degree of execution or
> taste of the several performers, but independent of these circumstances, to con-
> sider the person entitled to additional claim, who shall produce airs not to be
> found in any public collection, and at the same time deserving of preference,
> by their intrinsic excellence. It is recommended to any harper who is in pos-
> session of scarce compositions to have them reduced to notes: that the Rev Mr
> Andrew Bryson of Dundalk be requested to assist, as a person versed in the
> antiquities of the nation, and that Mr William Weare, Mr Edward Bunting and
> Mr John Sharpe be requested to attend as practical musicians.[10]

It is Bunting's name, of course, which leaps out from this account. The
Harp Festival was to be the source of his lifelong preoccupation with Irish
music; conversely, it was through his work that the festival achieved its potential. In his three published collections of Irish music, and especially in the first
(1797) and the third (1840), Bunting repeatedly adverted to the impact which
the event had upon him. It is not too much to say that his innate abilities as
a musician were realised by his exposure to the ethnic repertory, nor that his
antiquarian zeal was fired by the example and precedent of literary research.[11]
But the festival itself, the confirmation which it provided that herein lay a

trove of remembrance, the relics of a culture all but extinguished, focused Bunting's mind permanently on the musical reality which he was called upon to record.

This act of preservation was central to Bunting's purposeful (and profoundly emotional) response to the music which he heard and notated in Belfast. Evidence was naturally prior to explanation, and Bunting's evidence was to be copiously drawn: *A General Collection of the Ancient Irish Music, containing a variety of admired airs never-before published and also the compositions of Conalan and Carolan, collected from the harpers, etc., in the different provinces of Ireland and adapted for the pianoforte, with a prefatory introduction by Edward Bunting* appeared in 1797.[12]

The solemn leisure of this title is worth a moment's reflection. Bunting distinguishes between 'Ancient' music and the compositions of Conalan and Carolan, but advises that both groups have been arranged for piano by the editor. However contradictory these discriminations may seem to contemporary scholarship, their literal function for Bunting was to clarify the kinds of air he had preserved and the manner in which he had done so. It is useful here to advert to Seamus Deane's persuasion that 'Gaelic could survive in English only in a "celtic" form'.[13] In musical terms, the underlying assumption which informs Bunting's collection is that Gaelic melody could likewise survive only in a 'tonal' form. It is a point of view which can be advanced with circumspection, if at all. One needs to distinguish between Bunting's apparent ignorance of modal structure and his reasonable supposition that the means to an intelligible communication of this music necessarily involved an act of 'translation' into the style and vocabulary of his own day. If anything, informed readers of the 1797 collection were struck by the untutored condition of some of the music, which despite Bunting's modernisations appeared crude and unacceptable:

> If we must object to anything in Mr Bunting's work it is to the frequent division of the Melody between the Treble and the Bass in many of Carolan's airs. We know that this was the composer's way of playing them, and that it would be impossible to arrange many of them otherwise. But in several there is no necessity for this mode of arrangement and it would surely be better to improve on what so evidently borders on barbarism.[14]

The 1797 collection is circumscribed, nevertheless, by Bunting's practical concessions to contemporary musical sensibility. The authenticity of music preservation makes a virtue of strict science only up to a point, and in Bunting's case this terminus was the keyboard: all three collections are 'arrangements' of airs for the piano. But the term which stubbornly persists in this assessment is 'translations'. There is a sense in which Bunting struggled to rationalise his duties as an antiquarian with his inclinations as a musician, insofar as his admiration for these airs was tempered by his commitment to their absorption by the musical community at large. Even in this respect, the style of his arrangements was vulnerable to the critique that they adhered too closely to the harp originals, that his 'translations', so to speak, were too literal and unrefined:

> We also greatly dislike the thin harp bases [sic] which he has given to others
> . . . However bearable the lengthened vibrations of our national instrument
> may have made such accompaniments, they will certainly never be tolerated on
> a piano-forte.[15]

As a preserver of these airs, it was Bunting's express intention to 'rescue them from oblivion'.[16] As an antiquarian, the condition and provenance of this music were his foremost concerns. As a musician, he was obliged to their being made intelligible to contemporary taste.

Each of these issues is rehearsed in the preface to the 1797 collection. Questions of style and provenance are especially prominent. Bunting not only distinguishes between the antiquity of the greater number of airs in the collection and the more recent compositions of Carolan in particular; he also seeks controversially to establish that the purest transmission of melody more easily accommodates its presentation in contemporary compositional practice than otherwise:

> The beauty and regularity, with which the tunes are constructed, appears sur-
> prising. The circumstances seemed the more extraordinary, when it was dis-
> covered that the most ancient tunes were, in this respect, the most perfect,
> admitting of the addition of a Bass with more facility than such as were less
> ancient. Hence we may conclude, that their authors must necessarily have been
> excellent performers, versed in the scientific part of the profession, and that
> they had originally a view to the addition of *harmony* in the composition of
> their pieces.[17]

At one level this represents the kind of wishful thinking representative of Walker at his worst; it can also, perhaps, be read as a young man's attempt to defend the integrity of his 'translations' from one musical discourse into another.[18]

These translations were quickly understood. If Bunting did not enjoy the financial remuneration which might have been his due (he was plagued by pirate editions in the first instance),[19] his 1797 collection nevertheless became the seedbed of antiquarian and creative endeavour in Irish music for at least half a century afterwards. Indeed it is precisely its seminal quality which writers have identified throughout the long history of its reception, a history which virtually extends to two centuries of commentary. Characteristic responses in 1816, 1847 and 1911 give some notion of the consensus which obtained as to the importance of Bunting's achievement:

...we allude to Mr Bunting – the first *musician* who had the good taste to admire the beauties of our music – the honesty and firmness to avow this admiration, regardless of the derision which it might excite – and the patriotism to devote his time and his talents to the preservation of what still survived the revaluations in government, and yet more important changes in manners and feelings, to which this Island has been subjected . . . The publication of Mr Bunting's first collection of airs was received with surprise by the *very* few who could be sensible of beauty in music that was not fashionable; The collection of Mr Bunting, . . . may be said to have given birth to several others whose titles are prefixed to this article.[20]

Of the excellence of the melodies in this first collection of Bunting's, it is scarcely possible to speak in terms too high . . . It has now been long out of print, and too generally forgotten; but the majority of its airs have been made familiar to the world by the genius of Moore, to whom it served as a treasury of melody, as may be gathered from the fact, that of the sixteen beautiful airs in the first number of 'The Irish Melodies', no less than eleven were derived from this source.[21]

The book stands . . . as the earliest standard authority on this department of study. Viewed with regard to its after effect in popularizing and saving Irish music, it must be classed as an epoch-making book. Not that its circulation was very extensive, for indeed it brought little profit to the young man who gave it to the world.[22]

Three themes recur in the reception of Bunting's early work: the attractiveness of the melodies, the crucial part which the book played in the redemption and rehabilitation of the ethnic tradition, and the creative debt which Thomas Moore incurred in his extensive use of the collection. The last of these was certainly ramified by matters of wider significance than personal acrimony, but the sense in which Bunting's subsequent collections were conditioned or modified by Moore's success is assuredly part of the cultural history of Irish music in the first half of the nineteenth century:

It is most probable . . . that considering the dilatoriness of Bunting's habits, the appearance of this [second] volume was somewhat hastened by the publication and extraordinary success of the first and second numbers of Moore's 'Irish Melodies', and it is certain that a natural spirit of emulation excited him to attempt a vain rivalry with it by the adaptation of English words to most of the vocal airs, and by a more successful one, by an expensive splendour of typography, not to be found in the musical publications of that poet – for it is easier to command good paper, engraving and printing, than good poetry.[23]

George Petrie made this observation in 1847; as a close collaborator and scholarly associate of Bunting's in later years, he was particularly well-placed to understand the inadequacy and misprision of Bunting's response to the early numbers of the *Irish Melodies*. Bunting's appeal was antiquarian: it could not be improved by a rash emulation of romantic individualism. But the attempt to provide English texts in the second volume of 1809, *A General Collection of the Ancient Music of Ireland, arranged for the pianoforte, some of the most admired melodies are adapted for the voice to poetry chiefly translated from the original Irish songs by Thomas Campbell, Esq., and other eminent poets, to which is prefixed a historical and critical dissertation on the Egyptian, British and Irish Harp, by Edward Bunting*, was attenuated by other factors. Between 1797 and 1809, collections of Irish airs by Smollet Holden and Lady Morgan (among others) had somewhat reduced the novelty of Bunting's enterprise.[24] Of considerably greater importance was the fact that Bunting's scholarly endeavours in the preparation of the 1809 volume were compromised by an admixture of personal and political circumstances. Bunting was not a United Irishman, but he counted among his closest companions those who were. His loyalty to such friends must have been strained when his major collaborator on the second volume, Patrick Lynch, turned King's evidence against their mutual friend Thomas Russell (1767–1803), with the result that he was hanged for high treason.[25] Bunting had embarked with Lynch on an extensive tour of Connacht in 1802 where Lynch collected and transcribed the texts of some 150 songs, many of which were intended for inclusion in the 1809 publication. Although Bunting obliquely refers to these texts in the preface, insofar as he 'wished to annex the original poetry in the Irish character [to the songs]', he clearly did not do so.[26] This can only be explained by Lynch's betrayal of Russell and his subsequently bitter estrangement from Bunting.[27]

It is difficult to gauge the extent to which political consciousness affected the structure and content of Bunting's collections; what is certain is that he was intimately connected with those who promoted revolutionary politics in Ireland, above all with the McCracken family in Belfast, with whom he lived for some forty years. But the problems which surrounded the 1809 volume were personal as well as political – Lynch's wounding betrayal of Russell being an admixture of the two. It is equally important to suggest, as Petrie did, that Bunting was unnerved by the success of the early numbers of Moore's *Melodies* and that the focus of Bunting's volume was badly affected as a result. The inherent tensions between antiquarian probity and popular appeal were redoubled by the self-conscious attempt to emulate Moore; the abrupt discontinuity of the volume itself, at least in Bunting's mind, must have been a fresh source of pain. To have fair copies of so much (Gaelic) text to hand and yet to withhold that text from publication is sufficient evidence of Bunting's distress.[28] Whether or not all of this was complicated by a rejected offer from Moore to write verses to the new airs is open to conjecture. Petrie, however, insists that 'it is certain that he deeply regretted, when it was too late, that he had not secured the aid of the great lyrist'. He drily adds that 'it may be doubted that the two instruments so differing in character would have run long together in smooth harmony'.[29]

*The Ancient Music of Ireland, arranged for the Pianoforte. To which is prefixed a dissertation on the Irish harp and harpers, including an account of the old melodies of Ireland. By Edward Bunting,* appeared in 1840. It forms the culmination of Bunting's career as an antiquarian. Having returned to the limitations of the first volume, i.e. arrangements of tunes without text (for the most part), Bunting's preface fortified the importance he attached to the authentic preservation and transmission of the ethnic repertory. His discourse on musical terminology, vocal style and melodic structure is more emphatic than before, and the inclusion of chapters by Samuel Ferguson and Petrie, on the 'Harp and Bagpipe' and the origin of the Brian Boru harp respectively, confirms that the 1840 volume is an act of consolidation, in which Bunting's painstaking disposition, classification and arrangement of 150 airs (many of them collected before 1809) is ratified by his junior contemporaries.[30]

The 1840 volume also clarifies the distance between Bunting's conception of authenticity and the romantic understanding of Irish music as a preponderantly melancholic expression of dispossession and loss:

> The world have been too apt to suppose our music of a highly plaintive and melancholy character, and that it partook of our National feeling at the state of our country *in a political view*, and that three parts out of four of our tunes were of this complaining nature. Now there never was anything more erroneous than this idea. [my italics][31]

Such an observation implicitly repudiates Thomas Moore, whose romantic perception (and projection) of the ethnic repertory so antagonised Bunting, especially given that it affronted the plain evidence which he had laboured to provide. That Bunting should regard Moore's romanticism as a 'political view', however, clearly attests his own awareness of the proximity between music and politics in Ireland. The manner in which this proximity had recast musical meaning was of paramount importance in Bunting's efforts to distinguish between authenticity and the uses of tradition. As ever, the Belfast Festival was Bunting's irreproachable witness to the aesthetic truth he sought to preserve undiminished in his collections, against the tide of romanticism which had broken over the ancient music of Ireland:

> The fact was the tunes were played with a great degree of animation at this meeting, quite different from the common adopted mode, which made them assume a new character and approached nearest to the national manners of the Irish, a spirited, animated and highly lively style, which certainly and in truth accords more with the natural character of the Irish than the drawling dead, doleful and die-away manner in which all our airs were and are in many instances played and sung to this day. . .[32]

Thus Bunting unambiguously disavowed the expressive conventions which by 1840 had steadily grown to characterise the ethnic repertory in its romantic address. The immense prestige of that address had been cultivated by Thomas Moore.

* * * * *

If antiquarianism – the recovery of the past – was overtaken by romanticism – the ideology of the present – in the first decade of the nineteenth century, that movement was nowhere more clearly traced than in music. Thomas Moore's alignment of the ethnic repertory with his own poetic was the decisive episode in this process. Seamus Deane remarks that he 'took some of the fruits of antiquarian labour and processed them for general consumption' and that he formulated a version of ancient Ireland which contemporary audiences (English and Irish) were happy to accept.[33] It was a version which depended openly and brilliantly on the simple candour of the drawing-room ballad. The understanding of Ireland which Moore purveyed in his songs was one which gained admission to the contemporary English mind through an arch-romantic synthesis of legend, political allusion, personal sentiment and domesticated Celticism. The last of these was drawn, of course, from existing musical sources as well as from Moore's verse, and the popular appeal of Celtic or pseudo-Celtic elements in music and poetry was one which Moore and his publishers exploited through the media of the English language and the romantic ballad.

One of the great problems which attends a reading of Moore's achievement in Irish cultural history is the perception that he stole from the dull antiquarians a priceless trove of melody which was then burnished by his own poetic bravura and skill. It is true that he borrowed heavily from Edward Bunting in the first instance (although only 38 of the 124 melodies are taken from Bunting).[34] It is also true, as he acknowledged himself, that his own interest in Irish music was as a consequence of reading Bunting's first collection. [35] But it is equally true that, from the beginning, Moore was alert to the political transformation of expression which Bunting's collected airs would allow. If Irish nationalism and republicanism effectively date from the 1790s, the impact of these ideas upon music dates from the early issues of Moore's *Melodies* in 1807 and 1808.[36]

That Moore himself would be overtaken by a more strident nationalism which added militant immediacy and subtracted the aesthetics of art music is an issue which lies beyond the concerns of this chapter. What is of moment here is the distinctive note of transformation by which Moore eclipsed not only Bunting's antiquarianism but also the 'Hibernian strain' of those publications of Irish music which followed in the wake of the 1797 *General Collection*. The transformation of Moore in turn, from romantic agent of Irish emancipation (and specifically Catholic emancipation) to hated darling of the Victorian parlour, is one that belongs to the sectarian projection of Gaelic culture, which in part characterised the Celtic revival of the late 1870s. Between 1807 and the advent of the Famine, however, Moore's voice was the conduit of a romanticised political sentiment which had its origins in the United Irishmen, the failure of rebellion and the newly symbolic force of the music itself.

The United Irishmen were a formative influence in Moore's education as a (Catholic) student in Trinity College, Dublin, from 1794 until 1800.[37] The air in Trinity was thick with insurrection, and the college itself appears to have been a venue for covert dissidence. If it seems difficult now to accept the admixture of student rhetoric and violent rebellion, no one can seriously doubt the continuity of thought and action which existed between them. Moore was close to the centre of this maelstrom and his intimate companions were closer still. That the government in Ireland should seek to determine the existence or otherwise of a lodge of United Irishmen in Trinity in 1797 makes plain the climate of danger and conspiracy which prevailed in the wake of 1796 and the French fiasco which took place late in that year.[38]

Two United Irishmen in particular, Edward Hudson and Robert Emmet, were central both to the plans for rebellion and to Moore himself. It was Hudson who introduced Moore to Bunting's collection and to Irish music generally, in 1797. It was Emmet to whom Moore played from the collection, exciting the apocryphal response: 'Oh, that I were at the head of twenty thousand men marching to that air!'[39]

How reliable are Moore's memoirs in respect of such anecdotes is admittedly an open question. What is certain, however, is that Moore's personal association with Hudson and Emmet, the one imprisoned and the other executed, deeply informed his understanding of Irish music. His poetic transformation of Emmet's disgrace almost immediately passed into myth: an anonymously printed version of Emmet's Speech from the Dock was circulated in Dublin c. 1811 which bore as epigraph the first verse of Moore's poem 'Oh, blame not the bard';[40] the early numbers of the *Irish Melodies* published at the same time admit a preoccupation with the romanticised figure of Emmet as traduced hero. Moore, unlike Bunting, was not silent at the betrayal of his violent friends. His poetic voice, on the contrary, was manifestly inspired by them.

This inspiration proved decisive for Moore's aesthetic understanding of the music which he found in Bunting and elsewhere. The essence of this understanding was an association which Moore repeatedly drew between the *inherent* nature of Irish melody as he apprehended it and the historical conditions of oppression, lament and betrayal which he believed to be its source. Without labouring the point, the contrast with Bunting could scarcely be more extreme:

> The language of sorrow, however, is in general best suited to our Music, and with themes of this nature the poet may be amply supplied. There is scarcely a page of our annals that will not furnish him a subject, and while the national Muse of other countries adorns her temple proudly with trophies of the past, in Ireland her melancholy altar, like the shrine of Pity at Athens, is to be known only by the tears that are shed upon it . . .

> Surely, if music ever spoke the misfortunes of a people, or could ever con-
> ciliate forgiveness for their errors, the music of Ireland ought to possess these
> powers.[41]

This was not romantic posturing after the event: Moore published these remarks as part of an appendix to his political satire, *Intolerance*, which appeared anonymously in 1808. Moore observed of it that 'this fragment was originally intended to form part of a preface to the *Irish Melodies*; but for some reason which I do not now recollect, was thrown aside'. The reason may have been that this peremptory address upon the 'sad degrading truths' of Ireland's recent history which Moore included in the appendix to *Intolerance* would not sit well with the apparently innocent solicitations of a drawing-room *ballade*.

*Intolerance* itself fortifies the concept of Irish music that is so variously and winningly explored in the *Melodies*, which appeared in ten numbers published between 1807 and 1834. The poem savagely condemns the contemporary architects of imperial repression and penal tyranny, whose legal strictures are so purposefully advanced in the interest of a Protestant polity:

> Who, arm'd at once with prayer-books and with whips,
> Blood on their hands, and Scripture on their lips,
> Tyrants by creed, and torturers by text,
> Make *this* life hell, in honour of the next!. . .[42]

Moore also wagers here on the immanence of poetry and Irish music against these righteous cruelties:

> Oh! turn awhile, and though the shamrock wreathes
> My homely harp, yet shall the song it breathes
> Of Ireland's slavery, and of Ireland's woes,
> Live, when the memory of her tyrant foes
> Shall but exist, all future knaves to warn
> Embalm'd in hate and canonised by scorn.[43]

Moore's poetic was thus explicitly informed by a cultural understanding of Irish music (and poetry) that would speak to those themes of recent political history which had informed it in the first place. His musical understanding was of course reinforced by his own responsibilities as a musician, wherein lay the source of his protracted dispute with Bunting. His famous journal entry for 15 July 1840 on the receipt of the third volume of Bunting's collection tellingly discloses not only this enduring sense of responsibility, but also the sense of positive technical enhancement which was the abiding feature of his approach to the traditional sources themselves:

> Received from Cramers & Co. a copy of Bunting's newly-published Irish Airs,
> which they have often written to me about, as likely, they thought, to furnish
> materials for a continuation of the Melodies. Tried them over with some anxi-

ety, as, had they contained a sufficient number of beautiful airs to make another volume, I should have felt myself bound to do the best I could with them . . .
. . . the whole task of selecting the airs and in some respects shaping them thus, in particular passages, to the general sentiment, which the melody appeared to me to express was undertaken solely by myself. Had I not ventured on these very admissible liberties many of the songs now most known and popular would have been still sleeping with all their authentic dross about them in Mr Bunting's first Volume.[44]

In part, Moore's reaction here is relief (he condemns the 1840 volume as 'a mere mess of trash') and in part, defence: he cites Bunting's acknowledgement of his own achievement ('the most beautiful popular songs that perhaps have ever been composed by any lyric poet') and he clarifies his own responsibilities with regard to the alteration of Bunting's originals, as against Bunting's mistaken allocation of these to Sir John Stevenson. Beyond these discriminations, the passage makes clear in the candid terms of a journal entry the distance between antiquarianism and romanticism. Moore's observations apostrophise the romantic understanding of music which so powerfully and detrimentally would endure in the Irish mind for a century afterwards. He took it as virtually given that the pressures of an historically informed imagination should transform the object of Bunting's fastidious preservation (notwithstanding the latter's own modifications) into a source of *textual* expression. That this expression in turn would function as an agent of nationalistic self-determination was not part of Moore's immediate concern. His concept of Irish music remained strictly relative to the sources which he found in Bunting and elsewhere. But Moore's achievement was crucial in the gradual polarisation of Irish music, insofar as he himself was prepared to insist upon a distinction between the authenticity of tradition and the contingent immediacy of his own use of that tradition.

What is too little understood, perhaps, is Moore's creative dependence upon the ethnic repertory. His own poetic was uniquely stimulated by his exposure to it and the *Melodies* inaugurated a bitter quarrel between tradition and innovation which would long thrive in Irish musical discourse. The *Melodies* also proposed a constricting intimacy between artistic and ethnic modes of expression which was to inhibit the growth of musical thought: Moore quite deliberately mediated between the musical past and the political present with a romantic zeal which for a time all but exhausted the concept of creative music in Ireland.

Moore had never publicly disavowed his sense of duty towards 'the national airs of my country'. In a letter 'On Music' addressed to Lady Donegal in the third number of the Melodies (1810), he remarks that he has endeavoured to regain from the 'tasteless decorations' of 'our own itinerant musicians' the 'pure gold of the melody'.[45] In its way, this kind of effort is ironically reminiscent of Bunting's own arrangements. Moore merely took the concept of musical translation a step further.

Sir John Stevenson's part in this process had been a source of controversy from the beginning.[46] His contribution was on one level innocuous enough. As a competent but not especially original musician, Stevenson added brief preludes and postludes ('symphonies') to his piano harmonisations of the airs. An anonymous critic (George Petrie) in *The Dublin Examiner* in 1816 remarked that these additions possessed 'nothing kindred with the airs which they introduce' and bluntly suggested that 'they are too much in the common style of the second-rate composers of the day, whose works obtain a popularity by being adapted to the taste, as well as the fingers of the young ladies to whom more finished productions would be unintelligible'.[47]

Much else in this vein (and worse) attended criticism of Stevenson's work throughout the nineteenth century. As Moore's position as national bard was consolidated, Stevenson's accompaniments came to seem more repulsive than the 'authentic dross' which they sought to dispel. Two general observations comprise a modest defence of his position: one is that his symphonies stand scrupulously apart from the modest accompaniment of the airs, so that Moore's version of the melody in question is scarcely ever complicated by extraneous musical matter; there is also the quality of musical invention, insofar as Stevenson's contributions attempt an absolute expression of the mood of the verse by means of an independent, though motivically related pianism. That Stevenson should have sought in this way to provide more than a bland keyboard accompaniment does not perhaps seem as offensive now as it did to those contemporaries who regarded his interventions as 'tawdry and modern upholstery'.[48] There is a case to be made for these 'symphonies' as the musical correlative of Moore's ennobled syntax. But it is a weak case. There remains the insuperable deficiency of style which results from the abrupt discontinuity between the preludes, vocal settings and postludes. Melodic structure and verbal feeling powerfully coincide in the verses. The symphonies seem all the more disjointed as a consequence.

Stevenson's material aside, the Bunting 'originals' and Moore's *Melodies* when taken together can appear to contradict the disparities between them, given that the identification of such differences was to become such a conventional feature of hostile Moore criticism through the nineteenth century. 'Oh! breathe not his name' from the first number and its Bunting original 'The brown maid' offer a case in point. Moore's adaptation is all but exact, and his few alterations obviously are intended to facilitate the scansion of his verse. He omits the ornamentation indicated in the harp version (Bunting) and introduces a single grace note to accentuate the close of the penultimate vocal phrase. A few rhythmic alterations also improve the word setting. Otherwise, Moore follows the key, time signature, tempo and tonal harmonisation of Bunting's version. It is the words which materially distinguish the antiquarian from the lyric poet, at least in this instance. Moore's typically allusive contemplation of Robert Emmet, versed in 'soft imperatives' (Seamus Deane), finds an exactly apposite musical context in the tune transcribed and arranged by Edward Bunting. It is only the symphonies by the hapless Stevenson which sound gauche, impertinent, redundant. Moore's verse otherwise finds definitive projection in the melody itself. One can hear why Bunting should have been thought to be so distressed when this Moore–Stevenson version of 'The brown maid' appeared: not because it distorted the original, but because it so authoritatively transcended it.[49]

Moore's 'Oh! blame not the bard', published as the third air of the third number in 1810, carries a note which is reminiscent of the Walker–Burney controversy a generation earlier: 'We may suppose this apology [i.e. "blame not the bard"] to have been uttered by one of those wandering bards whom Spencer [sic] so severely, and perhaps, truly describes in his state of Ireland...'[50] The poetic intent is also clear:

> Then blame not the bard, if in pleasure's soft dream
> He should try to forget what he never can heal

Moore's favourite theme of art impoverished, even emasculated, by Irish history is plainly but nevertheless decorously rehearsed in these verses. We are far from the brutal truths of *Intolerance* or the satirical indictments which were to come in the novel *Captain Rock*.[51] It is just this quality of decorum which here gains Moore such memorable access to the drawing-rooms of London and Dublin. But unlike the cultural attritions of Lady Morgan's *Wild Irish Girl*,[52] Moore's songs collectively and individually attribute blame and seek restitution. If it is not too much to say that the *Melodies* 'formed the secular hymn-book of Irish nationalism',[53] one must add that these songs are well made and well bred: their popularity ought not to disguise these qualities. For Moore's contemporaries, moreover, they provided a cultural interface between the English mind and that Gaelic civilisation which the Ascendancy had so largely failed to comprehend.

Given Moore's proximity to both traditions, it is not difficult to regard the poetic voice of 'Oh! blame not the bard' as one which extends beyond the role of cultural interlocutor. The poem is at least an oblique *apologia pro vita sua*: it is as if Moore's poetic voice has been dislocated by the harsh facts of Irish political and social history which he castigates so exactly elsewhere. Moore's 'suppressed' preface to the first number of the *Melodies* supports this sense of dislocation, in that the contemporary poet therein is obliged by recent history either to speak by allusion or to give himself over to a celebration of 'Ancient Days':

> But the sceptic is scarcely to be envied who would pause for stronger proofs than we already possess of the early glories of Ireland; and were even the veracity of all these proofs surrendered, yet who would not fly to such flattering fictions from the sad degrading truths which the history of later times presents to us?[54]

We might suggest that Moore rationalised his own stance as an artist in 'Oh! blame not the bard' by advancing the same argument in poetry.[55]

Although Moore's word setting has sometimes been criticised for its poor emphasis,[56] the characteristically sensitive marriage of text and pre-existent melody (itself a reversal of the ordinary procedure) which his best songs enjoy is evident even in the use of harp tunes from the Bunting collection. Whatever the exact provenance of 'Kitty Tyrrell', Moore knew it as the arrangement of a harp melody when he took it from Bunting as the basis for 'Oh! blame not the bard'.[57] Bunting's arrangement and Moore's melody both strongly preserve the profile of a moderately paced harp air, notwithstanding the removal of triplets, trills and turns in Moore's version. Other than these modifications, Moore lowered the original pitch by a fifth to accommodate a medium vocal range and introduced passing notes and some intervallic alterations, notably the widening of the sixth, which so prominently features in Bunting's version, to an octave. This is not so much the removal of authentic dross as the technical accommodation of poetic sensibility. Moore's appeal in the text is conditioned by the musical terms of reference (Irish, Gaelic, authentic) which the melody defines. To juxtapose Bunting's version with the Moore–Stevenson arrangement is to confirm the continuity of cultural discourse between the two. Moore's poetic *apologia* gains inestimable impact by virtue of its lyric articulation: to observe as much amounts to a truism. What is not perhaps as immediately evident is that Moore's romantic individualism qualifies the antiquarian integrity of the Bunting originals. It was this which so distressed Bunting. Moore's success as the 'bard of Erin' transformed the *Ancient Irish Music* from antiquarian collection to romantic source. It was not a permanent transformation, and in antiquarian terms it remained an indefensible one. But we cannot disclaim the fact that Moore's poetic was advanced and developed by his fantastically successful recourse to the melodies which Bunting had so painstakingly (if intermittently) struggled to preserve. At the last, the difference between them was that Moore became interested in the past as an image of the present, whereas Bunting was committed to the past for its own sake.

This difference did not disrupt the perceived continuity between them which had been established almost immediately upon the publication of the early numbers of the *Melodies*. The response from Tory journals like the *Anti-Jacobin Review* to Moore was predictably severe: 'Several of them [the melodies] were composed with a view to their becoming popular in a very disordered state of society . . . They are the melancholy ravings of the disappointed rebel, or his ill-educated offspring.'[58] Otherwise, Moore's immense popularity in the drawing-room found an interesting critical parallel in those sections of the press constitutionally sympathetic to the idea of political reform. The long review-essay on Bunting, Moore and related publications by Petrie which appeared anonymously in *The Dublin Examiner* in August 1816 typifies the general perception of Moore as bardic redeemer of Irish music, fruitfully dependent upon the Old Testament of Bunting's endeavours: 'It was this work [Bunting], we understand, that excited the taste, and raised the ambition of our bard, to immortalise at once himself and our country.'[59]

The distinction between Moore and Bunting was not necessarily blurred by such encomia, even if the sense of Bunting having been overtaken by a movement which extended beyond the music itself tended to prevail in such assessments. Moore's arguments for the recent provenance of much Irish melody, however, which he emphatically associated with the privations of modern Irish history, were technically challenged by writers who took Bunting's side on the ancient and purely preserved condition of the music, which the latter had noted down.[60] For many writers, a recent provenance was all but incompatible with the authentic tradition of Irish music.

Moore's own voice would in turn be overtaken by the more strident claims of Young Ireland and by the balladry of Thomas Davis and his colleagues who contributed to *The Nation* newspaper. The *Melodies* would never lose their symbolic force as a cumulative petition for self-regulation; neither would they quite shake off the aura of the drawing-room. If Moore's art derived in significant measure from his personal association with the United Irishmen and his acute sense of political and social injustice, it also firmly belonged to a social milieu which disdained such preoccupations:

> 'And can this', thought we, taking up the 'Melodies' – 'can this be forgotten?' No; these songs are no longer as they were, popular only in the drawing-rooms of Europe and America; they are gradually becoming known to the middle classes in Ireland, and the Irish translation bids fair to reach the mind of our peasantry. It may be fault or excellence in them; but Moore's songs bear translation. They not only have appeared in every European language, but they supplied the Poles with their most popular revolutionary songs during the last war – the highest honour ever shown to a lyrist . . .[61]

It is instructive to find such lines being written as early as 1842 by Charles Gavan Duffy, a principal architect of Young Ireland. These sentiments eclipse the antiquarian–romantic debate in favour of a new concern with Moore as an ardent propagandist of nationalism in Europe, and by extension in Ireland. In such terms Moore becomes the well-spring of a nationalism in music which is functional, symbolic, ineluctably textual. The *Irish Melodies* begin to enjoy a cultural afterlife that is not confined to nostalgic remembrance. On the contrary, they establish a vibrant exchange between politics and Irish music which itself becomes conventional and well-nigh inescapable.

Moore's prestige was such that he permanently endowed the Irish mind with a sense of music that all but occluded the wider aesthetic of European norms in the nineteenth century. The very success of his transformation of the ethnic repertory inhibited an independent mode of art music, and the symbolic potency which his union of music and text achieved made it effectively impossible for subsequent composers to escape the supreme anxiety of his influence. This anxiety did not extend to Moore's own prowess as a musician; it rather concerned the preoccupation with 'folk song' which his *Melodies* had entered as an enduring obstacle in the development of creative musical thought in Ireland. He not only politicised the ethnic repertory: he also ensured that it would predominate in all considerations of music as a modern art form in Ireland.

# ANTIQUARIANISM AND POLITICS
## Davis, Petrie, Hyde and the Growth of Music in a Sectarian Culture[1]

Music is the first faculty of the Irish, and scarcely anything has such power for good over them. The use of this faculty and this power, publicly and constantly, to keep up their spirits, refine their tastes, warm their courage, increase their union and renew their zeal is the duty of every patriot.[2]

This awful, unwonted silence, which, during the famine and subsequent years almost everywhere prevailed, struck more fearfully upon their imaginations, as many Irish gentlemen informed me, and gave them a deeper feeling of the desolation with which the country had been visited, than any other circumstance which had forced itself upon their attention; and I confess that it was a consideration of the circumstances of which this fact gave so striking an indication, that, more than any other, overpowered all my objections and influenced me in coming to a determination to accept the proposal of the Irish-Music Society.[3]

In a society made inert by repressive authority, the work of art becomes the quintessential deed.[4]

The contingent relationship between music and Irish political and cultural history in the nineteenth century was of such intensity that it may be said to have determined the central aesthetic difficulties of music as an emancipated art in Ireland. The antiquarian restoration of music as a fact of the past, a past radically endangered by the Famine, rather than as an image of the present (as in Moore), is necessarily a primary consideration in the perception of music in Irish cultural history. And set against this antiquarianism was the dependent growth of balladry as an expression of the politics of Young Ireland and of nationalism in general. The strength of this association between political aspiration and musical expression is one which all but eclipsed the possibility of independent musical growth. The art tradition lapsed into mediocrity or silence. In its stead, the preoccupation with an identifiably 'Irish' music was such that a bifurcated development (music as folklore, music as political propaganda) endured in the Irish mind to the extent that the Celtic revival of the 1890s for the most part accommodated not music *per se*, but music as a symbol of renascent Irish culture.[5]

In this chapter, I should like to consider that development in terms of its two principal constituents: the consolidation of antiquarian research as the expression of a Gaelic musical culture, and the exponential growth of the ballad tradition as an agent of political and cultural nationalism. The projection of music as a symbol of sectarian culture and its simultaneous development as a utilitarian function of political aspiration entailed fateful consequences for the understanding and reception of the art throughout the nineteenth century and most of the twentieth century in Ireland. The self-conscious re-animation of ethnic musical expression and the subordinate but powerful medium of ballad singing occluded any other significant mode of musical development. In particular, the European aesthetic of art music could not survive the polarisation of musical norms in Ireland which were circumscribed and defined by political and cultural associations. The failure of genres, ideologies and styles of musical expression which did not reflect the demands of Celtic revivalism or nationalism is self-evidently of concern in this study of music and Irish cultural history. But the claims of nationalism and antiquarianism themselves enjoy prior urgency. These were the forces which respectively depended upon and advanced the concept of a palpably *Irish* music. This concept in turn determined all other musical issues in its wake.

\* \* \* \* \*

Oliver MacDonagh distinguishes between the doctrinaire republicanism of the United Irishmen (and of Wolfe Tone in particular) and the aspirations of the Young Ireland movement of the 1840s in this way:

> There were apparent similarities in the two cries to break the connection with England and in the two declarations that Catholic, Protestant and Dissenter formed a single flock. But Tone's and Davis's words had very different provenances and contexts. The apparent or verbal similarities should not blind us to the revolution which Romanticism had really wrought. The new emphasis was on cultural division and cultural hostility; on emotion rather than rationality; on group rights rather than individual; on a subjective and creative rather than a formal and negative concept of independence; and of course, in the very long run, on race and language, as in the Fatherland. In essentials, Young Ireland was the harbinger of Ireland after Parnell, of the New Ireland of the 1890s.[6]

It is not difficult, perhaps, to read modern Irish history as a succession of phases which alternate constitutional reform, romantic nationalism and outright rebellion. But there is difficulty in the pre-eminence of cultural sectarianism which MacDonagh perceives as the essence of the Young Ireland movement. The difficulty is at least religious and linguistic, if not racial. Rejected by European nationalists because of the language question, the Young Irelanders nevertheless articulated a powerful condition of feeling which differed clearly from the loyal emotions of Daniel O'Connell's massive following and the armed agitations of Fenianism and the Irish Republican Brotherhood.[7]

They channelled that feeling by means of periodical debate and propaganda. However fractious their relationship with O'Connell, however dependent (at least initially) on the principles of his immense popularity, the Young Irelanders eventually understood their proper domain to be the weekly journal which they founded in 1842, *The Nation*. Roy Foster estimates its readership in 1843 as 'possibly 250,000', and he singles out the celebration of violent resistance to England ('so long as it was safely in the past') as a recurring trope in the material which it published.[8]

Cultural separatism may have (in part) been an outgrowth of European romanticism; the cult of violent struggle, sectarian demeanour and Anglophobia was, however, more local in origin: 'Young Ireland took to logical extremes the feelings that O'Connell alternately pandered to, and conjured away again.'[9] This characterisation of O'Connell as panderer (rather than as constitutional reformer) throws into sharp relief the apparently naive ardour of the Young Ireland movement by contrast.[10] However crudely programmatic its political agenda, Young Ireland harvested a wider movement of the spirit which flourished principally by means of rhetoric, leisurely analysis and verse. The group of writer-activists who centred upon *The Nation* – preeminently Thomas Davis (1814–45), Charles Gavan Duffy (1816–1903) and John Blake Dillon (1816–66) – were not merely purveyors of doggerel verse, even if they did attract to *The Nation* a whole sub-genre of ballad poetry devoted to the politics of repeal and (ultimately) the cult of Catholic nationalism. At the least, they were political ideologues whose genius for popular sentiment was realised by periodical literature.[11] The success of *The Nation* (its explicit manifesto being 'to create and foster public opinion and make it racy of the soil') provided a cultural context in which the nationalist debate could be effectively conducted. Gavan Duffy, writing in 1890, recalled that the journal was an immediate sell-out on its first appearance, and that its original contributors included not only Davis and Dillon, but also the antiquarians John O'Donovan and Eugene Curry. Gavan Duffy continues:

> The form and appearance of the journal were new in Ireland; political verses were printed among the leading articles and claiming equal attention, and there was a distinct department for literature. The first leader declared . . . we would recognize only two parties in Ireland – those who suffered by her degradation and those who profited by it. Clarence Mangan proclaimed our second purpose – to be the emancipators of the trampled peasantry.[12]

It is useful to regard *The Nation* as part of that tradition of periodical discourse represented in nineteenth-century Ireland by such journals as the *Dublin Review* and *The Dublin University Magazine*, the latter brilliantly characterised by W. J. McCormack as 'the supreme archive of Irish Victorian experience'.[13] Much of *The Nation's* structure and content were clearly dependent on this tradition, its 'National Gallery', for example, a distinct echo of the 'Portrait Gallery' in *The Dublin University Magazine*; its cogent and politically charged appraisal of Irish literature and other periodicals a succinct reworking of more leisurely considerations published elsewhere, as in the essays on Moore, on the novels of Charles Lever and on *The Dublin University Magazine* itself which *The Nation* carried in 1842 and 1843.[14]

The presence of music as an integral force is strikingly apparent in both *The Dublin University Magazine* and *The Nation*, even if the latter brought to its consideration of music a degree of utilitarian urgency hitherto unknown in Irish periodical literature.

Urgency was in effect the keynote of *The Nation's* address as the organ of Young Ireland, and the cultural separatism which it preached was a vital preliminary to its romantic vision of Ireland as a politically independent entity. This vision was immediate and clear, not least because the radical sense of history which Young Ireland embraced was predicated upon a commitment to the nation state which eclipsed Catholic emancipation and repeal of the Union. The emphasis which *The Nation* gave to matters of race and language, and the explicit programme of nationalist opinion which it fostered, entailed a remarkable appropriation of cultural history towards the political climate which it endeavoured to influence.

Thomas Davis was foremost in this enterprise. Roy Foster laconically observes that the Young Irelanders 'cherished a certain cult of Carlyle, reading Sartor Resartus while undertaking rapt tours of the Irish landscape'.[15] Their prodigiously romantic awareness, however, did not languish in impotent self-regard. On the contrary, the influence which they exerted on the political complexion of the arts in Ireland endured long after the voice of *The Nation* itself had faded into silence. The rhetorical energy of Davis's contribution in this respect was such that he encompassed in prescriptive detail the functions of music as well as poetry, and his peculiar achievement was to affect profoundly the perception of music as a special form of political address in Ireland. That music should be hospitable to political history, that it should voice the aspirations of the politically aware individual, was a cliché of romantic nationalism and of music generally after the French Revolution. That music should be cultivated *expressly* to foster a climate of political opinion was Davis's special form of belief, and one which vividly enlisted the ballad tradition of which his verses were a part.

This distinction in Davis's musical thought – that cultural history in the making should influence, rather than be influenced by politics – is a significant development in the projection of Irish music as the outgrowth of a sectarian culture. *The Nation*, together with its offspring *The Spirit of the Nation*, conveniently locates the articulation of this thought.

Gavan Duffy's famous apostrophe, 'Davis loved and sang the whole Irish people', succinctly characterises the thrust of this thinking.[16] The imperative sweep of Duffy's judgement is much nearer to Davis's own conception of his ambition, which was not to cultivate music for its own sake, but to endow it with an inherently programmatic function. The equally utilitarian motivation of his prose and poetry makes this clear:

> It would be unjust and unskilful criticism to judge the verses Davis wrote in intervals of his busy and stormy life by the canons we apply to a poet in his solitude. They altogether mistake his character, indeed, who regard him as distinctively a poet or a writer. His aims were far away from literary success: All his labour, tended only to discipline and stimulate the people. He looked to share in guiding the counsels of a nation he had prompted into action and marshalled to victory. The place he would have loved to fill was not beside Moore or Goldsmith, but beside O'Neill, Tone and Grattan.[17]

Duffy, Davis's intimate friend, his close colleague on *The Nation* and his biographer, exactly understood the prescriptive function of Davis's verse and cultural commentary. Both derived from the absolute belief in nationalism not as an ill-defined aspiration but as the terminus of systematic and programmatic change. Davis enlisted every material and spiritual entity of which he could conceive in the service of this programme, which embraced a bewildering assortment of subject matter, on which he was prepared to pronounce, often with compelling rhetorical finesse.[18]

If it is fair to suggest that Davis's reading of music was chiefly as a matter of political resource, it is equally fair to propose that his own sense of Irish music was not altogether crudely propagandistic. Three essays from *The Nation* – 'Irish Music and Poetry', 'A Ballad History of Ireland' and 'Irish Songs' – offer a conspectus of Davis's musical thought which clarifies his remarkable sense of music not merely as an adjunct but also as an instigator of political change. That Davis was keen to locate Irish music within the history of Irish ideas is beyond doubt: his review of John O'Donovan's translation of *The Tribes and Territory of Hy-Fiachrach* includes the characteristic observation that the antiquarianism of Walker and his peers 'smoothed the reception of Bunting's music, and identified Moore's poetry with his native country'.[19]

'Irish Music and Poetry' typifies the blend of persuasive chauvinism and pragmatism which informs Davis's reading of the condition of music in Ireland.[20] He traces explicitly narrative or descriptive functions in the ethnic repertory ('The hunter joins in every leap and yell of the "Fox Chase"; the historian hears the moan of penal days in "Drimindhu"'); and he condemns the influence of European music, specifically art music: 'paltry scented things from Italy'. Davis justifies the 'popularity and immense circulation' of *The Spirit of the Nation* on the grounds that 'almost all of the Irish political songs [prior to its appearance in 1843] are too desponding or weak to content a people marching to independence'.[21]

The 'little sixpenny book' which appeared in March 1843 as *The Spirit of the Nation* was regarded by Davis as a symbol of renascent nationalism in Ireland, and the verses it contained required 'new music to be sought for them':

Not on their account only was it to be sought. We hoped they would be the means of calling out and making known a contemporary music fresh with the spirit of the time and rooted in the country.

Since Carolan's death there had been no addition to the store. Not that we were without composers, but those we have do not compose Irish-like music, nor for Ireland. Their rewards are from a foreign public – their fame, we fear, will suffer from alienage. Balfe is very sweet and Rooke very emphatic, but not one passion or association in Ireland's heart would answer to their songs.[22]

There is barely a discrimination here offered between 'Irish-like music' and music 'for Ireland'. Davis is not incapable of responding aesthetically to Balfe, but the extreme chauvinism of his sense of Ireland, in a phrase, his cultural separatism, excludes the work of such composers from any significant part in the nation state which he constantly envisages. This would not be of much moment were it not that Davis was so successfully to polarise and germinate the idea of Irish nationalism. Under the aegis of this idea, his conception of music was widely and enthusiastically adopted.

'A Ballad History of Ireland' reinforces both Davis's sense of music in Ireland as an ideally functional concept in the service of political and (morally) prescriptive norms and his utilitarian attitude to the music itself:

In olden times, all ballads were made to music . . . Printing so multiplies copies of ballads . . . that there is less need of this adaptation to music now. Moreover, it may be disputed whether the dramatic effect in the more solemn ballads is not injured by lyrical forms. In such streaming exhortations and laments as we find in the Greek choruses and in the adjurations and caoines of the Irish, the breaks and parallel repetitions of a song might lower the passion.[23]

There is no sense here that Davis wishes to dispense with the prior condition of music; if anything, his understanding of Irish music as a legacy, as an inheritance for the benefit of the Irish people, is strikingly naive and simplistic: the corpus of Irish airs exists for Davis in the same way that the mountains and valleys exist. The topography of Ireland, the sensibility of being Irish and the cultural stasis of 'Irish music' are all of a piece to him and all are vulnerable to the same purposeful exhortations ('A man who has not raced on our hills, panted on our mountains, waded our rivers . . . is not master of all a Balladist's art.'). But in the composition of ballads, expressly for the purpose of relating 'the past, present and future, in words so perfect that generations shall feel and remember', the programmatic objective may thoughtfully exclude the cultivation of music, even Irish music, for its own sake.

Davis is the first ideologue of significance to *prescribe* the cultural placement of music in Ireland, and his reading of 'Irish Songs' represents his most sustained contemplation of this issue.[24] In this essay he projects anthologies respectively entitled 'Songs of the Irish Nation' and 'Songs for the Fields and

Streets', 'to be published with music, either in parts or in single songs' (Davis's ital-ics). This project is envisaged as an original enterprise and not as a recapitu-lation of Bunting and Moore. Davis takes pains to distinguish between three categories of Irish song: the lyrics of Moore, the 'Songs of the Irish-speaking people . . . composed during the last century' and contemporary ballads:

> It may be said that Moore is lyrist enough for Ireland. We might show that though he is perfect in his expression of the softer feelings, and unrivalled even by Burns in many of his gay songs, yet, that he is often deficient in vehemence, does not speak of the sterner passions, spoils some of his finest songs by pretty images, is too refined and subtle in his dialect, and too negligent of narrative.[25]

Of songs in the native tradition:

> Their structure is irregular, their grief slavish and bombastic, their religion bit-ter and sectarian, their politics Jacobite, and concealed by extravagant and tire-some allegory.[26]

Ballads, finally, are characterised by:

> Some humour, some tenderness, and some sweetness of sound; but you will certainly find bombast, or slander, or coarseness, united in all cases with false rhythm, false rhyme, conceited imagery, black paper, and blotted printing.[27]

Such discriminations, which are textual rather than musical ('It is not needful for a writer of our songs to be a musician'[28]), nevertheless circum-scribe Davis's reading of Irish music in the past as imperfect to the require-ments of the present. The criticism of Moore echo a general impatience on the part of Young Ireland with 'the wail of a lost cause'; they also affirm the naively programmatic perception of cultural history which is endemic to Davis's romantic nationalism, in which prevailing responsibilities to narrative and ideology occlude aesthetic understanding.

'Narrative' is worth a moment's further reflection. As with Moore's set-tings, Davis (in this instance) finds in the ethnic repertory a style of language distorted by sectarian hatred and extravagant conceit. For Davis, the purpose of song is to bring 'Love, Courage and Patriotism' to every heart and in every department of life: 'Fair and Theatre, Concert and Drawing-room, Road and Shop'.[29] These prescriptions, at least in 'Irish Songs', assume that the condi-tion of the music itself is inherently of the past, the 'great heritage of national music'. The method of songwriting proposed in this essay – 'to learn an air for the purpose of writing words to it' – supposes that music exists as a resource for the propagation of political ideology, a *prior* resource which is incapable of any other function or independent growth. Davis, in short, cannot accom-modate a music which is not subordinate to ideology and which is removed from the 'heritage' of Bunting and Moore.

These incapacities partly explain the artless condition of music in *The Spirit of the Nation*. In style and appearance, the 1845 edition, which includes music for many of the songs, resembles the collections of Moore and Bunting. In effect, its intention was to 'supersede the miserable street ballads'.[30] *The Spirit of the Nation* occupied a midway point between the drawing-room and the highway; its immense popularity appeared to signify that it represented 'the hopes and passions of the Irish people',[31] and its persistently martial strain (exemplified by 'Clare's Dragoons', 'Step Together' and 'A Nation Once Again', all by Davis) appeared to fortify the hope expressed in the preface that such songs would be played by the temperance bands and sung by 'young men, ay, and the young women' who would 'chorus them till village and valley ring'.[32] The rhetorical energy of these remarks, as of the songs themselves, echoes the good heart of Davis, whose prescriptive zeal ignites the simplistic but potent ardour of the whole collection.

As hymns of romantic nationalism, the songs in *The Spirit of the Nation* exemplify the function of music in a bi-cultural society. Bland but expertly marked piano accompaniments support the original or parodistic Irish airs, which are themselves secondary to the projection of political and cultural propaganda. Davis and his collaborators knew Moore well, but they were scarcely in a position to emulate him, except insofar as they added original texts to pre-existent melodies. Moore's songs and the battle-hymns of *The Spirit of the Nation* do not otherwise profit by comparison: we do better to respect the avowed intention of Davis and Duffy to move decisively beyond the wail of a lost cause towards 'the virile and passionate hopes of a new generation'.[33]

That the writers associated with *The Nation* could not distinguish between Moore and their own achievement (except in terms of feeling) betrays not only a degree of aesthetic naïvety but more tellingly a sense of music which remaindered it firmly to the past. Music became the resource of nationalist sentiment and the trove of cultural remembrance under the duress of romantic idealism. In Davis's essays, in his songs, in *The Spirit of the Nation*, it is this trope of musical remembrance which prevails. Davis was not ignorant of antiquarian musical research and the collections which this research had nurtured: on the contrary, he divined in the collections a *status quo* which rationalised both his own perception of music (within the nationalist credo he so firmly espoused) and a functional role which music might enjoy in the new Irish nation. Davis's belief that musical prowess was endemic to the Irish and that its cultivation in the service of patriotism was of primary importance apostrophises two fundamentals of Irish music reception history: that the Irish were profoundly musical, and that their music ought principally to be a conduit of socio-political aspiration. Neither of these fundamentals originates with Davis, but he more than any other consolidated them both.

\*   \*   \*   \*   \*

The development of cultural nationalism did not belong exclusively to Young Ireland. That Davis should regard music as a means of mobilising political opinion was remarkable, but it was not of absolute significance. Two other elements were required to complete this powerful admixture of cultural consensus as to the growth and perception of music in the later nineteenth century. These were the regeneration of antiquarian research in the post-Famine period and the projection of cultural absolutism associated with the Gaelic League. The ultimate condition of music in Ireland would only become clear with its failure to function within the otherwise abundantly fertile terms of the Celtic revival except as a symbol of renascent Irish culture. In the meantime, that is, between the 1840s and the 1890s, the impact of antiquarianism, romantic nationalism and cultural absolutism was such that *the growth of music itself* became secondary to the nurturing of these interrelated ideas.

The cultural discourse of pre-Famine Ireland laid the foundations of this intimate communion. As a counterpart to the unbridled patriotism of *The Nation*, *The Dublin University Magazine* was at least occasionally hospitable to writing about music, and its Tory demeanour did not occlude vigorous discussion of the burgeoning interest in traditional song, as we have seen.

Samuel Ferguson's lengthy review of James Hardiman's *Irish Minstrelsy; or, Bardic Remains of Ireland, with English poetical translations* (1831) appeared in *The Dublin University Magazine* in 1834.[34] Ferguson's position in the history of Irish literature is perhaps too well-known to bear detailed rehearsal here, but the climate of musical opinion which he helped to foster, not least in this review, most certainly warrants appraisal. This essay on Hardiman, commonly regarded as the *locus classicus* of Ferguson's early critical voice (in addition to his verse polemic, 'A Dialogue between the Heart and Head of an Irish Protestant'), signals a crucial perception in the cultural understanding of music in Ireland.[35] Ferguson drew back sharply from the aspirations of his Trinity colleague Thomas Davis, but he espoused a cultural praxis which in the Hardiman review is located between the new-found integrity of Irish letters and music, and the radical politics to which these gave rise:

> These are the songs before us – songs such as the speakers of the English language at large have never heard before, and which they could not see and hear but for the pious labours of a man, who, however politically malignant and religiously fanatical, has yet done such good service to his country in their collection and preservation, that for her sake we half forgive him our own quarrel, and consent to forego a great part of its vindication.[36]

> We will look in vain for the chasteness, the appositeness, the antithetical and epigrammatic point, and the measured propriety of prosody, which delight the ear and the judgement, in a song by Thomas Moore, among the rude rhymes which accompanied the same notes two centuries ago, but the stamen and essence of each is interwoven and transfused through the whole texture and complexion of the other – for sentiment is the soul of song, and sentiment is the one imprescriptible property of the common blood of all Irishmen.[37]

Mr Moore's idea that the point of honor and its effects were done away with by
the Relief Bill is utterly fallacious. Mr Hardiman's book is a striking illustration
of the truth of our assertion. He had written the greater part of his notes and
comments previous to Catholic emancipation [1829], and in them, he freely
indulged in what those who agree with Mr Moore would denominate natural
indignation against England and the English. The work, however, is not published till 1831, two years after all cause for that obstinate hatred in which Mr
Moore thought himself justifiable, had been removed. But what effect has this
on Mr Hardiman? He does not bate a jot of his most indignant obstinacy, he
does not expunge an expression of his most invertebrate and unexchangeable
hatred for Clan Luther, and the Saxon, but disfigures the book, and disgraces
himself by his flinging in the teeth of his manumission, the whole miserly
hoardings of his hatred when a slave.[38]

Although it is tempting to regard Ferguson here as the intelligencer of
high Tory indignation, the anxiety which lies near the surface of these passages stems from a concern to redeem Irish literature – specifically, Gaelic
poetry translated into English – from the purview of repeal politics. Ferguson's intemperate regard for the ideology of Hardiman's *Irish Minstrelsy* was
exact, insofar as he queried not only the interpretations offered by Hardiman
but also the quality of translation itself. His own versions from the Irish,
appended to the final part of the review, 'have made Ferguson one of the rec-
ognized initiators of a specifically Anglo-Irish tradition in poetry', as Peter
Denman succinctly reminds us.[39]

These versions also authorise his attempt to distinguish between the
refined lyrics of Moore, the original Irish texts and the airs themselves. Ferguson is motivated by more than authoritarian zeal: the whole burden of his
fiction and poetry was to recuperate in English the literature of Gaelic civilisation. He expressly believed that literature to be part of his own conception
of modern Ireland, in terms of a cultural nationalism which was pro-Union
and politically conservative, just as Davis's version was anti-Union and politically separatist.[40] But the romanticism of Ferguson's reading of Gaelic culture
– exhaustively sustained and articulated in collections such as *Lays of the
Western Gael* (1865) – could not survive the impact of modern Irish history,
except as a myth of the literary revival. Rehabilitation of the original texts
themselves, meanwhile, was destined to end in sterile cultural absolutism.

The essential metaphor which recurs in Ferguson's meditations on Irish
culture (as it does in the work of his fellow contributors to *The Dublin University Magazine*) is song. The song as an expression of Gaelic civilisation, as the
source of cultural regeneration in Ireland, attains to such symbolic strength
that the music itself is taken as a *donnée*, to be adapted or pragmatically emulated at will. Music lives in the shadow of its own symbolic incandescence.

With the collapse of Young Ireland and the death and emigration of mil-
lions as a consequence of the Famine, the sectarian projection of Irish culture
is fortified by the drastic reorientations of Irish politics. The gulf between

Ascendancy and Catholic interests seems to represent the paradigmatic structure of political and social disharmony in modern Ireland. Similar gulfs, similar struggles for power between landlord and tenant, between constitutional reformer and Fenian, between the Roman Catholic Church and the Irish Parliamentary Party, between the Union and Home Rule, would appear to characterise the complexion of politics between 1850 and 1890. And in the same period, another kind of struggle is maintained in order to establish a continuity of cultural experience with the past. The consensus of restoration which distinguishes all shades of romantic nationalism before the Famine gains a special form of authority in the wake of that catastrophe. We might suggest that the experience of the Famine decided the reception and projection of Irish culture in its aftermath. As before, the recovery of music predominated in this development.

* * * * *

The Society for the Preservation and Publication of the Melodies of Ireland was founded in 1851 with George Petrie as its president.[41] Its only publication was the first volume of the *Petrie Collection of the Ancient Music of Ireland* in 1855.

At first glance, we seem to be on familiar ground: the very titles of the Bunting and Petrie collections echo. We know Petrie, moreover, as a critic of Bunting, as his collaborator and as the person on whom the mantle of Bunting was to fall, to use Aloys Fleischmann's metaphor.[42]

The introduction to Petrie's volume affords a recapitulation of his own career as a collector of Irish music, but it also signals a crucial distinction between the antiquarian research of the past and the exact motivation which spurred Petrie (an avowed musical amateur, but the doyen of Irish archaeology, topography and local history[43]) to cohere, arrange and partly publish his collection of some 1,582 airs.[44] Petrie's conviction that the entire corpus of traditional music lay imperilled by the Famine moved him to 'gather from amongst the survivors of the old Celtic race, innumerable melodies that would soon pass away for ever; . . . such exertion should be immediate'.[45]

Petrie's conception of the effects of the Famine, the 'calamities, which, in the year 1846–7, had struck down and well-nigh annihilated the Irish remnant of the Great Celtic family',[46] is crucial to our sense of Irish music at mid-century. In fact, Petrie's use of 'Irish' as a subset of 'Celtic' is the key term which explains his supra-nationalistic reading of cultural history in language which adumbrates, however faintly, Matthew Arnold and the Celtic revival itself. If, in this reading, 'Standish O'Grady, Pearse and Daniel Corkery come to mind as readily as Yeats and Synge', it is because, in Seamus Deane's winning formulation, 'The mutation from the Celtic to the Gaelic Revival is quick, subtle, and, in the end, sectarian.'[47]

It is not Seamus Deane, however, but George Petrie who remembers the disappearance of the peasantry during and after the Famine. It is Petrie who is moved to rationalise his preoccupying commitment to the preservation of music, after a lifetime's devotion to the Ordnance Survey, to archaeology and to the widest conceivable cultivation of Celtic *analecta*, by an appeal to the here-and-now of Ireland in the 1850s. It is Petrie, abetted by his close colleagues in the Royal Irish Academy, who changes for ever the socio-political significance of the collector in Ireland by preserving the cultural artefacts of a civilisation at once remote from and subversive of good government in Ireland. If Petrie can be regarded as the centre of an arch which spans the collection of folk music in the nineteenth century, from Edward Bunting to Patrick Weston Joyce (1827–1914),[48] he can also be advanced as the link in the chain of thought which joins the broad conception of Celtic culture, with its attendant connotations of benevolence, to the more narrowly defined issue of a nearly depleted Gaelic civilisation.[49]

In Petrie, the consolidation of music as a fundamental of sectarian culture is almost complete. This is not to denigrate the inherent achievement of the collections (published and unpublished), but rather to read their wider cultural significance.Unlike Bunting, the Petrie collections did not proceed to the drawing-room and the transliterations of Moore. Unlike Bunting, whose enthusiasm was also inspired by the imminent disappearance of the tradition he sought to record, Petrie belonged to an Ireland in which antiquarianism had become so imbued with political resonance that the recovery of the past could not but signify immediate implications for the present. And in a present determined by the aftermath of famine, by violent struggle and by land reform, the Petrie collection argued the existence of a cultural discourse radically at odds with the Union and conversely at one with the more widespread claims of an indigenous civilisation.[50]

Such claims were not slow to accumulate in the latter part of the nineteenth century, although there is nothing in Petrie's work which expressly advocates a challenge to the political *status quo*. His own sense of cultural revival, and of the role of the collector therein, nevertheless embraced a critique of the political constituency of which he himself was a part:

> Could music penetrate their stony hearts, the melodies of Ireland would make them weep for the ills they were the means of perpetrating on this unhappy land, and they would embrace the ill-treated people with a generous affection, anxious to make reparation for past injuries.[51]

Here it is Moore's reading of Irish music rather than Bunting's which endures, and the understanding of this music as an agent of social (if not political) redress is one which achieves conventional status in Petrie's work. This equation between the preservation of a dying culture and the rehabilitation of social and political well-being in Ireland is one which individual collectors after Petrie were to draw on as a virtual axiom of Irish musical thought.[52] Petrie's position as vice-president of the Royal Irish Academy, moreover, meant that his collections became part of a coherent scholarly endeavour to

represent the culture of Gaelic Ireland and to establish in particular the grammar of the Irish language even as its use rapidly declined after the Famine.[53]
In this context, the growth of 'Irish music' ineradicably tended towards a
distinctiveness almost as acute as that between the Irish language and the
English language. In Petrie and in the work of the collectors who followed
him, the cumulative effect of the ethnic repertory was such that no significant
development beyond it seemed possible or desirable. Despite the history of
censure which attaches to his competence as an editor,[54] Petrie's significance
as a collector lies not only in the sheer volume of music which he accumulated, but also in the conventional understanding of Irish music which these
collections established. The equivalence which his work achieved so firmly
between Irish music and Gaelic culture was one which would profoundly
inhibit the emancipation of music in Ireland, especially when that culture was
eclipsed by new forms of artistic consensus, above all by the literary revival
itself.[55]

This inhibition is at the heart of the matter: as the sheer accumulation of
ethnic music continued into the 1880s, it was fortified by the wider growth
of language revival and the alignment of cultural distinctiveness with political
self-determination. The founding of the Society for the Preservation of the
Irish Language in 1876, and of the Gaelic League in 1893, mark well-known
stages in this progression. As the collection and preservation of music continued, music itself became detached from the cultural shift from Gaelic literature written in Irish to Irish literature written in English. The Irish Folk Song
Society (1904) simply co-ordinated the effort to edit the repertory inherited
in the prints and manuscripts of the preceding century. Gaelic music, unlike
Gaelic literature, had no means of access from one language into the next, or
from one tradition (ethnic) to the other (art).

Seamus Deane's opinion that the antiquarians and ideologues who struggled to preserve the literature of Gaelic Ireland in English 'helped to consign
Gaelic poetry to the bookshelf' may allow us to clarify this difficult issue.[56]
Deane argues that the translations of Hardiman, of Ferguson, Mangan, Hyde,
'were little more than obituary notices in which the poetry of a ruined civilisation was accorded a sympathy which had been notably absent when it was
alive'.[57] His understanding is that the desiccated condition of Gaelic culture
was idealised and transmogrified by Yeats – who cross-fertilised elements of
it with the romanticism of Young Ireland and with a fertile misunderstanding
of Ascendancy culture – but that the ruined civilisation was (and is) a fact of
cultural history nevertheless. Two issues derive from this reading. One is that
this transcendence of Gaelic culture by means of the literary revival was not
replicated in music.[58] The second is that the preservation of the musical artefacts of this 'ruined civilisation' compelled an association between cultural
and social reform (as I have argued here) which consequently denied significance to the concept of inherent *musical* development. On the contrary, it was
the very consolidation of Gaelic cultural thought which copperfastened the

sectarian projection of 'Irish music' as exclusively a matter of the Gaelic past. Ideologues of Irish culture, and of Irish music itself, forcefully upheld this cultural stasis.[59] As the literature of Gaelic Ireland fed into the complex of Celtic revivalism in English, the music of Gaelic Ireland became ever more distinct and unaccommodating of acculturation and assimilation. As the transmutations of Yeats's poetry and Synge's drama helped to establish an original literature in English which was ineluctably Irish, the cultural divide between the ethnic repertory and whatever else there was of music in Ireland became effectively impossible to bridge. Music itself had become by the 1890s so closely identified with and symbolic of the culture of Gaelic civilisation that it became useless to consider the concept of 'Irish music' in any other meaningful way. To detach part of the ethnic repertory in an effort to make it hospitable to the norms of art music (to arrange an Irish folk melody, or to score a song) was merely to display the shibboleths of an alien culture. Or a ruined one.

The writings of Douglas Hyde exemplify the projection of Gaelic culture as the proper representation of Irish music in the late nineteenth century.[60] Hyde's position as an ideologue of Gaelic civilisation stemmed from his own conviction that 'the nation which once was, as everyone admits, one of the most classically learned and cultured nations in Europe, is now one of the least so'.[61] The keynote of his thinking is brilliantly struck in his lecture delivered to the National Literary Society on 25 November 1892, 'The Necessity for De-Anglicising Ireland'. The rhetorical continuity of thought which Hyde espoused in this lecture is in essence racial and linguistic, and explicitly reminiscent of Thomas Davis. Hyde's curious amalgam of loosely defined Unionist politics with a cultural nationalism of the most stringent and radically programmatic kind combines to offer a vision of Ireland which peremptorily ignores the racial and cultural complex of the embedded religious divide in favour of a linguocentric ideal which is loud in its explicit recommendations against 'anglicisation' but which in its reading of political and cultural history is partisan to the point of absurdity. To read the lecture a century after it was delivered is to recognise the static chauvinism of Hyde's Ireland: a nation drilled in every department of the life and mind to conform to some dreadful programme of cultural identity, vice-like in its grip:

> Every house should have a copy of Moore and Davis. In a word, we must strive to cultivate everything that is most racial, most smacking of the soil, most Gaelic, most Irish, because in spite of the little admixture of Saxon blood in the north-east corner, this Island is and will *ever* remain Celtic to the core, far more Celtic than most people imagine, because, as I have shown you, the names of our people are no criterion of their race.[62]

This image of cultural regeneration, impossible to contemplate now without irony, given what we know of enforced 'cultural revolution', was contained in its own day by the practical considerations of an Anglo-Irish polity not nearly as ill-disposed as Hyde to the influence of 'anglicisation', and yet more determined than he upon the course of Irish political autonomy.[63]

Much of Hyde's passionate advocacy stops short of the splenetic enthusiasms and prescriptions which so memorably characterise 'The Necessity for De-Anglicising Ireland'. Hyde's insistence upon originality of thought and his call for cultural rather than (merely) political modes of independence voice a consensus of opinion (nourished by organisations such as the Gaelic League) which extends beyond his own rhetorical extremes. But the price of such consensus was to prove high. The repudiation of things English ('books, literature, music, games, fashions and ideas') was also a repudiation of things European, especially where music was concerned. In fact, Hyde's unconditional association between Irish music in particular and the cultural profile of Gaelic civilisation in general conversely implies a similarly unconditional association between English music and the vulgarities of the music-hall:

> Our music, too, has become Anglicised to an alarming extent. Not only has the national instrument, the harp . . . become extinct, but even the Irish pipes are threatened with the same fate. In place of the pipers and fiddlers, who, even twenty years ago, were comparatively common, we are now in many places menaced by the German band and the barrel organ . . . If Ireland loses her music, she loses what is, after the Gaelic language and literature, her most valuable and most characteristic expression. And she is rapidly losing it . . .
>
> For the present, then, I must be content with hoping that the revival of our Irish music may go hand in hand with the revival of Irish ideas and Celtic modes of thought which our Society is seeking to bring about, and that people may be brought to love the purity of *Siubhail Siubhail*, or the fun of the *Moddereen Ruadh* in preference to 'Get Your Hair Cut', or 'Over the Garden Wall', or, even if it is not asking too much, of 'Ta-ra-ra-boom-de-ay'.[64]

Not only does Hyde modify here the politically motivated reading of the ethnic repertory offered by Davis: he unambiguously ranks music as highly as possible in the cultural spectrum of Ireland. But this ranking is confined to the music of the past, and it points to the recurring problem so fruitfully resolved in literature by means of the English language itself. The musical language of European art music is an anathema to Hyde, just as the English language is. The former cannot be admitted in any consideration of the cultivation of Irish music, just as the latter cannot be allowed to impinge on the revival of Irish manners, customs, place-names, personal names or literature. Hyde excludes the art tradition in music as firmly as he excludes, over and again, the continued use of English as a *modus vivendi* (still more as a cultural resource) in Ireland. For Hyde, the two – music and language – so obviously go together.[65]

As with Davis, Hyde's exhortations would not be of much concern were it not for the immensity of his influence in the formation of cultural opinion at the turn of the century. For all its bombast, Hyde's rhetoric is less intemperate than the most extreme perpetrations of the 'Irish Ireland' view of cultural discourse, and the awareness of Gaelic culture which Hyde stimulated, through the agency of the Gaelic League, was profound. Hyde failed to de-anglicise Ireland, but he did revive far more than an antiquarian sense of Gaelic culture. He imbued the Irish mind with a permanent sense of Ireland which was and remains radically distinct from English or European discourse, and which continued to countermand the literary revival in English throughout the twentieth century. If the revival took its place in the international domain of letters, the Gaelic League (and Hyde's role therein) established a cultural domain that belonged exclusively to Ireland.

Hyde's cultural nationalism is clearly significant to this study because he espoused music as a prime symbol of Gaelic (and therefore Irish) culture. But two limitations circumscribed this espousal. The first is that Hyde's concept of music was primarily textual and verbal; the second is that it was static. 'Irish music', a fact of antiquarian research, became for Hyde and his contemporaries a petrified object precisely by means of the cultural renascence which it helped to stimulate. To revive Irish music for those who subscribed to 'the philosophy of Irish Ireland'[66] was to revive a cultural past inherently unresponsive to the imaginative resources of the present. This was for Hyde a satisfying state of affairs.

It is fair to say that those most intimately concerned with the revival of Irish music at the turn of the century shared in large measure the cultural separatism which Hyde so vigorously espoused. Richard Henebry, Charlotte Milligan Fox and Alfred Perceval Graves, all of them prominent members of the Irish Folk Song Society, disdained to a greater or lesser degree the possibilities of musical cross-fertilisation between ethnic and art traditions. Their will was to preserve music in *both* senses of that verb: to make it available and to protect it from corruption by the European aesthetic: 'The more we foster modern music the more we help to silence our own' was Henebry's formulaic response to the prospect of contemporary developments, even within the sphere of traditional music itself.[67] His colourful atavisms merely exaggerate the fundamental chauvinism of much writing on Irish folksong in the early 1900s, a trait which was to survive throughout the twentieth century.

Henebry's *Irish Music* (c. 1903) and *Handbook of Irish Music* (1928) are compelling sources for the notion of 'musical purity' which echoes Hyde's rejection of English culture in general. So determined was Henebry to achieve a correlative definition of 'Irish music' (correlative to the Irish language) that he rejected Carolan on the grounds that his compositions betrayed an infectious corruption of taste which undermined the very notion of Irish music:

> And so with the decay of taste we can understand how a harper named Carolan
> gained notoriety in the seventeenth century amongst the gentry . . . by his per-
> formance or rather composition of concertos, etc., and how through the
> patronage of his admirers he attained to a certain amount of prestige amongst
> the vulgar. A little later certain people in Dublin prided themselves upon being

the first to appreciate Handel's music. That will show the spirit that was moving the fashionable musical world at the time in Ireland and enable us to discount the title of the last of the bards innocently bestowed upon Carolan. Indeed, his tunes . . . show him to be no Irish musician.[68]

This rejection of Carolan is obviously of Henebry's own eccentric making, but it signifies a process of musical sectarianism which was not peculiar to the *Handbook of Irish Music*. Not only is the romantic impulse of antiquarianism and Young Ireland overtaken by a more aggressively separatist philosophy of culture (as in Hyde and the 'Irish Irelanders'), but the process of musical acculturation itself is sternly condemned. Henebry's repudiation of Carolan is metonymic of the widespread quest for a degree of musical distinctiveness (and 'purity') which would match that of the Gaelic language.

That Irish music should be lodged for ever within a hermetically sealed cultural past was the ideal thus evinced by the Gaelic League. The literary revival would absorb this past into the processes of a new literature written in English. Why similar processes of acculturation – specifically with reference to an aesthetic of Irish art music – could not take place to any significant degree is a central query in this study. Why could not Ireland achieve what Poland achieved in the nineteenth century and Hungary in the twentieth: an art music of international currency underwritten by a tangible corpus of ethnic melody?

*  *  *  *  *

These questions return us to Davis and the narrative structure of Irish music in the nineteenth century. The continuity of cultural discourse between the romanticism of Young Ireland and the sectarian principles of the Gaelic League was especially pronounced in the perception of music as an agent of political expression. If the objective of *The Nation* was expressly to 'foster public opinion and make it racy of the soil',[69] then this objective was most purposefully exploited through the use of music, and in particular by means of the ballad tradition. The literary imitations of street balladry which Davis and his colleagues cultivated in *The Spirit of the Nation* fortified the popular understanding of music as a functional resource, which repeatedly and insistently advanced the cause of Irish self-determination. We have seen that Davis repudiated the commonplace vulgarity of street ballads, but he did not disdain the central influence which they exerted upon the formation of public opinion.

In his exhaustive study of political street ballads in Ireland, Georges-Denis Zimmerman adverts to the intimate communion between this tradition and the circumstances by which it was maintained:

> We may admit that the political street ballads had some influence on the attitude of the Irish people, and therefore on the course of Irish history, although we cannot say precisely to what extent. They were effect and cause at the same time . . . [They] were a nearly collective expression of commonly held beliefs

or prejudices and of political aspirations, and we may regard them as a running commentary on Irish political life.[70]

Had not the narrative force of this tradition been refined by Davis, its significance in terms of the development of art music in Ireland would perhaps be nugatory. But the fact remains that Davis, Mangan and the Young Ireland movement reified the narrative condition of balladry to the extent that music became a secondary issue in the process. Notwithstanding another form of continuity by which *The Spirit of the Nation* produced a host of imitations as the changing complexion of Irish politics demanded, its cultural significance depended on the idea of music as a source of political growth, rather than the reverse.[71] That music should function as an exclusive and potent metaphor of political and cultural aspiration, that it should both symbolise and nourish the condition of nationalism in particular, was an explicit belief central to Davis's own ideology. When we juxtapose this belief with the strongly held impulse to preserve the ethnic repertory, an impulse satisfied over and again both before and after the Famine, we gain some notion of the degree to which the contingent and culturally static perception of 'Irish music' became entrenched in the nineteenth century.

In this climate of cultural entrenchment, the concept of music as an independent 'work of art' was necessarily diminished. The 'quintessential deed' by which George Steiner denotes the art work in a society 'made inert by repressive authority' became so thoroughly indentured to political and cultural propaganda that it could not long survive as an independent entity. The projection of Irish music either as a textual adjunct in the service of romantic nationalism or as the symbol of a sectarian ideology of culture tended to eclipse the possibility of a music sufficiently emancipated from these burdens to develop freely of them.

Some degree of comparison between the respective condition of music in Poland and Ireland in the nineteenth century helps to secure this argument and to press home one of its primary implications, namely that the condition of art music could only thrive at one remove from the immediacy of socio-political ferment. The parallels between Irish and Polish history are not hard to discover: both Ireland and Poland were colonised countries in the nineteenth century, both countries endured the crushing aftermath of insurrection (Poland in 1794, 1831 and 1848; Ireland in 1798, 1803 and 1848) and in both countries the cult of romantic nationalism flourished under similar conditions of political deprivation. As one historian expresses the matter, ' "Poland" as an abstraction, could be remembered from the past, or aspired to for the future, but only imagined in the present.'[72] This is a formulation we might usefully apply to Ireland.

Zofia Chechlínska's recent observations on Polish musical nationalism also sound familiar in the context of Irish music:

> The concept of nationalism in art . . . fell upon particularly fertile ground in
> Poland. As a result of the loss of national independence in 1795, art was one of
> the few areas in which a sense of Polish national identity could be displayed
> and preserved. The postulate of music's national character dominated the
> whole of Polish musical culture of the day, and the saturation of compositions
> with a national element became an essential criterion in their appraisal.[73]

In a country preoccupied throughout the nineteenth century and long afterwards by the materials of its ethnic musical culture (some seventy thousand
folk melodies were collected in the post-1945 period alone, according to *The
New Grove*), the central national identity of Polish music was at least as powerful as its counterpart in Ireland. And on the surface, it does appear as if cultural as well as political parallels existed between the two countries. The
influence of Thomas Moore on Poland's most prominent advocate of nationalist literature in the first half of the nineteenth century, Adam Mickiewicz
(1798–1855), was such that Mickiewicz not only admired and translated
Moore's verses but also imitated his lyric style. And the history of Moore
reception in Poland would suggest that both countries reciprocally fostered a
sense of cultural identity founded in part on the mutual aspiration to independence.[74]

But this identity is one of contrastive rather than shared parallels in the
domain of music. The more precisely a comparison between Ireland and
Poland is drawn in this respect, the less easily it functions. There is irony in
Moore's position here as the seminal figure against which Young Ireland
asserted its own romantic understanding of music, especially given his influence on Mickiewicz, whose literary nationalism stands behind the development of Polish musical nationalism. To contemplate the ballads of Thomas
Davis in *The Spirit of the Nation* by comparison with the *ballades* of his close
contemporary Frédéric Chopin (1810–49) is to understand the fundamental
difficulties in cultural context which so profoundly affected the growth and
perception of music in either country.

Recent Chopin literature is careful to distinguish between the history of
Chopin reception in Poland (where the composer's music was immediately
and permanently understood as the essence of the 'Polish soul') and the
impact of nationalist ideology on Chopin himself.[75] Jim Samson under-
stands the matter of Chopin's 'professional exile' expressly in terms of this
distinction:

> [Chopin's] approach to the principal national dances – the polonaise and the
> Mazurka – changed significantly following the early years in Warsaw. In a man-
> ner that strikingly anticipates later nineteenth-century developments, he trans-
> formed these dance elements from colourful exoticisms (available to all) to
> potent evocations of Poland, and specifically a Poland oppressed. A compari-
> son with Liszt is instructive. Both composers cultivated images of their native
> lands and used musical symbols to convey these images, albeit only in selected

works. *At the same time they combined national material with the most advanced
contemporary techniques of European music, fusing, as it were, nationalism and modernism. Their music derived energy from national material but was not confined by
it nor indeed by a nationalist aesthetic.* Unlike Moniuszko in Poland or Erkel in
Hungary, they worked in the world at large. [my italics][76]

I cite Samson at length here because he identifies precisely that which the
cultural matrix of music in nineteenth-century Ireland excluded: a fusion of
the ethnic with the European, and, as important, a transformation of nationalistic elements which by its very emancipation from the immediacy of cultural
context produced powerful evocations of 'a Poland oppressed'. It is surely not
too much to add that Chopin's evolution of a new genre – the *ballade* – reflects
the narrative structure of the Polish ballad in particular, and that its 'end-
directed' structure implies a narratology of political events which are subsumed by the music's distance from these events. This argument, cultivated in
Chopin scholarship, does not contradict the absolute integration of Chopin's
compositions into the wider context of European art music in the nineteenth
century.[77] If Chopin's music 'came to symbolise the national struggle, helping
to cement the Polish spirit at a time when the country was without political
status',[78] then in his case the work of art *was* the 'quintessential deed'. This
symbolism remained strictly subordinate to the reception of Chopin's music
beyond Poland, where, if anything, it drifted from the Slavonic to the Salon.
In either case (Chopin as bard of Poland, Chopin as Parisian cosmopolite), the
cultural response was not so extreme as to inhibit the composer's emancipated
condition, notwithstanding his private reservations and meditations. That a
sense of Poland ('Poland oppressed') profoundly informed the shape and substance of Chopin's musical thought can scarcely be doubted, however one
might want to espouse a revisionist reading of his achievement as a composer.
But neither can one doubt the means by which this sense of Poland came to
life: the means of infrastructure (the Warsaw conservatory, where he absorbed
the techniques of the European aesthetic), the means of exposure (the concerts
in Vienna, Munich, Stuttgart, Paris and London, early in his career) and, above
all, the means of exile (his life in Paris).

Exile was decisive. It offered Chopin an opportunity to contemplate
Poland at a distance, an opportunity at once to cultivate and to objectify his
sense of Polish nationalism. Paris was not merely the centre of a Polish *émi-
gré* enclave (by which his nationalism was sustained), it was also, and self-evidently, at the heart of musical Europe. If Chopin's works permanently endow
the repertory of European art music with an irreducibly Polish voice, they do
so in terms of a cultural nationalism crucially removed from the direct sphere
of political engagement. Moreover, Chopin's music would suggest that 'exile'
was a vital precondition for his synthesis of art and ethnic traditions, insofar
as his purpose was to create new music rather than to preserve the musical
past of his country intact. However vulnerable to nationalistic symbolism,

Chopin's music existed (and exists) independently of the sources which gave it original force.

Thus to 'work in the world at large' was to partake of a cultural nationalism at once more productive and less politically engaged than that which confined the imaginative space of those who remained at home. Jim Samson compares Chopin to Liszt. For our purposes, I shall compare him to James Joyce, whose preoccupation with Ireland stood in ironic and inverse proportion to his refusal to return there after 1904. Joyce's exile was also self-imposed and his work, as with Chopin's, represents the same fusion of indigenous and modern materials by which his vision of Dublin in particular was attained. There is more to Joyce than the fact of his being an Irish writer (as there is more to Chopin than his Polish nationalism). But in either case the national qualification is essential. Joyce altered the strategies of fiction, Chopin crucially enlarged the expressive range of piano music: exile in both cases fortified the ineluctable degree of Irishness and Polishness respectively in their work.

No such comparison is tenable between Chopin and any Irish composer, between Chopin and John Field (1782–1837), for example. And this is obviously because in Field's case the fact of Irish birth and the potential of Irish culture were of no significance whatever to his English background and training. Thus his life in Russia was not (in creative terms) an exile, but an immigration, complete and unabridged. To describe John Field as an *Irish* composer in the context of cultural history, particularly for the purposes of essaying a comparison between him and the *Polish* composer Chopin, is to offer a false cognate.

No true cognate is available: this chapter has sought to explain why this should be so. If nationalism inspired music in Poland, we might evenly respond that music inspired nationalism in Ireland. The complete dearth of educational infrastructures, the cultural divide between the ethnic and art traditions (a divide which in Poland was pragmatically bridged), the ideological weight of musical preservation and the projection of music as a badge of sectarian culture, second only to language, collectively made the development of an emancipated compositional voice in Irish art music an impossibility. Instead, the preoccupation with 'folksong' (increasingly the term used to describe the ethnic repertory), not as a resource but as a *substitute* for the art tradition, hindered the transformation from Gaelic to modern Irish modes of musical expression in the second half of the nineteenth century.

# HEINRICH BEWERUNGE AND THE CECILIAN MOVEMENT IN IRELAND

> What I would like to suggest is that the devotional revolution which took place after the famine satisfied more than the negative factors of guilt and fear induced by that great catastrophe. There may indeed be something worse than the fear of being destroyed – the mounting terror in the growing awareness that one is being destroyed. The Irish, after all, had been gradually losing their language, their culture, and their way of life for nearly a hundred years before the famine. Education, business, politics, and communication in the written word, even more than in the spoken word, were all increasingly geared to English as the Irish were being effectively Anglicised, or, perhaps, more appropriately, West Britonized . . .
>
> The devotional revolution, I would argue further, provided the Irish with a substitute symbolic language and offered them a new cultural heritage with which they could identify and be identified with one another. That is why, for example, Irish and Catholic have become almost interchangeable terms in Ireland, despite the attempts of Nationalists to make Irish rather than Catholic the inclusive term.[1]

The cultural history of music in Ireland inevitably embraces the history in turn of Irish Roman Catholicism. If the terms 'Irish' and 'Catholic' became synonymous in the minds of many nationalists after the Famine, the identification of one with the other reinforced that spirit of cultural sectarianism which so prevailed in Irish affairs from the second half of the nineteenth century onwards. Of course, the equation between religious affiliation and national identity remained complex, especially in the light of Fenianism, with its ideological commitment to political as well as cultural separatism and its tense regard for church–state relations.[2] Nevertheless, the consolidation of a bourgeois Catholic communion with pretensions to political power is evidently a vital factor (of urban life especially) in post-Famine Ireland. The principal affairs of Irish political life – land reform, education, the language question and party political representation at Westminster – were collectively and individually expressive of a new *status quo*, however tenuous and hard won. The sense of every question in Ireland being a religious question and every religious question being a political one enjoyed a striking revival in the second half of the nineteenth century.

This *status quo* is difficult to summarise except in one respect: the powerful condition of influence exercised by the Irish hierarchy in virtually every department of life, especially after 1850. If, as Emmet Larkin argues, the Roman Catholic Church did provide a 'substitute culture' for many Irish people, it did so in the interest of consolidating its power not only as a protective agency of religious freedom but also as the controlling force of social, cultural and political progress in Ireland.

This notion of the Catholic Church as an agent of cultural reform in Ireland is clearly circumscribed by the boundaries of socio-political and religious thought which the hierarchy variously attempted to establish from the middle of the nineteenth century onwards. The appointment of Paul Cullen (1803–78) as archbishop of Armagh and primate of Ireland in 1850 was critical in this development, and Cullen's absolute commitment to a species of church policy in which papal authority ruled supreme in all matters of ecclesiastical procedure and discipline was perhaps the central force in the remarkable programme of consolidation and reform which he spearheaded for almost three decades.[3] That Cullen succeeded in reconciling the political ambition of his fellow archbishops with his own drive to rehabilitate a wholly romanised clergy is beyond doubt.[4] However fractious his relationship with certain elements of the Irish church (including Maynooth), Cullen was uniquely placed to initiate a programme of ecclesiastical reform unprecedented in Irish church history. His influence was especially apparent in the appointment of bishops sympathetic to his own unshakeable belief in ultramontanist principles, in the building of churches, convents and educational establishments designed to cohere the religious practice and intellectual formation of the Irish faithful and in the promulgation of synodal acts and decrees by which the policies of the hierarchy in general could be rescripted by Rome should these contradict Cullen's own priorities and desires. In this last respect, Cullen's insistence upon the foundation of a Catholic university and his unremitting opposition to the Queen's Colleges established by the British government in 1845 were reinforced by the strategy of synodal legislature.[5]

This pattern of legal ratification fortified by the exercise of personal influence was one which carried music in its powerful wake. As part of the devotional reform initiated and implemented by Cullen, music was to feature in the first national synod convoked in Ireland since the twelfth century. The synod of Thurles, which effectively comprised Cullen's first step towards the imposition of a regularised clerical and liturgical practice upon the church in Ireland, included two decrees on music which thereafter signified the Irish hierarchy's commitment to the Roman ideal of a Latinised sacred music. The question of an indigenous mode of liturgical musical expression was not to be seriously countenanced. Instead, these decrees ratified the means by which church music in Ireland would develop as an expression of aesthetic ideals formulated elsewhere. Irish church music, in brief, was to become the local species of a wider European movement.

The Thurles decrees tersely clarified this intention:

> 38. No singing is to be carried out in the churches unless it is solemn and Ecclesiastical in nature. The Rectors of seminaries must ensure as a primary

responsibility that their students are well instructed in chant so that they may properly learn the sacred ceremonies.

    39. During solemn masses, nothing but Latin may be sung, neither is anything to be found outside of mass in churches, unless it is contained in the approved Ecclesiastical books, or permitted by the Ordinary.[6]

These decrees did not originate *ex nihilo*: they rather stemmed from a general movement, brilliantly advocated by Cullen, towards a uniform, stabilised mode of aesthetic and artistic expression in the service of divine worship. In this respect it is useful to cite from a report of the opening ceremonies of the Thurles synod which took place on 22 August 1850. Laurence Forde, master of ceremonies, wrote that 'The Mass was celebrated by the Primate himself with full solemnity – all the arrangements were modelled as far as possible on the plan of the Papal Chapels – the music too was *Ecclesiastical* – the Mass was the old Irish College Mass in four parts quite in the Palestrina style.'[7]

    It is the phrase 'Palestrina style' which is significant in Forde's account. It denotes an awareness of that widespread movement for reform in church music which dominated liturgical thought in Europe throughout the nineteenth century and which stemmed in turn from the frail but unbroken tradition of *stile antico* composition which was carefully regenerated, especially in Rome and Vienna, before the French Revolution. The development of church music in Ireland between 1850 and 1900 was in part a general recovery of this awareness, by which the aesthetic parameters of European liturgical reform would determine the thinking of Irish ecclesiastics in remarkable detail. Indeed, Cullen's zealous adherence to the romanisation of the Irish church would find a detailed correlative in the romanisation of Irish church music, and the climate of conservatism which he so powerfully fostered would enable this process to flourish with unprecedented success, at least for a time. The Thurles decrees on sacred music adumbrated exactly an episode in Irish cultural history in which music was removed from the immediacy of political ferment. Instead, its cultural context was determined by a consolidation of doctrinaire aesthetics and religious fervour. This potent admixture produced a reform movement in Ireland which for once drew its inspiration directly from European sources. Uncomplicated by the corrosive divisions of political history, the extraordinary profusion of decrees, journals, debates, festivals and societies which characterises church music in Ireland between 1850 and 1900 speaks instead of a cultural context which was at once Irish and European in complexion. This context in turn reflects a wider cultural consensus or cultural matrix, namely, the consolidated mass of Irish Roman Catholics, obediently reformed by the hierarchy in the nineteenth century.

*   *   *   *   *

Although the history of church music in Ireland between 1850 and 1875 (the year in which Cullen's second national synod reaffirmed the Thurles decrees[8]) remains largely undocumented and unresearched, three major texts alert us to the fact that Irish ecclesiastics were aware of the need for reform and instruction in the matter of church music in general and of chant in particular for a considerable period prior to Rev Heinrich Bewerunge's arrival in Ireland in 1888 as the first professor of sacred music at the national seminary for the education of priests, St Patrick's College, Maynooth. Rev Nicholas Donnelly's translation of the *Magister Choralis* by F. X. Haberl (1877), the first run of the journal *Lyra Ecclesiastica* (1879–93) and Rev William Walsh's *Grammar of Gregorian Music* (1885) each testifies to a thoroughgoing concern with church music reform in Ireland from the mid-1870s onwards.[9] Nicholas Donnelly's determined erudition in the matter of church music was a consequence of several visits which he made to Regensburg – epicentre of the European revival of scholarly and pragmatic interest in chant and polyphony – between 1873 and 1878.[10] The culmination of this interest was the formation of the Irish Society of St Cecilia in October 1878, with direct links to the founding German association of the same name.[11] Even prior to this activity, the publication of Rev L. J. Renehan's *Grammar of Gregorian and Modern Music* in 1858 (newly edited and enlarged by Rev Richard Hackett in 1865 and 'compiled chiefly for the use of the students of St Patrick's College, Maynooth') shows that in Maynooth, at least, the church was disposed to recognise the necessity for some measure of formal instruction in sacred music, as prescribed by the Thurles decrees.[12]

Donnelly's translation of the *Magister Choralis* was at once the most influential of these publications in international terms and the apparent catalyst for the journal (*Lyra Ecclesiastica*) and the 1885 *Grammar* (Walsh) which followed it. Donnelly undertook his translation 'with the author's [i e Haberl's] permission and under his personal direction'[13] and the work appeared under the imprint of the official publisher to the German Cecilian Society, Frederick Pustet, in Regensburg, New York, Cincinnati, London and Dublin. It thus achieved the status of an official translation of Haberl's seminal text, undertaken by a priest of the Cathedral Church of the Immaculate Conception in Dublin

Donnelly's translation carries a warm letter of approbation from Cullen (now cardinal archbishop of Dublin) dated 5 February 1877. The prefatory material also includes a number of important references to documents in which Haberl's edition of the chant is ratified by the Irish clergy. Chief among these is the thirteenth decree of the Maynooth synod of 1875.[14] Donnelly also cites other Irish publications which had appeared in response to the Regensburg edition of the chant, notably in the *Dublin Review* (July 1874) and the *Irish Ecclesiastical Record* (August 1875). His translation is characterised by occasional 'references . . . to local uses or abuses, as the case may be, with a view to calling attention to them that they may be corrected in accordance with the standard editions now available'.[15]

Having worked closely with Haberl, who revised the musical content 'note by note', Donnelly thus combined the twin objectives of the Cecilian movement in his translation of the *Magister Choralis:* textual accuracy and pragmatic reform. The second of these objectives predominates in the journal

*Lyra Ecclesiastica*, which was edited by Donnelly and was first published as the 'monthly bulletin of the Irish Society of St Cecilia' in October 1878 (for the sake of convenience the collected yearly volume was dated from 1879). The opening numbers sought to establish the scope and purpose of Cecilian activity in Ireland.

The first issue of *Lyra Ecclesiastica* featured a leading article on 'What is the Cecilian Society and What does it Propose?', which comprised an attempt to clarify what the society was not, as much as an effort to convey what it was: 'We begin then, by correcting various misapprehensions, and by clearly stating what the Cecilian Society is *not.*' Three main points followed:

> (1) It is *not* a society of musicians . . . whether professionals or amateurs. It is a society in which all may take part who are zealous for the decorum and splendour of Catholic worship. But it is expected, and earnestly hoped, that all Catholic musicians, especially those holding appointments in our churches will cordially join in this effort to reform and give the promoters the benefit of their advice . . . in establishing this 'much-wanted' society.
>
> (2) The 'Society of St Cecilia' as proposed, does not contemplate the use of Gregorian chant in our church services to the *exclusion* of all figured and harmonized music. The Society . . . favours and supports and furthers – 1st The Gregorian chant above all; 2nd The ancient and *modern* polyphonic vocal music, if *suitable* for ecclesiastical art and liturgical; 3rd Instrumental music, if it complies with the laws of the Church and is used to *support* the singing.
>
> (3) The proposed Society of St Cecilia does not counsel the exclusion of female voices from our choirs, or any violent interference with existing arrangements.[16]

Donnelly's article also rehearsed other 'Cecilian' themes, which were already familiar from the Continent:

> How many of our great composers . . . were guided by those principles [of 'prayerful constraint'] when they sat down to write a mass? How many of them ever consulted the requirements of the liturgy in their so-called compositions? and must not every clergyman officiating at High Mass be often-times puzzled to decide whether he is in a church or in a concert-room?[17]

Thus the position of the Irish Cecilian movement, in its advocacy of Gregorian chant and sixteenth-century polyphony to the virtual exclusion of all else (with the notable exception of the contemporary reanimation of Renaissance models) was expressly clear and unambiguous from the first page of the first number of *Lyra Ecclesiastica* onwards. It was a position which closely adumbrated that of Heinrich Bewerunge, whose own writings bear out exactly the tone and content of these early statements of the Cecilian movement in Ireland.

*Lyra Ecclesiastica* offered its readers considerably more than general exhortation. It published the papal approval of the German Cecilian Society bestowed by Pius IX in 1871 (with an English translation); it provided a detailed account of sister societies throughout Europe, and it instituted a regular column entitled 'Cecilian Intelligence' which initially included episcopal endorsements from members of the (Irish) hierarchy, in the form of letters to Father Donnelly. *Lyra* also published a *Monthly List of Sacred Music* forthcoming from the firms of Pustet in Regensburg and M.H. Gill and Son in Dublin.

The Cecilian Society directed its activities at every level of music and music education in Catholic Ireland, and through the columns of its journal it urged the assimilation of the music and associated pedagogical methods which it promulgated in Irish schools, seminaries, convents and churches. The journal reported on the annual general meetings of the society in Ireland (the first such meeting took place on 21 November 1878 in the Aula Maxima of the Catholic University of Ireland), and it reprinted germane articles from other periodicals.[18] It also censured what it took to be unsuitable or profane music in church:

> One of the objects of the Cecilian Society is to banish from our churches what
> is certainly known to be *profane* music. Occasionally the words [of the liturgy]
> are tortured in the most painful fashion, and rendered perfectly unintelligible,
> in order to fit them to that charming air from 'Der Freischutz' or that charming
> duet from 'Maritana' . . . The editors of the *Lyra Ecclesiastica* will consider it part
> of their duty to publish in each number a sort of *Index Expurgatorius* of these
> forbidden adaptations, and so endeavour gradually to eliminate them from our
> choirs and organ galleries.[19]

Expurgation, reformation, regulation: the impact and pervasive appeal of the Cecilian movement in Ireland knew no precedent in terms of its ecclesiastical support and its congruence with similar movements throughout Catholic Europe and the United States. *Lyra Ecclesiastica* affords detailed documentation of the enormous success which this movement enjoyed in its efforts to reclaim for Irish Catholicism a musical *modus operandi* which would match the reinvigorated conservatism of the church in Ireland. Nicholas Donnelly, several years in advance of Bewerunge's arrival in Maynooth, brought from the Continent, and specifically from Regensburg, a code of musical aesthetics which could not but flourish in the climate of ultramontanism so strongly nurtured by Paul Cullen and his successors to the see of Dublin.[20]

The publication of William Walsh's *Grammar of Gregorian Music* in 1885, some three years prior to Bewerunge's appointment, also supports the view that the Cecilian movement was a well-established and predominant factor in Irish church music by the mid-1880s. Walsh published his book as president of Maynooth: later that year he would succeed Edward McCabe as archbishop of Dublin. The *Grammar* carried a *nihil obstat* from one Carolus Maher, an officer of the Irish Cecilian Society, and its preface established the debt which Walsh owed to Haberl's *Magister Choralis* and its translation by Donnelly.[21] The prefatory material to Walsh's book also includes several references to his own articles in the *Irish Ecclesiastical Record* from 1883 and 1884, which addressed the scholarly achievements of Haberl's chant research.[22] As with Donnelly before him, Walsh thus prepared the ground for similar articles published by Bewerunge in the same journal.

Walsh was careful to ratify the authority of the Regensburg edition of the chant, which had recently been reaffirmed by a decree promulgated by the Sacred Congregation of Rites in April 1883 and published in the *Irish Ecclesiastical Record* in July of the same year. The greater part of Walsh's *Grammar* is a practical primer or instruction manual as its title implies, and in this respect it calls to mind the Renehan *Grammar of Gregorian and Modern Music*, an important precedent for all three texts discussed here.

From all of these publications we can conclude that the pattern of didactic commentary, scholarly translation, pedagogic instruction and learned criticism which characterised Heinrich Bewerunge's published work was in the main already well-established by his predecessors and immediate contemporaries in Ireland. Such a conclusion does not detract from the magnitude and significance of Bewerunge's achievement, but it does significantly modify the hitherto accepted assessment of that achievement, which conventionally attributes to Bewerunge a *pioneering* role in the development of the Cecilian movement in Ireland.[23] That movement was well-established prior to Bewerunge's arrival, and it can properly be regarded as an outgrowth of cultural history which derives from the consolidation of the church's power in Ireland in the closing decades of the nineteenth century. The success of Cullen's attempt to romanise the Catholic Church in Ireland is reflected in the unprecedented enthusiasm with which its musical articulation was greeted by the (approximately) eleven hundred members affiliated to the Dublin branch alone of the Society of St Cecilia in 1886.[24]

\* \* \* \* \*

Heinrich Bewerunge has long been recognised as an outstanding figure in the history of the Cecilian movement in Ireland. As a pedagogue, as a forceful and illuminating exponent of the Cecilian ideal and as an internationally acknowledged authority on the chant, Bewerunge ranks as a vital contributor to the history of musical thought not only in Ireland, but throughout Europe, especially in terms of the reanimation and controversial development of Roman Catholic church music in the late nineteenth and early twentieth centuries. His own career, indeed, mirrors the upward curve and subsequent decline of the Cecilian movement, especially in Germany, which achieved the greater part of its influential work between the appearance of the Regensburg edition of the chant in 1871–8 (*Editio Medicaean*) and the promulgation of *Motu proprio* by Pius X in 1903, which ratified the preparation and publication of the *Editio Vaticana* of the chant between 1905 and 1923.[25] This latter edition, prepared by Dom Pothier of Solesmes, effectively signified the dominant influence of French Gregorian scholarship (notwithstanding the central contribution of German scholars, including Peter Wagner) unconnected with the aims and ideals of the Cecilian movement. Although the movement continued its activities for some years beyond the appearance of the Vatican edition, it no longer occupied a central position in the scholarly study of chant manuscripts, which, in part, had distinguished those activities from 1870 onwards.[26]

Heinrich Bewerunge was born in 1862 at Letmathe, in Westphalia.[27] His family moved to Düsseldorf in his early youth, and he made his intermediate studies in a classical gymnasium in that city. He thereafter entered the university of Würzburg (Bavaria) as a student of theology. In the summer of 1885, he was ordained at Eichstadt. During his studentship at Eichstadt he also enrolled at the Royal School of Church Music at Würzburg, and after ordination he studied with F. X. Haberl in Regensburg. On his return to the Rhineland, Bewerunge was appointed secretary to the vicar-general in the diocese of Cologne and chanter in Cologne cathedral.

On 26 June 1888, a chair of 'Church Chant and Organ' was established at St Patrick's College, Maynooth, and the trustees of the college (the Irish hierarchy) invited Bewerunge to accept the newly established professorship on the recommendation of F. X. Haberl.[28] Bewerunge took up his position that autumn and retained it over a period of some thirty-five years. In 1914, he was appointed to the chair of music at University College Dublin, but the outbreak of war prevented his taking up this position, and he lived in Cologne from the summer of 1914 until his return to Maynooth in 1920. Bewerunge then resumed his professorial duties there, although his health had visibly declined during and immediately after the war years. He died at Maynooth on 2 December 1923.

During his tenure at Maynooth, many of Bewerunge's activities were practical rather than exclusively academic. His responsibilities centred upon the reformation and training of the college choir and the systematic instruction and training of all seminarians (about six hundred in number) in the elements of chant. Bewerunge also established a smaller, specialised *schola cantorum* for the performance of the more complex parts of the chant repertory and of sixteenth-century polyphonic mass and motet settings. To this end, he also arranged the works of Palestrina and his contemporaries for male-voice choir, and he introduced to Maynooth the works of Cecilian composers (pre-eminently Haller) who wrote in the so-called 'Palestrina' style.[29] Bewerunge's extensive knowledge of organ-building led him to commission the magnificent Stahlhut instrument which was installed in the equally imposing and recently constructed college chapel in 1890.

Apart from his writings on church music, music education and the history of the chant and its editions, Bewerunge's non-professorial activities were directly related to the propagation of the Cecilian movement in Ireland. From 1891 to 1893 he edited *Lyra Ecclesiastica*, and he participated in several Cecilian festivals in Maynooth, Dublin and in Continental Europe. As a member of the Dublin Feis Ceoil committee and the Incorporated Society of Musicians,

Bewerunge was a frequent and lively correspondent in newspapers and journals on several aspects of music in Ireland. He also introduced to Ireland German organists who filled positions in cathedrals and larger churches throughout the country, even as he strongly advocated the training of musicians born in Ireland for the same purpose.

His influence, in brief, on the course and development of church music in Ireland was immense. It was also problematic and, notwithstanding his Maynooth professorship, it was short lived. But his translations, writings and editions (published and unpublished) in the field of sacred music are of paramount importance, in terms of both their intrinsic value and their national and international relevance.

*   *   *   *   *

Bewerunge's writings may, for the purpose of this assessment, be conveniently divided into two distinct groups. The first of these comprises the essays and reports which he undertook in his capacity as editor of *Lyra Ecclesiastica* until its demise in 1893, although few of these writings actually appeared in that journal. Many of the unsigned reports may probably be assigned to Bewerunge, but in this context it is best to confine ourselves to those signed pieces which appeared in the *Irish Ecclesiastical Record* and the *New Ireland Review*. In these publications, Bewerunge established himself as a sometimes tendentious intelligencer of Cecilian reportage, but also as a focus for those issues of aesthetic crisis by which the whole Cecilian movement would ultimately be undone. In addition, Bewerunge's predilection for debate drew him naturally into contention with a number of musicians who opposed the Cecilian aesthetic in Ireland. His writings in this respect widen the cultural context of Irish church music beyond the parameters of the Cecilian movement.

The second group of writings comprises the major essays on the Vatican edition of the chant which appeared initially in *Irish Ecclesiastical Record* and which were subsequently published as separate pamphlets in French and German translations. We need also to acknowledge associated essays on technical aspects of the chant which appeared in the *Irish Theological Quarterly*, the *Irish Ecclesiastical Record* and the *Catholic Encyclopedia*. The essays in this last publication relate to writings by Bewerunge on organ-building technique and on tonality in Gregorian chant which first appeared in the Cecilian journals *Kirchenmusikalisches Jahrbuch* and *Musica Sacra*.[30]

As with Donnelly before him, Bewerunge's reputation was initially established as a translator, although the works which he published in this capacity were in fact unconnected (strictly speaking) with music in church: a version of Hugo Riemann's *Katechismus der Musikaesthetik* which appeared in 1891 and a version of the same author's *Vereinfachte Harmonielehre*, published in 1896. The pedagogical cast of these writings typifies the tone and purpose of much of Bewerunge's own work, but the point to observe here is that Bewerunge's technical competence extends beyond the domain of sacred music and encompasses, at least in part, the work of the foremost German musicologist of the day.

As a propagator of the Cecilian movement, Bewerunge's work as editor of *Lyra Ecclesiastica* and the papers which he published on church music in Ireland and abroad are obviously of the first importance. His lengthy report on the thirteenth general meeting of the German Society of St Cecilia, held in Graz from 24 to 26 August 1891, exemplifies the blend of admonitory criticism and factual observation which characterised Bewerunge's music journalism throughout his tenure as editor of *Lyra*. Preliminary to the report itself is an account of Bewerunge's visit to the Hofburgkapelle in Vienna, in order to hear a mass by Mozart:

> I was greatly disappointed. There was a great noise of instruments – of the brass especially – and through this noise the singers tried in vain to make themselves heard. How much better do they perform in the opera house! But for the church anything seems to be good enough. From a liturgical point of view I should condemn the performance still more. Those meaningless flirting violin figures! Those dance-like rhythms which make one smile against his will! No, Mozart, we venerate thee as a musical genius of the first rank, but let them spare us thy masses! After the Credo I left the Hofburg-Kapelle and went to the Hofpfarrkirche of St Augustin. There I heard another credo of Mozart's which made a still worse impression on me.[31]

Lesser composers were given even shorter shrift.[32] It would be a mistake to regard these comments as unique to Bewerunge's admittedly forthright and trenchant style of criticism: the tone of his remarks, on the contrary, compares closely with that of his predecessors in the pages of *Lyra*, as we have indicated here.

Bewerunge gives praise in this report when he feels it is due: a rendering of Palestrina's mass *Ecce ego Johannes* during the Graz festival is described as a 'magnificent performance', while other, more modern works come 'dangerously near the concert style'. Bruckner's 'Ave Maria' is 'a good composition, but rather straining after effect, and I should not recommend it as church music'.[33] The point of such observations, along with other detailed comments on the quality and type of choirs and organs to be found in the churches of Graz, was to underline the extent to which the music adhered to or deviated from the aesthetic norms of the Cecilian ideal, namely, a corpus of music and a style of performance which would enhance and respect the liturgical demands of the religious service in question. Those demands for Bewerunge almost invariably meant the use of the chant and/or vocal music of the High Renaissance.

Bewerunge's extensive assessment of 'Palestrina and Orlando di Lasso' appeared in the December 1894 issue of the *Irish Ecclesiastical Record*. In this essay his emphatic preference – in aesthetic as well as liturgical terms – for the works of the Counter-Reformation is definitively Cecilian in temper:

> But their [Palestrina and Lassus] principal importance lies not in this, that they, in their time, advanced musical art a considerable step, and that their works continue to be a worthy object of study and imitation for the earnest student of music, but in the fact that, as Church musicians, they have created works which have never been surpassed, and which must still be regarded as the ideal model of all church music written in parts.[34]

This reformulation of the Cecilian ideal, itself an aesthetically inhibiting one, is fortified in 'Palestrina and Orlando di Lasso' by a precise disclosure of the facts of (then) recent musical scholarship, particularly with regard to Haberl's work on the biography of Palestrina.[35] Bewerunge devotes considerable space to a biographical account of both composers which is informed by this scholarship, but he also distinguishes between them in critical terms which illuminate his persuasive reading of musical style:

> Then the Mass is the more perfect form of church composition and it is the perfection of the formal, the full and consistent development of the musical idea that is characteristic of Palestrina's style. Orlando's strength . . . lay principally in the power of direct and vigorous expression, in the invention of striking and characteristic musical ideas. And for this he had more scope in the form of the motet, in which . . . each phrase of the text was to receive a new musical formation suitable to express the peculiar mood suggested by the words. In a word, Orlando possessed what we now call dramatic power . . . Haberl compares Palestrina with Raphael, Orlando with Albrecht Dürer. I should feel inclined to compare them with Bach and Handel. Lasso and Handel are both masters of the polyphonic style . . . but they do not care so much for logical development, and are always prone to follow the unrestricted flight of imagination, rather than by reflection deepen their work. Like Giants they proceed, and in a few bold outlines, draw a picture overpowering us by the grandeur of its conception and the strikingness of its expression . . . Palestrina and Bach . . . no less fertile in invention . . . constantly, like Gothic architects, try to give us their conception of a strictly logical form; they glory in carrying out a musical idea to its extreme consequences; they strive to explain the full meaning of their thoughts by following them out into their most profound depth.[36]

If the notion of cultural history which underlies these stylistic observations appears naïve or simplistic in the late twentieth century, we do well to remember that such comparisons were validated by musical historiography long after 1894: neither Gustave Reese's concept of Renaissance style nor Manfred Bukofzer's formulation of the musical baroque, for example, would seem to be radically at odds with Bewerunge's discrimination between Lassus and Palestrina vis-à-vis Handel and Bach. On the contrary, we find in Bewerunge's discussion an attempt to rationalise forms of musical imagination in terms which accommodate both the didactic and religious ends of Cecilianism and the inherent aesthetics of the music itself, independent of liturgical function and meaning. Such discriminations bespeak a sensitive response to the concept of musical style.

Bewerunge advocates three reasons in this essay for the revival and imitation of High Renaissance polyphony. The first reason is that polyphony is 'a higher form of art when all the parts are imbued with melodic interest than when one part absorbs it all, and leaves the rest devoid of it'.[37] The second reason depends on the 'purely vocal character' of the music itself, which for Bewerunge renders it especially suitable for liturgical purposes. The third reason is more complex and controversial:

> It is an undeniable fact that the music of the last three centuries has been mainly used for the expression of profane sentiments, of secular enjoyments, and worldly passions. Composers poured out in tones all the manifold feelings of their heart, or illustrated dramatically the sentiments of imaginary personages. Sexual love is the subject of a great deal of our music, and dance music not only increased to a large amount, but also influenced considerably the development of musical forms. Far be it from us to blame music for the course which it has taken. As a pure art it has achieved great things, which we must gladly enjoy. But we cannot overlook the fact that the expression of religious sentiments has been lost to a considerable extent; and to recover it, therefore, we must go back to a time when it was known, and we must study the masters who wrote before it was lost.[38]

This argument clarifies, in uniquely candid terms, the aesthetic *raison d'être* of the Cecilian movement.

In Ireland, as elsewhere, it met with considerable opposition. Bewerunge sought to establish opera as the central expressive force in Western music from the seventeenth century onwards, in order to show that the formulation of an independent mode of expression for church music was essentially incompatible with this force. In 'Palestrina and Orlando di Lasso', Bewerunge is careful to distinguish his acknowledgement of and admiration for the expressive norms and concerns of secular music, so that his insistence upon the loss of a corresponding sacred norm – justifiable from the vantage point of Palestrina's achievement, for example – may be all the more plausible. Notwithstanding the integration of sacred and secular materials in the Lutheran traditions of the German baroque, it is not hard to concur with Bewerunge's argument, if we limit ourselves to Roman Catholic music. It is a point of view which historians of musical culture have formulated and reformulated to the present day.[39] Within the domain of Catholic church music, the controversies over modern style which dogged Monteverdi's sacred and secular works, the wholly secular idiom of the Viennese court mass in the hands of Mozart or Haydn, and the appropriation of the text of the mass ordinary and other liturgical texts as a means of individuated romanticism (as in Beethoven, Liszt, Verdi) all support the basic thrust of Bewerunge's reasoning. Bewerunge writes from the point of view of one for whom the liturgical texts of the church represent and embody doctrinal truths, disclosed at a fixed point in human history. That music should adorn and illuminate these truths, Bewerunge takes for granted. That it should *appropriate* them, solely in order to widen the scope of individual thought or expression, he rigorously rejects.

Bewerunge's arguments in turn were rejected by those who opposed his reactionary reading of the state of sacred music in the Catholic Church beyond the sixteenth century. The *New Ireland Review* sought to rehearse these arguments and counter-arguments in a series of articles which clarified the controversy, although they notably failed to resolve it. Rev George O'Neill, in two papers respectively entitled 'Musicians in Controversy' and 'Sacred Music as a Living Art', summarised an exchange of letters between Bewerunge and three correspondents, 'C.Sharpe', F. Maguire and 'J.B.', which had appeared in the *Daily Nation* in 1899. This correspondence, O'Neill sardonically observed, 'lay somewhat above the ordinary range of newspaper discussion'.[40]

The correspondence concerned the 'aesthetico-liturgical' considerations which might be brought to bear on the use of contemporary idioms in church music. O'Neill, paraphrasing 'C.Sharpe', formulated the objections to the Cecilian argument in this way:

> Church music ought to be modern, living and as much in harmony with our mental and moral contribution in this current year of grace as are the secular works of Dvořák and Brahms. But the sacred music of the sixteenth century is *not* modern, living and as much in harmony, etc., etc. Therefore it is not what church music . . . ought to be.[41]

F. Maguire put the matter in similar terms:

> In modern music, dramatic or other, we have progressed during this century from the comparatively restricted harmonic effects of Handel and Haydn to the immeasurably bolder, richer, more passionate effects of Wagner, Dvořák, Grieg, etc. Musical critics may not agree that the highest type of music has been reached, but unquestionably the vast bulk of listeners find that in such music the directest and keenest appeal has been made to their own likings and emotions. Then why should our religious emotions be chilled and restricted by a style of music which we have outgrown, for which we feel at best a certain admiration, but not sympathy? . . . Father Bewerunge, while holding that Palestrina's music ought to be 'intelligible' to me because of that much-discussed 'inherent relation' between our aesthetic faculties and musical expression in general, holds that I ought to like it because of its 'artistic excellence and liturgical fitness' . . . but what has been strongly questioned is whether Palestrina's artistic excellence is of a kind that makes any appeal to a modern congregation and whether 'liturgical fitness' requires that we should limit ourselves . . . to absolutely Palestrinian compositions, or (with Father Bewerunge) to modern works, moving within much the same limits as the Palestrinian.[42]

This *argumentum ad hominem* found support, according to O'Neill, in 'many musical utterances which bear out the view of Father Bewerunge's opponents, that music not only finds, like every other art, its very life in perpetual change and development, but is more than any art a creature of mutability.'[43] O'Neill cites Hermann Helmholtz, Eduard Hanslick, Edmund Gurney, Jean-Jacques Rousseau and J.R. Lowell on the inevitability of musical change: a strategy which is intended to reinforce the literate and well-informed persuasions of Bewerunge's detractors. One of these persuasions, as we have seen, was that the music of Counter-Reformation Italy could not satisfy the aesthetic demands of nineteenth-century Ireland. Another was that newly composed church music in a proto-Renaissance style must be artistically defunct. Robert Dwyer, professor of Irish music at the Catholic University of Ireland, put the case even more strongly:

> The recent movement among a few leading Church-musicians and others more or less responsible for our liturgical performances, in favour of a 'purer style', and in opposition to what they have termed the 'theatrical style' of Haydn, Mozart, Beethoven and their contemporaries, has had, as most things have, its disadvantages. One of these has been the production of a great deal of music which is feeble, half-matured and oppressively dull. It seems intended to give satisfaction to the contemporary Cecilian mind; but how such music could minister agreeably to the taste or devotional feeling of anyone at all given to the contemplation of things either divine or simply beautiful is indeed to me a mystery.[44]

All such 'imitations of Palestrina' (the title of Dwyer's essay) were repugnant to the aesthetic and progressive criteria by which Bewerunge's opponents assessed the question of music in church. The distinction which Bewerunge and the Cecilian movement at large wished to make between sacred and secular modes of artistic endeavour seemed essentially false and untenable to Dwyer and his contemporaries.

Bewerunge, however, remained implacable. In a final statement on the 'C.Sharpe' controversy (as O'Neill termed it), he repudiated the arguments ascribed to him by Maguire and others with respect to his supposedly exclusive concern with chant and sixteenth-century polyphony. He also cleverly maintained that the 'antiquity of Gregorian chant cannot be argued against its capacity to live', by drawing an analogy between the chant and the revival of Irish melodies which 'it is thought . . . contain within them the germ that may be developed into a fresh luxuriant growth of Irish music'.[45] Given his command of musical history and his sheer ability to pursue an argument to its conclusion, it is not surprising to find that Bewerunge easily and impressively dismissed the attacks of his opponents. But those attacks bespoke a socio-religious climate of feeling which was inimical to the scholarly and devotional rigour of the Cecilian movement at its innately conservative extreme. Bewerunge urged the wholesale reanimation of sixteenth-century polyphony for the sake of its 'devotional qualities' not in any simplistic sense, but because that music, along with the chant, culminated the artistic quest for a liturgical mode of musical expression. Such a belief was clearly incompatible with the opinion of his adversaries and Bewerunge finally conceded as much:

> In conclusion, I may say that I do not promise myself very much advantage from discussions of this kind. Arguments brought forward against what I consider the right view I have tried to refute, and shall try to refute in the future. But this is only negative work, and the positive work is of far greater importance.[46]

For Bewerunge, that work lay not only in the advocation of training and education for Irish church musicians,[47] but also in the astringent and scholarly elucidation of the preservation, history and publication of Gregorian chant. In this domain too he was to prove intransigent and controversial.

*   *   *   *   *

Bewerunge's writings on the chant seem in fact almost pervasively negative in tone, if positive in intention. His seminal response to the Vatican edition of the chant, which first appeared in three papers published in the *Irish Ecclesiastical Record* in 1906 and afterwards in French and German translations, justifies such an assessment of his contribution to the history of sacred music.[48] If we leave to one side the implications of the Vatican edition for the Cecilian movement as a whole – to which I return at the close of this chapter – we can perhaps gain some notion of the methods and observations which Bewerunge brought to bear on the whole question of chant scholarship.

Five factors characterise Bewerunge's reading of the Vatican edition of the chant. The first of these is a summary of the papal legislation which led to its inception and to the corresponding withdrawal of the former decrees in support of the Regensburg (Medicaean) edition.[49] Bewerunge quotes extensively from *Motu proprio* of 25 April 1904 in order to establish that the forthcoming Vatican edition was to be based on a comparative scrutiny of the extant codices of chant material:

> But then something unexpected happened. By a letter of his Eminence, Cardinal Merry del Val, dated 24 June 1905, Dom Pothier, the President of the Commission, was made the sole judge of the version of the new edition, and the other members were reduced to the position of his helpers . . . Dom Pothier, as soon as he had got a free hand, set to work vigorously, and at the Gregorian congress in Strasbourg last August [1905], it was announced that the last sheet of the 'Kyriale' had got the final *Imprimatur*. At the same time, the Commission, that is to say, the majority of the members present in Strasbourg, declared that the 'Kyriale' represented the fruit of the long and enlightened labours of the monks of Solesmes. We shall see how much truth there is in this.[50]

This controversial beginning to Bewerunge's assessment predicates a second critical strategy: his visit to the Isle of Wight (Appuldurcombe), where the Benedictine collection of chant manuscripts was then deposited, in order to compare Dom Pothier's edition with the manuscripts themselves. His findings there resulted in a detailed catalogue of 'misreadings' which he discerned in the Vatican edition. Bewerunge compares, detail for detail, note formations, melodic formulae and modal structures to be found in French, German, English and Spanish codices, as against those printed in the Vatican edition. This second, central factor enables Bewerunge to fortify his general censure of the Vatican edition with a specific textual critique of considerable authority and even plausibility.

Bewerunge's general observations on these misreadings focus upon the whole question of editorial procedure:

> It would be difficult to see any definite principle in all the cases where Dom Pothier has defied the evidence of the MSS. In some cases, as we have seen, he followed a special current of tradition against the general tradition, in others, a morbid fear of the tritone made him introduce changes. But for most cases the only actuating principle that could be assigned is his 'aesthetic taste', or shall we say, his whim? In any case it is clear that he has given up his role as restorer of the ancient melodies, and has joined the ranks of the 'reformers'.[51]

Anger and indignation notwithstanding, this scrutiny of editorial principle, original sources and printed text in Bewerunge's reading of the Vatican edition of the chant represents positivistic criticism of a high order, and it belongs to the (then) comparatively recent tradition of German musicological methodology. Bewerunge's third strategy, the condemnation of Dom Pothier as a 'discreditable' editor, depends on this examination and to some extent is justified by it.

Bewerunge, moreover, finds the Vatican edition to be the 'saddest spectacle of all' (i.e. of all editions of the chant) because no other edition is the outcome of an act 'of the central authority of the Church'. This last point represents the fourth factor in Bewerunge's reasoning against certain editorial procedures in the Vatican edition: 'If the *Vaticana* [Vatican edition] cannot stand on the strength of its intrinsic excellences, no artificial propping up by decrees will prevent it from tumbling down.'[52] Bewerunge is concerned here not only to insist upon the primacy of scholarly rigour over papal authority, but also to acknowledge that such authority in itself does not guarantee the inherent usefulness of any given edition, a point he readily concedes with regard to the Regensburg texts. However harsh these strictures, Bewerunge's fifth and final point with regard to the Vatican *Kyriale* is that 'of all existing editions it is the best'.[53]

In his review of the *Commune Sanctorum* of the Vatican edition, also published originally in the *Irish Ecclesiastical Record* in 1906, Bewerunge finds that he 'cannot say the same of it'. Using an exactly similar means of criticism and comparative reference to the Solesmes manuscripts and the edition itself (which entailed a second visit to the Isle of Wight), Bewerunge intensifies his charge against Dom Pothier, namely, that the latter has largely ignored this vast corpus of source material and has instead wilfully introduced changes into the Gregorian melodies without any firm scholarly basis for having done so. One brief excerpt will illustrate the specific nature of Bewerunge's observations in this regard:

> The melody of the Alleluja verse *Hic est sacerdos* is one which recurs frequently. On the neuma of the Alleluja Dom Mocqereau published a special dissertation in the *Rassegna Gregoriana* of May–June 1904, page 311. From a careful examination of eighty-six codices, giving some 700 or 800 notations of the melody, he proves conclusively that the five notes c d f d f form one group. Notwithstanding, the *Vaticana* still separates the last f from the preceding group. It seems clear, then, that the editor does not want to act even on the most convincing evidence.[54]

Bewerunge's criticism of the Vatican edition is technically astringent, well-informed and unremittingly precise. It openly depends on textual scrutiny and on extensive secondary reading. It would be fatuous to contend, however, that his critiques were and are not vulnerable to subsequent modification, even if he himself found this difficult to accept.[55] Nevertheless his writings on the chant are remarkable in at least two general respects: they establish Bewerunge's own authority as a textual critic of significance on the *musicological* aspects of the chant question (as distinct from the ideological concerns voiced in his 'Cecilian' writings), and they confirm the virtually anomalous achievement of this Maynooth professor in the scholarly recension of church music. We have already seen that this achievement was adumbrated in the work of Donnelly and Walsh, but Bewerunge's penetrating mastery of paleographical techniques, which his criticism of the Vatican edition amply demonstrates, stands alone in an Irish context. His use of materials from *Paléographie Musicale*, his contributions to theories of note formation and metrical theory and his essays in organology extend decisively beyond the domain of informed response.[56]

\*   \*   \*   \*   \*

Karl Gustav Fellerer has observed that the withdrawal of the decrees in support of the Regensburg edition of the chant dealt a critical blow to the Cecilian movement.[57] Although Fellerer imputes an even greater seriousness to the inner aesthetic crisis of the movement, which effectively constituted a resistance to the impact of contemporary modes of musical thought on the liturgy, it seems clear that the Cecilian movement could not survive in its former strength because it was deprived of a meaningful role in the pursuit of chant scholarship with the advent of the Solesmes school. Deprived of its intellectual authority, it lapsed into aggrieved debate or silence.

In Ireland, this crisis was sharply apostrophised in the person and career of Bewerunge himself. An exhaustive reading of *Lyra Ecclesiastica* has shown that Bewerunge not merely presided over its demise in the two years during which he edited the bulletin, but that his critical castigations and strikingly insensitive demeanour gradually eroded whatever enthusiasm remained for a concerted Cecilian movement in Ireland.[58] His own response to this diminished interest was to turn his attentions elsewhere, and precisely to a scrutiny of the new chant editions. Moreover, Bewerunge's location as professor of sacred music in Maynooth meant that he was necessarily removed from that network of Dublin churches which had fostered and realised the objectives of the Cecilian movement from 1878 until 1903. In the last ten years of its existence (1893–1903) the Dublin Diocesan Committee [of the Irish Society of St Cecilia] functioned independently of Bewerunge, from whom it was effectively estranged. There is some irony in this development, given that it was Nicholas Donnelly's passionate admiration for Regensburg which led to Bewerunge's appointment at the forefront of Irish Cecilianism. Bewerunge's exacting aloofness to one side, the movement could not adequately reconcile its principles of uniform, ultramontanist liturgical music with the claims of individual freedom of expression.

In James Joyce's 'The Dead', another complication sets in:

> Aunt Kate turned fiercely on her niece and said: ' I know all about the honour of God, Mary Jane, but I think it's not at all honourable for the pope to turn out the women of the choirs that have slaved all their lives and put little whipper-snappers of boys over their heads. I suppose it is for the good of the Church, if the pope does it. But it's not just, Mary Jane, and it's not right.'[59]

Joyce is referring here to the expulsion of women from church choirs which was uniformly demanded throughout the Catholic Church as a result of the promulgation of the 1903 Motu proprio, a drastic move justified on the grounds of historical and expressive authority. And Aunt Kate's outraged sense of natural justice on behalf of her sister begs this question of individual rights as against the demands of a controlled, romanised liturgical music. In Joyce's case, the question is circumscribed by multiple ironies, one of which is that 'Mary Jane' in the story is the main provider of the household because 'she had the organ in Haddington Road'.[60] Women were not forbidden to play for choirs (or to conduct them, for that matter), only to sing in them. It probably never occurred to Pius X that such a situation would arise, that women would actually hold paid positions as church organists or choral directors. The Pauline chauvinism of Motu proprio (mulier tacet in ecclesia) was born of the same sense of prior commitment which enfranchised the Cecilian movement; it simply took to logical extremes the aesthetic and liturgical parameters of Cecilianism:

> The Holy Father has spoken, and matters which were regarded as subjects for discussion have been removed from the region of controversy to the region of obedience . . . The day for individual expression of opinion has happily gone forever.[61]

It was this sense of finality that persuaded many Cecilians that the cause of the reform was won. The waning authority of the German movement certainly diminished the impact of Cecilian principles in terms of organised societies throughout Europe, even if the afterlife of reform continued to be felt in institutions such as Bishop Donnelly's choir guild and the Palestrina Choir, endowed by Edward Martyn in the pro-cathedral in Dublin.[62] Nevertheless, with the disintegration first of *Lyra Ecclesiastica* and then of the Irish Society of St Cecilia itself, the implications of the 1903 *Motu proprio* seemed to signal the virtual demise of this self-contained episode in Irish cultural history. Those implications would not have been enough to thwart the great triumvirate of Walsh, archbishop of Dublin and passionate advocate of European musical culture, Donnelly, Cecilian *extraordinaire*, whose refined sense of aesthetic necessity also went hand in glove with his membership of the hierarchy, and Bewerunge, Maynooth professor and ardent (if intemperate) perpetrator of the scholarly positivism of German musicology. But other events intervened and the mere force of personality could no longer sustain an aesthetic ideal which itself was increasingly untenable in the face of early twentieth-century Irish history. The First World War destroyed Bewerunge's health; the claims of nationalist politics distracted Walsh from his prior commitment to music, and the attractions of local history finally attenuated even Donnelly's loyalty to a cause to which he had given over half of his long lifetime.

At the last, those issues of doctrinaire policy-making and the exclusion of artistic individualism which characterised the Cecilian movement were remaindered by the broader, more imperative demands of church–state relations in the first decades of the twentieth century. As Ireland changed, the spoken liturgy of the Roman Catholic Church admirably met the spiritual–nationalist synthesis of the new state. Church music, meanwhile, accommodated itself to an ever wider degree of compromise which embraced a range of musical philistinism intermixed with the remnants of chant and polyphony which survived: *Tantum ergo*, *Panem de coelo*, the *Missa de Angelis*. And alongside these shibboleths, there were the cloying sentiments of a new hymnology which loudly proclaimed the musical banalities of congregational religious feeling: *Soul of my Saviour*; *I'll Sing a Hymn to Mary*; *Sweet Sacrament Divine*. Without the infrastructures of widespread musical education, nothing could stem the tide of mediocrity which was to follow. The Catholic Church in Ireland would for decades after *Motu proprio* hang fire on the question of music as an art. It would largely content itself with music as the conduit of popular (religious) sentiment. In this respect, it followed the new state.

\* \* \* \* \*

Yeats remarked in *Explorations* that the *Playboy* riots signalled an end to the 'Celtic Movement' and a beginning to the 'Irish Movement' which took its place. The disappearance of romantic Ireland and in its stead the terrible beauty of 1916 are conventional markers not only in the development of

Yeats's aesthetic but in the cultural history of Ireland as a nation state. It is not too much to say that the Cecilian movement, and more especially the espousal or cultivation of an art music aesthetic, was decisively eclipsed by this progression. At best, a curious aftermath of debate lingered on: proponents of 'Irish Ireland' sought to derive the modal quality of traditional music from the structures of Gregorian chant.[63] This intersection between the causes of church music and those of Irish nationalism (personified readily by Edward Martyn, Annie Patterson and Richard Henebry at the turn of the century) did not produce much of significance: it is a mistake, as a consequence, to read the history of Cecilianism in Ireland as an expression (however muted) of nationalist politics. Instead, it is preferable to see the movement for what it was: an attempt to consolidate the 'devotional revolution' in terms which might reflect the consensus of an Irish Catholic middle class. Of course it was no less Irish for that. Even if we concede that this peculiarly Continental mode of Irish Catholicism was overlaid by an ethos of 'Victorian respectability' (one thinks again of Joyce), there is no reason for the cultural historian to disdain it. To do so is to suppose that the only version of Irish history – cultural or otherwise – that matters is one which reads into the 1880s and 1890s the spirit and substance of 1916. *After* 1916 the redoubled energies of a Catholic–nationalist synthesis excluded the development of art music not only within the church but beyond it. Thereafter, it was not *motu proprio* but the essential irrelevance of art music in Ireland which proved decisive. And a synthesis between church and state which produces *Faith of our Fathers* does not (and did not) hold out much promise of artistic regeneration. That state of affairs, too, belonged to the new Ireland.

# MUSIC AND THE
# LITERARY REVIVAL

William Butler Yeats is, perhaps, the only absolutely original man we have in our midst. Certainly, as far as published work enables us to judge, he is the only absolutely original poet we have. Folklorists, framers of many-sided fiction, classic commentators, historians, new humorists, weavers of graceful lyrics, are beginning to tune up more frequently for our pleasure and edification than was the case erstwhile. I do not put the suggestion in any spirit of irreverence or cynicism . . . but if a plague of silence were to fall upon each and all of the aforementioned tomorrow, *would our lives lack much music in consequence?*[1]

It may be maintained . . . that we already have a school of national music. We have – in a sense – just as we have a school of local folklore, but the one cannot be taken as the final goal beyond which there could be no advance any more than the other. No one would have our legends and tales remain for ever at the stage of development which suited our remote ancestors. But we have amongst us those who consider that Irish music should stop short in its development, who ask us to remain content with traditional tunes and melodies, and who anathematise all such modern inventions as Cantatas, Overtures, Symphonies, Sonatas, etc., as so much waste of energy, misplaced matter utterly unsuited to the Irish temperament and genius.[2]

I think I may claim in all modesty that I was the first to translate the hidden Ireland into musical terms. And all this I owed in the first place to Yeats, for his was the key that opened the gate of the Celtic wonderland and his the finger that pointed to the Magic Mountain whence I was to dig nearly all that may be of value in my own art. Neither does my debt to that great man end there, for his poetry has always meant more to me than all the great music of the centuries; all the days of my life I bless his name.[3]

It is a commonplace that the most significant event in modern Irish cultural history is the literary movement which stemmed directly from the Celtic revival of the 1890s. Between the death of Parnell in 1891 and the Easter Rising of 1916, a body of Irish literature written in English changed utterly the complexion of cultural life in Ireland and once more threw into sharp relief the relationship between Irish political aspiration and political expression. The phrase 'changed utterly' of course belongs to W. B. Yeats,[4] and it was Yeats's own writings that imposed coherence on the literary revival as a movement which bypassed the bourgeois politics of the Irish Parliamentary Party and the ethnocentric atavism of the Gaelic League. The cultural nationalism which Yeats gradually espoused under the aegis of a Celtic renaissance he interpreted principally as an act of transcendence: 'an illogical blend of radical fervour and occult yearning, mingled with an evangelical certainty and excitement'.[5] Given Yeats's explicit sense of himself as high priest and mentor of revivalist discourse (no more exactly formulated than in the query 'Did that play of mine send out/Certain men the English shot?'[6]), it is not too much to say that every other significant writer in the revival was to a greater or lesser extent his acolyte: John Synge, Lady Gregory, AE (George Russell), Padraic Colum and even George Moore.

The Yeats vision of an Irish poetry and drama in English, forged from an idealised version of Ascendancy values and a nationalist culture liberated from quotidian politics, was one which these writers brilliantly and variously sustained. The Celtic myths of the revival were not merely the imposition of a late romantic exoticism; they were not simply a fertile reworking of the stories and legends of ancient Ireland (as in Standish O'Grady's immensely influential *History of Ireland: Heroic Period*, 1878–80). Instead, the group of writers around Yeats and pre-eminently Yeats himself regarded the romanticising of the Celt as an inadequate process, one which took account of the folk tradition but which excluded the small pantheon of eighteenth-century Anglo-Irish writers so dear to Yeats's sense of himself. Seamus Deane remarks that 'the most seductive of all Yeats's historical fictions is his gift of dignity and coherence to the Irish Protestant Ascendancy tradition'.[7] This bestowal of significance upon Berkeley, Burke, Swift, Goldsmith and Sheridan lends precedence and authority to Yeats's own attempt to understand Irish history as a repudiation of the 'filthy modern tide' which he intended to stem. Yeats understood the Anglo-Irish as an aristocracy which might be in fresh communion with the Catholic peasant, both united in their rejection of bourgeois mercantilism. In short, Yeats energetically misconstrued and mythologised history in the service of his own poetic vision.

That vision, however, was essential to the success of the revival: it lent it the desirability of a Celtic tradition which was at once aristocratic and individualistic and which manifested a unity of cultural purpose in the face of contemporary Ireland at large:

> The authentic Celtic tradition, in such a view, was organic and coherent, aristocratic and individualistic. As such, it could be exploited . . . as a powerful symbolic corrective to the sectarian, exclusivist, democratic and collectivist doctrines of Irish Ireland and Modern Irish political nationalism.[8]

This notion of the Celtic tradition as a 'corrective' to the condition of modern Ireland is one which polarised the literary revival in relation to the Gaelic League. The central difference between the two (revival and League) turned on the language question. For Hyde, as we have seen, the symbolic status of

Irish culture was inextricably bound up with the Irish language itself, and the forms of cultural nationalism which he espoused in the Gaelic League primarily depended upon the re-creation of that language as the pre-eminent means of intelligible artistic expression. For Yeats, this effort to rehouse Irish as the central agency of artistic discourse was completely at odds with his own vision and realisation of an Irish literature in English. His virtual creation of the National Literary Society in 1892 and of the Irish Literary Theatre (with Edward Martyn, Lady Gregory and George Moore) in 1898 confirmed his divergence from Hyde (notwithstanding their continued collaboration in certain ventures).[9]

The differences between Hyde and Yeats, as between the Gaelic League and the National Literary Society, were only part of a spectrum. The 'battle of two civilisations', in D.P. Moran's famous phrase,[19] between those who purveyed the 'Celtic note' and those who contended the superior claim of a wholly 'Irish Ireland', took place in a wider context in which the essential political issue, Ireland's relationship with Britain as an emergent nation state, appeared to lie dormant after the split in the Irish Parliamentary Party on Parnell's death. Thus the redoubled association between Catholicism and Gaelic culture which Hyde disavowed but which nevertheless drew strength from the Gaelic League, the actively conservative climate of Roman Catholic Church politics between 1890 and 1922 and the convergence of Sinn Féin and the Irish Republican Brotherhood collectively rank as vital developments in Irish history of the period.[11]

Another vital component was Ulster. 'It was Ulster that blocked the way in 1912–14, and helped channel nationalist energies into what became Sinn Féin; it was Ulster resistance that should have provided the target for advanced nationalist aggression in 1916. The leaders of 1916, however, preferred . . . to ignore the reality of Ulster Unionism in favour of a mirage of "cultural unity" based on such irrelevancies as memories of Hugh O'Neill, and the Red Branch cycle'.[12]

The principal question to be raised here is the extent to which Irish cultural history produced and then rejected the literary revival in favour of a Catholic–nationalist synthesis. The 'blood-sacrifice' of Thomas MacDonagh, Joseph Plunkett and Patrick Pearse (all participants in the 1916 rebellion) was, to an extent, derived from the myths and narratives of Celtic Ireland which the Gaelic League and the literary revival shared in common (hence the authentic – if histrionic – scruple of 'Easter 1916'). And the aspirations towards cultural autonomy expressed by both sides invariably shaded into expressions of political freedom: this was as true of Yeats's *Cathleen ni Houlihan* (1902) as it was of Pearse's essay 'The Coming Revolution' (1913). That Yeats should publish 'Easter 1916' during the Anglo-Irish war of 1919–21 testifies further to this sharply contingent rapport between the sources of Celtic revivalism and the politics of the day. It is no great matter to suggest that Yeats was prepared to adjust and interpret his vision of the Celtic past in the wake of Pearse's 'terrible beauty'.[13] What is of account here is that his poetic sensibility accommodated the hostile divisions of revolution and social disintegration to the extent that the events of 1916 came to seem continuous with Yeats's original exploration of Celticism. Under the pressure of these events his high aesthetic of Celtic revivalism not only became more politicised, it also helped to define the Irish Rising as a redemptive force in European culture.[14]

That Yeats's development as a poet should have been co-terminous with the wider mutation from cultural to political unity of purpose (notwithstanding the thorn of Ulster Unionism) is a matter of central significance in this reading of Irish cultural history. The conflict between 'Irish Ireland' and the Anglo-Irish literary revival which his writings voiced was overtaken by the preoccupations of the new state after 1921. It can be argued that these preoccupations (in the main with a Catholic–nationalist synthesis of unparalleled intensity but also with the business of emergent independence) occluded Yeats, just as he had borne witness to the disappearance of Romantic Ireland in the poem 'September 1913'. But the contours of Yeats's poetic are extremely complex, and it is perhaps more useful to affirm simply that the vision of Celtic regeneration espoused in his plays and poems between 1890 and 1910 was sharply vitiated by a host of related events. Beyond 1921, Ireland could no longer remain completely hospitable to his imagination.

It is a truism to observe that no writer other than Yeats embodies so comprehensively the concept of literary revival in Ireland. What is not perhaps as immediately apparent is the consequence of this for music in Irish cultural history. Yeats's absolute indifference to music (with a few, notable exceptions)[15] would not be of moment were it not for the pervasive influence of his poetry in the formation of an Irish cultural aesthetic. This being the case, however, it is necessary to press home implications which arise in relation to music as a neglected source of *creative* endeavour in the revival except in one respect: its metaphorical resonance as a symbol of the literary imagination. This is a matter which bears especially upon Synge and Joyce in ways which relate to linguistic invention as a *substitute* for musical composition in Ireland. The impact of music upon the Irish literary imagination, in short, can seem more significant than the impact of music *per se*.[16]

This assertion, however, does not exhaust the question of music as a force within the terms defined by the Celtic revival. On the contrary, the revival itself helps to explain why the concept of art music failed to develop in any significant way at the turn of the century. We have already seen how the collection and preservation of the ethnic repertory was partly subsumed under the aegis of the Gaelic League and how that music came to be permanently regarded as a symbol of sectarian cultural discourse. It is useful to consider ways in which this repertory both inhibited and stimulated the prospect of an art music in Ireland answerable to the aesthetic of Celtic revivalism. In addition, we can examine the claim offered by Arnold Bax that Yeats's Celticism could provide a source for such an art music unrelated to ethnic traditions.[17]

The difficulties here are legion. Four principal questions, however, would seem to predominate. Firstly, there is the question of art music as an impoverished force in Ireland throughout the nineteenth century and especially after the Famine. Secondly, there is the tangle of associations between the folk music collections, art music based on these, and the aspiration of individual composers to conceive a style of Irish music. There is also the difficulty of historical perspective: whether to regard the concept of Irish art music as an integral force in Irish cultural history or as the expression of local colour within the broader terms of British music.[18] There is, finally, the perception of art music from within the cultural debate itself.

Each of these issues can be surveyed in order to try the case of music in relation to the literary revival. Alongside them, however, is the question of music as a preoccupation of that Catholic middle class which Yeats either repudiated or ignored in his writings. This issue does admittedly surface in relation to Irish periodical literature, and we have already seen some manifestation of it in the confined context of the Cecilian movement in Ireland. But it is a troubling fact of Irish cultural history that two individuals intimately involved with the revival – Edward Martyn and his cousin George Moore – appeared to fortify Yeats in his indifference to music, despite their much vaunted absorption of its influence.[19] Martyn's virtual obsession with liturgical music, moreover, increased upon his withdrawal from the Irish Literary Theatre, so that he too reinforced the cultural assumption that art music could exist in Ireland only as an expression of conservative pietistic fervour. His endowment of the Palestrina Choir in Dublin's pro-cathedral could scarcely have been more remote from his endorsement of Yeats's theatre. If anything, it represented instead a firm commitment to the culture of those who prayed and saved.[20]

\*   \*   \*   \*   \*

> Berkeley, Swift and Burke composed for Yeats an Irish Ascendancy tradition of 'idealism' which he then associated with the folk tradition in Ireland, claiming that each refuted science by its apprehension (although differently articulated in each case) of mystery and death. The peasant and the aristocrat, kindred in spirit but not in class, united in the great Romantic battle against the industrial and utilitarian ethic.[21]

The Ascendancy tradition in music was meagre: 'it left little in the way of practical estate'.[22] The idealism which Yeats discerned in the history of Anglo-Irish letters, especially with regard to that espousal of intimacy between aristocrat and peasant, was not one which accommodated music. To confront art music in Ireland during the nineteenth century is to reckon with atrophy. Whereas the ethnic repertory was absorbed by antiquarianism, by literature and by the politics of Young Ireland, the history and practice of art music relapsed into a strange provincialism, incapable of any significant artistic ferment. To an extent, this torpid condition reflects the wider malaise of British music for much of the nineteenth century; the mediocrity of Irish art music can also be explained otherwise. It is true that opera maintained a considerable presence, but preponderantly in terms of the performance and enthusiastic reception of an ever smaller number of works which enjoyed a degree of static popularity symbolic of the pervasive creative apathy: these works, or excerpts from them, passed into the bloodstream of fond (sometimes literary) remembrance, particularly in Dublin, but they attested more to the conservatism of bourgeois taste and less to any significant level of musical creativity.[23] The popularity of light romantic opera was insufficient to counter a quite remarkable degree of cultural musical stagnation.

Three institutions dominated the musical profile of Dublin for much of the nineteenth century: Trinity College and the two metropolitan (Established Church) cathedrals of Christ Church and St Patrick's. What little musical development there was emanated from these sources insofar as they provided the opportunity for experience, education and performance. The communion of cultural interest which they represented was effectively colonial and imperialist, which is not to gainsay the fact that those few individuals who made a sustained impact on the cultivation of art music also reflected a wider constituency of interest more plentiful in Britain than in Ireland. In brief, the Trinity–Christ Church–St Patrick's fulcrum produced a continuity of musicians whose professional commitment to church music accommodated in turn the cultivation of analogous secular genres in which large-scale choral music was pre-eminent.

This development was not immediate. The passing of the Act of Union in 1800 appeared to confirm the impoverished state of Ascendancy culture, at least in respect of music. James Culwick, writing to O. J. Vignoles c. 1898, confirms as much:

> In an Irish magazine, dated 1800, there is a review of the state of music at the opening of the century . . . There appeared to be some tuneful glee singing, and tasteful rendering of sentimental songs among the better class of musicians; but though Handel at his visit (1742) could find an orchestra and a band of musicians more than able to satisfy him, yet, in 1800, instrumental music of all sorts, it would seem, had almost vanished. Music had ceased to be a serious art having for its object pure ideals and elevation of thought . . . and our University had long ceased to count music as worthy of serious consideration.[24]

Throughout the nineteenth century, this dearth was never to be wholly overcome. But that slender continuity of commitment represented by Sir John Stevenson, Joseph Robinson (1815–1898), Sir Robert Prescott Stewart (1825–1894) and James Culwick himself (1845–1907) was vital to the more widespread regeneration of music after the Famine.[25]

There were important differences between these four: Stevenson was the only one among them to engage seriously (if unhappily) with the ethnic tradition (notwithstanding Culwick's important papers on Irish music delivered in 1897 to the National Literary Society); Robinson's contribution was not primarily as a composer but as organist (to the two cathedrals) and pre-eminently as soloist and conductor with the Dublin Philharmonic Society (founded in part by members of his family in 1826), and as founding director of the 'Antient Concerts' in 1834. His seminal contribution to the success of the Royal Irish Academy of Music (1848) and his choral-orchestral association, the Dublin Musical Society (1876–99), ensured the strength of his influence almost to the turn of the century.

Stewart trailed a similar path. His early musical training was as a chorister in Christ Church Cathedral and he subsequently became organist in Christ Church, the Chapel of Trinity College and St Patrick's Cathedral. In 1846 he accepted the post of conductor of the University of Dublin Choral Society and in 1862 he was appointed to the chair of music in Trinity. Throughout his multifarious career he emulated the pattern of organist–educator–composer so successfully established by his British contemporaries and immediate predecessors. He replicated, in effect, that commitment to public performance which characterised the Victorian church musician as instrumentalist, conductor and teacher.[26] A memoir of his conductorship of the Bray Philharmonic Society vividly conveys the extent of this commitment:

> Under his supervision, we undertook Handel's *Acis and Galatea*, Mendelssohn's music to the *Midsummer Night's Dream*, Locke's music to *Macbeth*, Mendelssohn's unfinished opera of *Lorelei*, and many other classical works. At the Bray concerts he was here, there and everywhere – now at the piano, now seizing the baton of the conductor, even singing himself to fill up a gap or taking a turn at a huge violoncello. . .
>
> His own cantata, *The Eve of St John*, was performed at one of the Bray concerts . . . His own music roused in him a pleasure half akin to pain. I believe it made him think how much more he might have done in this higher department of his art if he could have devoted more time to it. . . He told us that one day he had given twenty lessons at the Academy of Music, and none of his pupils, he added, with a smile, were interesting! Fancy the wear and tear of this, and of training choirs, and then his Sunday duty: the service at the College Chapel at a quarter to ten o'clock, then hurrying off to Christ Church at 11.15, then to the three o'clock service at St Patrick's.[27]

Stewart's professional obligations offer an extreme instance of the Victorian composer under the duress of multiple occupations. Notwithstanding certain rare exceptions in the theatre (as in the case of Arthur Sullivan), the British composer in the nineteenth century became intelligible to his public not as an independent artist but as a mouthpiece for the Establishment understanding of music. This meant in Ireland as in England a preponderant obligation to write music for public occasions, or more modestly, for the Established Church. Stewart's anthems and services, his cantatas (1858 and 1872) and above all his setting of George Savage-Armstrong's *Ode for the Tercentenary Festival* (of Trinity College in 1892) collectively answered this obligation. His regular contact with British and European festivals of music (from 1857 onwards) and his close connection with English contemporaries fortified Stewart's sense of provincial duty to a united, imperial concept of music. It was this sense of duty which in turn determined his response to the immediacy of his Irish surroundings. His remark in a letter dated December 1892 apostrophises the understanding which he had of the *status quo* of an Irish polity under pressure:

> We are in a great state of anxiety lest Gladstone's revolutionary Bill [to grant Home Rule or 'local autonomy' to Ireland] should become law, for that means widespread damage to Synod, Trinity College, and every interest of our Episcopal Church.[28]

For Stewart, musical composition was necessarily an outgrowth of this conception of Ireland. He was loyal, imperial, even colonial in outlook, and the occasional inclusion of stylised indigenous material in his compositions was a matter of exotic colour rather than distinctive identity, musical or otherwise. It was not that Stewart was unaware of the ethnic tradition: his censure of Petrie demonstrates otherwise, but rather that the ethnic tradition was effectively irrelevant to his understanding of art music, as the greater population of Ireland was to his own explicit Establishment view.[29] His letters show him to be a full-blooded, late Victorian musician absorbed not only by high church traditions but by Wagner, whose music dramas he heard in Bayreuth.[30] Intensely committed as he was to the tradition of European art music, he became a force in Irish music as one wholly conversant with that tradition and prepared to impart it to others. Having to conduct, play, teach, supervise and instruct to the extent that he did, Stewart's impact as a composer was necessarily restricted; as an educator, however, his range of influence was profound.

This sphere of influence is difficult to measure other than to point to the sheer force of his presence as a teacher and performer, especially in Christ Church and Trinity College. His long tenure consolidated the position of music as a permanent resource (however poorly financed) among that wider community of the Church of Ireland which had little to do with the Ascendancy itself. He was not solely responsible for this development: Joseph Robinson's stewardship of the Antient Concerts and the Dublin Musical Society rivals the significance of Stewart's achievements. Both men ensured the passage of music in Dublin from the sporadic recreation of a landed nobility to the preoccupation of a wider constituency, namely, the university and the middle classes of the Church of Ireland. Nevertheless, that constituency was narrow in terms of the entire population of Dublin (to say nothing of Ireland), and it is salutary to recognise how confining the extent of musical education and performance was to remain for the greater part of the nineteenth century. Stewart's own career, for example, began with a performance of *Israel in Egypt* by the University of Dublin Choral Society, given in February 1847 for the relief of victims of the Famine.[31] Forty-five years later, it closed with the Trinity Tercentenary *Ode*. Enclosed by the university and the cathedrals, it was Stewart's achievement to have cultivated these institutions so as to broaden the base of art music in Dublin. Had he not done so, there would have been few structures to sustain its growth as a force in public life.

'Public life' is worth a moment's scruple. If Robinson and Stewart nourished the cultivation of Handel, Beethoven, Mendelssohn and a host of lesser composers, they did so under the guidance of a sectarian divide. This is a matter which demands research both as to the repertory performed in Dublin during the nineteenth century and as to the extent to which opportunities for such performance embraced the Catholic middle class of the city. Joseph Ryan has recently advanced the argument that musical organisations such as John William Glover's Royal Choral Institute, which was established in 1851, represent 'the Catholic response to earlier Protestant initiatives'.[32] The public advertisement of its first concert, indeed, espoused the hope that the Royal Choral Institute would establish a large body of choristers 'composed chiefly of the working classes, capable of performing the best classical works, the performance of which is at present confined to private societies'.[33] If this notice argues the desire for a music 'more appropriate to their position than an unlearned oral tradition associated with the language and civilisation of servitude',[34] it also confirms a division of resources within the sphere of art music. This division was inevitably one of class and religious denomination. It was a division which was healed as the century closed, but not completely. The dissipation of slender means by which musical organisations duplicated activities better coordinated was to remain a feature of Irish cultural history well into the twentieth century.[35]

This was particularly true of music education. If anything hindered the development of a secure base for art music in Ireland it was the impoverished condition of music literacy and of music education in general throughout the country. The record of provision – again insofar as current research permits – is dismal. Commissioners' reports from the mid-1850s onwards suggest that the introduction of sight-singing classes (based consecutively on the methods of John Hullah and John Curwen) into Irish primary schools was slow and sparse: in 1851, of 204 schools examined only 6 were teaching music; in 1870, of 6,332 schools inspected, 688 were found to include the subject. If late in the century individual inspectors such as Peter Goodman advanced the cause of school music significantly, the First World War greatly reduced the standing of the subject in the primary school curriculum.[36]

The availability of formal musical instruction of any kind was scant throughout the first half of the nineteenth century: in a country which loudly proclaimed the inestimable resource of its corpus of folk music, the subject itself was all but ignored. This neglect was significantly redeemed by the institution of the Irish (afterwards Royal Irish) Academy of Music in 1848.

In several respects the founding of the Academy was the most crucial event with regard to music and Irish cultural history in the immediate aftermath of the Famine. It provided a focus for disparate energies in that it addressed the fundamental question of education; it drew together the resources of Robinson, Stewart and the host of (largely European) expertise which they were able to muster in its cause; it identified music as a constituent factor in Irish urban culture, and it promoted the idea of music education in ways which simultaneously drew for inspiration from Britain and the Continent. In this last respect it is useful to advert to similar institutions in London – notably the Royal Academy of Music (1822), the National Training School for Music (1876; afterwards the Royal College of Music [1883]), Trinity College of Music (1875) and the Guildhall School of Music (1880). At first glance it would seem that the Royal Irish Academy of Music, expressly intended 'for the children of respectable Irish parents', simply reflected that mid-Victorian tendency to impose a coherent academic agenda upon the hitherto uncertain process of music education. In part, it did. But whereas the complexion of musical awareness in Britain was at least comparatively healthy – and the proliferation of choral societies throughout the country and at every level of society bears witness to this – no such comparable substructure existed in Ireland.[37] There, the cultivation of art music remained the preoccupation of a small minority. The Academy furthermore could not hope to resolve the pervasive anomalies which continued to attend music in Ireland: a populace for the greater part musically illiterate in possession of an ethnic repertory which *de facto* had little or no place in government educational policy. It is true that by the last decade of the century some redress was attempted in that a Dublin Municipal School of Music was established under the aegis of the Academy to make 'provision for the musical instruction of the working classes'. The new institution was at first distinguished from its parent in musical as well as social terms: its brief was to offer instruction in woodwind, brass and percussion instruments. It thereby addressed the band movement in Dublin city which itself comprised a musical subculture effectively remote from the concerns of the Royal Irish Academy of Music. But the Municipal School began to offer classes in piano and stringed instruments by the turn of the century and replicated the work of the Academy, in the process 'losing sight of the concept of complementary institutions which together could furnish a wide range of skilled executants capable of peopling orchestras and ensembles'.[38] In short: more dissipation of resources.

Nevertheless, the Academy and the Municipal School advanced the condition of music to the extent that it was significantly freed from the Trinity–cathedrals enclave, even if personnel from the latter institutions continued to figure prominently in performance and education. It is tempting to suggest that the neo-Ascendancy origins of the Academy as against the nationalistic origins of the Municipal School reflected not only the explicit division of bourgeois *versus* working-class interests which respectively characterised both institutions, but also the polarities of musical culture in Ireland as a whole. But this is to exaggerate. What can be safely asserted is that both institutions consolidated the concept of art music as one which could transcend the colonial–ethnic divide. The old alignments of class and musical tradition (as between art music and the upper classes and traditional music and the peasantry) shifted in favour of new affiliations, as between ethnic music and nationalism on one side and a middle-class consensus for art music on the other. But this affiliation was subject to constant modification (as for example in the case of Edward Martyn, discussed earlier in this chapter).

If the Academy promised the hope of a more mature cultural base for music, it was slow to appear. The gap between instruction (now that it was available) and reception only appeared to widen:

> While . . . it is quite true that the greatest quickness and capacity for receiving musical ideas and impressions is common among the Dublin public, it is equally true that there are few places of importance where musical education is so disastrously backward. By musical education we do not in the least mean technical education. Of this latter we have plenty, and our fair share of distinguished and capable professors; but of that musical education which implies a thorough acquaintance with the best works of the best masters, Dublin folk, as a rule, know little or nothing.[39]

There is some irony in this critique, published as part of a review of the Dublin 1881 musical season in the journal *Hibernia*. Had not Stewart, Robinson and their colleagues expanded the range of musical performance in Dublin through the middle decades of the century, the impetus to establish education on a secure footing could not have been mustered. But the city could not seem to overcome those obstacles of class division which entailed at best a needless duplication of resources and at worst outright cultural stagnation:

> For what did and does our musical year generally consist? Taking last season as a fair average specimen we shall find something like the following – Two pianoforte recitals by Anton Rubinstein; three or four oratorios; twelve nights of opera in English (of which four were devoted to the *Bohemian Girl* and *Maritana!*); two or three ballad concerts, by so-called Italian artistes, and with programmes cursed with the immortality of the Struldbrugs; three very inadequately attended chamber concerts; a few performances, vocal and instrumental, by pupils of the Royal Irish Academy of Music; a sprinkling of that saddest of all sad things, amateur opera; small concerts, whose name was legion, by some half-dozen very well known amateurs; and the opening of a couple of new pianoforte warehouses – these are about the most notable events in the history of the last season.[40]

This gloomy catalogue speaks for itself. The reliance on Michael Balfe (1808–70) is noteworthy (compounded by the irony that benefit performances of *Maritana* led directly to the financing of the Academy twenty-five years earlier). So also is the apparent indifference to the quality of performance suggested by the *ad hoc* juxtaposition of a small number of professional musicians with their abundant amateur counterparts. If music flourished occasionally in Dublin, it did so casually. By the early 1880s it would seem that this indifference extended to the repertory itself:

> When we become more explicit, and add, that there was not a single first-class orchestral performance in our city; that not one of Mozart's symphonies or Beethoven's immortal nine was given (nor, has been for years!); that many works of the first rank, such as Mendelssohn's *Elijah*, lie practically on the shelf, that not a single public organ recital by any well-known performer was heard . . . and that our local societies, with the exception of that newest favourite [St Patrick's Oratorio Society, founded in 1880]), whose field of action is in St Patrick's Cathedral, are not supported at all as they should be by the public – when these things are so, it will hardly be conceded that all is right . . .[41]

These dismal findings convey the *status quo* of art music in Dublin: its depleted condition appeared to be permanent, even if sporadic surges of activity contradict the general sense of atrophy. Thus the existence of opera as a dynamic in the city's cultural life up to the 1830s enjoyed a long afterlife in actual revivals of Balfe, William Vincent Wallace (1814–65), Julius Benedict (1804–85) and Italian opera of the period, in the second half of the century. These works enjoyed another kind of afterlife in the communal memory of the Catholic bourgeoisie, an existence brilliantly characterised and exploited by James Joyce.[42] But the level of serious musical commitment was (otherwise) low. Celebrity recitals and short seasons by European luminaries of grand opera were self-serving, they did not contribute to a wider cultivation of art music *per se*. Charles Villiers Stanford's judgement on Stewart reflects this tenuous state of musical affairs:

> It was hard, even for one gifted with so brilliant a brain, to live in a circle of half-baked musicians without being affected by their standard, and still harder to occupy a position in which he had no rival to excel or learn from. He left his mark, however, on the 'melancholy island', which was responsible both for his witty and versatile gifts and for the lack of opportunity to give value and effect to them.[43]

This estimation brings us to Stanford himself.[44] Stanford's compositions – indeed his whole career – illustrate the difficulty of conceiving adequate terms for the understanding of music in Irish cultural history. A product of that Anglo-Irish synthesis of Trinity College and the cathedrals (insofar as he received his early musical education in part from Robinson and Stewart), Stanford was at once pivotal in the emancipation of British music from the Victorian claim of 'musico-social respectability' (Percy Young) and the victim of it. He was the first composer to address in any significant way the resources of Irish music and yet his response to the ethnic repertory was circumscribed by a fundamental disengagement from Ireland, except as a province of the United Kingdom. Unlike Yeats, who was born within the same generation, Stanford interposed a crucial distance between himself and Ireland, preferring instead to interpret the question of 'Irish music' as a matter of local colour within the spectrum of European music in general. His attempt to rationalise Irish folk music within the parameters of the European aesthetic is at the heart of the matter. Bernard Shaw, his *bête noire* in this respect, was quick to recognise this:

> As for Mr Villiers Stanford's Irish Symphony [1887], it is only an additional proof that the symphony, as a musical form, is stone dead. Some such structure as that used by Liszt in his symphonic poems would have admirably suited Mr Stanford's fantasia on Irish airs. The effect of mechanically forcing it into symphony form has been to make it diffuse and pedantic. Since Bach's death, the rule as to fugue has been 'First learn to write one, and then don't.' It is time, and has been ever since Beethoven's death to extend the rule to the symphony.[45]

However mercurial and quixotic in judgement, Shaw could perceive the essential dichotomy in Stanford's music which he characterised as a conflict between the Celt and the professor.[46] This annoying formulation oversimplifies the case, and Shaw used it as a stick with which to beat Stanford as an eminence of British music in general, but it does identify a problem in Irish music which in effect originated with Stanford. His thorough absorption of the European aesthetic was delimited – and revivified – by his imaginative debt to the German symphonic tradition. He also sustained an unprecedented commitment to the ethnic repertory, which enriched his own lyric impulse and determined the expressive range of a great deal of his instrumental writing. The difficulty is that neither element could be satisfactorily reconciled with the other. Shaw was not unique in seeing that this was the case, but it would be an obvious error of cultural history to suggest that this difficulty existed in any serious way for Stanford himself. There is no reason to suppose that Stanford attempted to create an 'authentic national style' in music, especially given that 'national' in this sense was politically and culturally repugnant to him.[47] But Stanford's music does exemplify a crucial miscalculation nevertheless, and that is the assumption that the traditional airs themselves (or edited versions thereof) could be absorbed into art music as the basis of an authentic *Irish* style. Joseph Ryan's argument that 'the very splendour of indigenous music, and the attention it has commanded, has inhibited the emergence of any substantial school of composition'[48] cannot really be applied retrospectively to Stanford. Stanford was not inhibited: he assumed if anything an attitude of benign, colonial appropriation with regard to his use of the ethnic repertory. It lent his music colour, a distinctive 'Irish note' and a

pitch of lyric intensity, with varying degrees of success. He diligently if errat-
ically researched and edited it as a corpus of music fundamentally exterior to
his own habits of mind and (musical) syntax.[49] He explored its resources not
to embody a definitive idea of Irish art music but to imbue his imaginative
response to the European aesthetic with a sense of place. The mere record of
his Irish works is unerring in its appropriation of a Celticism to be assumed
or discarded at will. The 'suffocating burden of tradition' hardly existed for
him in such terms.[50] Stanford drew upon Brahms and the folk collections
with the same uncomplicated gusto. To contemplate the *Irish* Symphony is to
bear out the validity of this assertion.[51]

The issue is a delicate one. The tendency has been to read back into Stanford's work that complicated history of aesthetic failure which was the outgrowth of music as a polarised and bifurcated resource in Irish cultural
history.[52] His special case is to have encountered the music independently of
its cultural context, as a composer whose professional focus was fixed whole
and entire on London. To read Stanford as an Irish composer somehow cor-
rupted by the European aesthetic is to misread the essential premise of his art.
Arnold Bax's famous critique apostrophises the extreme formulation of this
point of view:

> Stanford was not Irish enough. An Irishman by birth, he belonged to that class
> abominated by Irish Ireland, the 'West Briton'. There are intimations in some
> of his work that he started not without a certain spark of authentic musical
> imagination, but quite early he went a-whoring after foreign gods, and that
> original flicker was smothered in the outer darkness of Brahms.[53]

Similar indictments by Percy Young and Shaw complete the terms of this
adjudication.

> He was a kind of Anglo-Irish Dvořák, whose talents, however, rarely reached
> the fulfilment that they often seemed to promise. Stanford was a patriotic Irish-
> man. As such, he believed in the superiority of the Irish to the English, but,
> because of his social origin, felt obliged to associate himself with those among
> 'the English who held it as a high responsibility to keep the majority of the Irish
> in subjection. Thus Stanford's Irishness was vitiated by a disbelief in any vital
> form of national expression. He fell back upon watery legends and comfortable
> fancies to please drawing-room gatherings. Thus he trod some of the way pre-
> viously covered by Tom Moore. But before Ireland made any obvious impres-
> sion on his music he had thoroughly schooled himself in styles that were
> antithetical to all that truly Irish was. And, for that matter, to everything that
> English music should have been.[54]

> But as it is [1890], Mr Stanford is far too much the gentleman to compose any-
> thing but drawing-room or class-room music.[55]

The last of these three statements (from Shaw) closes Young's assessment of
Stanford in *A History of British Music* (1967), and it apostrophises the former's

reading of the English 'musical renaissance'. Stanford as the whipping-boy of English music is a sufficiently familiar habit of British music historiography not to require analysis here, but that Young should connote Stanford's failure in terms of *Irish* music does call for comment.

Young's argument would appear to be that Stanford by class and origin sold his birthright not for a mess of potage but for a knighthood. He thus excluded himself from the reality of Ireland and peddled instead a dilettantish exoticism which graced his own commitment to a central European aesthetic 'antithetical' to Ireland and the well-being of English music. Three flaws in this reading concern the position of Stanford's music in the aftermath of Irish cultural history. First, it was precisely his musical ability which necessitated his departure from Ireland, where, given the circumstances outlined in this chapter, it would have floundered. Second, the issue of 'nationalism' as a force in musical thought was inherently irrelevant to Stanford: 'Irishness' in this sense formed no part of the equation between indigenous and art music in his case. Third, his encounter with the indigenous repertory itself was not a matter solely of piecemeal opportunism. He certainly did not 'fall back' on it: his significance as an Irish composer in fact is that he positively tried to *incorporate* it in a number of substantial works. Young is prescriptive and motivated by his reading of British music at the turn of the century as a (largely) misdirected force blazing the trail of late Victorian pomposity. I am not concerned here to deny this reading (nor, for that matter, the stinging rebuff by Shaw which is used to support it) except in one central respect: the definition of 'Irishness' which lies behind it. I would argue that it is a definition inadequate both to Stanford's case and to the riven polity which he left behind him in Ireland. For Stanford, 'Irishness' was a remarkably simple (and commonplace) idea. It comprised the quotation of folksong. His own lyric impulse agreeably sustained this notion, with the result that many of the 'Irish' compositions have recourse to entire melodies which are arranged rather than recomposed into the musical fabric. The best known of the orchestral rhapsodies, for example, repeatedly shows this to be the case.[56] Over a career which spanned four decades, Stanford assumed this understanding of 'Irishness' again and again. The corpus of melody upon which he drew was for him self-contained, apolitical (except in terms of the mildest satire) and integral.

This is what makes Bax's charge of 'corruption' so untenable. Bax conceived all too clearly that Stanford was by class and social origin wholly removed from the 'Irish Ireland' syndrome, yet he condemned him for this fact and illogically asserted that his music had been overwhelmed by the European aesthetic and in particular by the precedent of Brahms. For Bax, degrees of Irishness ('not Irish enough') are degrees of authenticity, and the 'West Briton' is thus less authentic than the 'Irish Irelander'. But this reasoning collapses on two counts. First, it is underpinned by the chauvinistic assumption that Stanford's Anglo-Irish heritage obscured his access to the 'hidden' Ireland, and second, it assumes nevertheless a continuity of cultural discourse between this 'Irish Ireland' and the background to which Stanford belonged. The truth is more prosaic. The mere fact of Stanford's having been born into the Ango-Irish community would not have been enough to deflect his access to 'Irish Ireland' had he been so inclined to seek it: Douglas Hyde, for one, reveals the implausibility of that assumption. But had Stanford been born beyond the privileged class to which he belonged, had he in fact been 'Irish enough', his access to any form of musical education commensurate with his talents would not have been possible. Stanford, in short, was as Irish as he wished to be.

In this respect he resembles that entire tradition of Ascendancy writing which Yeats pressed into service of his Celtic revivalism. Like Yeats, Stanford had no command of the Irish language, but his knowledge of Irish airs was patently extensive. The fundamental difference between them in cultural terms is that whereas Yeats created an Irish literature as it passed from one language into the other, Stanford harvested Irish music strictly as a means of defining his response to a prevailing European aesthetic. We do not inquire, 'Was Yeats Irish enough?', although such questions stand behind the attacks made upon him by Moran in *The Philosophy of Irish Ireland*. With Stanford, too, the question is not one of Irishness but of ambition: the quotation of folk melody aside, his professional orientation and choice of texts declare the cultural context for which his music was (largely) intended. In simplest terms, Stanford wrote for an English audience indifferent or hostile to the cultural (and ultimately political) implications of a pervasively Irish art. Again the comparison with Yeats is instructive. Yeats's early plays, particularly *The Countess Cathleen* (1899) and *Cathleen ní Houlihan*, self-evidently and self-consciously address a crucial episode in Irish cultural history: the formation of a national theatre as the intelligencer of literary revival and all this might represent. Stanford's contemporary essay in Irish opera, *Shamus O'Brien* (1896), sets a romantic comedy adapted from a text by Sheridan LeFanu in which the London stereotype of Stage Irishman is ebulliently revived. No art work could be more decisively removed from the Celtic revival and remain recognisably Irish. Like the choral setting *Phaudrig Crohoore* (another LeFanu text), *Shamus O'Brien* proclaims at once its absolute innocence of (then) contemporary Irish cultural sensibility and its accomplished (if not especially memorable) mastery of English operetta. It could not but prove of little consequence for the cultural history of Irish music. It was to prove of no consequence whatever for the history of Irish culture in general.[57]

This tone of dismissal cannot uncritically apply to Stanford's work as a whole. Put negatively, Stanford's legacy was to have reinforced the stultifying precedent of folksong as the hallmark of Irish art music. It was a habit of mind which grew independently of Stanford's own cultural assumptions and beliefs: indeed it served for long afterwards as the definitive arbiter of a work's being Irish in any meaningful way. The reliance on folksong was to prove acutely burdensome not only because it engendered a creative cul-de-sac (in terms of structural development), but also because it betokened the redundancy of an art music thus circumscribed by literal representation of the indigenous repertory. And if the cult of nationalism which attached itself to that repertory was to have any address upon art music, it would only be in terms of repudiation on the grounds of irrelevance. Put positively, Stanford's achievement was seminal in one respect. It raised the issue of an Irish art music, especially in terms of examining the question of cultural discourse between two distinct traditions. It established the challenge of an Irish art music in the first place and it clarified the central difficulty which perforce it had to overcome. For those who remained in Ireland, it functioned as a means of exploration and perhaps as an exemplar which proved the urgency of cultural engagement if the concept of Irish art music was to survive into the twentieth century.

*    *    *    *    *

Engagement, like education, was a slow and uncertain process. It is useful here to return to the quotations from the *New Ireland Review* which open this chapter. Because of its association with D. P. Moran, author of the definitive 'Irish Ireland' tract *The Philosophy of Irish Ireland* (1905), the *New Ireland Review* occupies an uncomfortable position in Irish cultural history. Moran edited it for two years (1898–1900), before he founded his own journal of hostile, propagandistic nationalism, the *Leader*.[58] But the *New Ireland Review* embraced a wider and more tolerant spectrum of opinion than Moran's editorship might suggest, and its early recognition of Yeats betokens this. The decisive tone of appraisal which characterises the excerpt cited at the head of this chapter is, for our purpose, less striking than the consistent recourse to music as a metaphor appropriate to Yeats's lyric power and to the enterprise of poetry in general. This apparently conventional association between music and poetry (poetry as music) is strangely revivified when applied to Yeats. The impact of his voice was to regenerate and not to disperse the strength of this association, which was to entail such interesting and fateful consequences for music itself. What need or hope of a new music when the literary renaissance was to be so received, as an essentially lyric impulse? Given the difficulties which engulfed music itself, given its aesthetic divisions of style, purpose, meaning, expression, what rival claim to poetry could it hope to enter in the wake of Celtic revivalism? The danger was that the Celtic revival would permanently consign music in Ireland to the limbo of scholarly preservation. Music might function as an atmospheric adjunct to the principal business of language (as in certain of Yeats's plays), but it would not escape that servitude in any significant way.[59] Music in Ireland would struggle between Hyde's vision of 'de-anglicisation' (itself a repudiation of the European aesthetic) and the feeble contingencies of an art form both parasitic upon the ethnic repertory and incapacitated by it. Located precariously between the Gaelic League and the Royal Dublin Society, music itself appeared to diminish in inverse proportion to its metaphorical prowess.[60]

These anxieties would seem to inform the appearance of music in the *New Ireland Review*. The journal maintained a sporadic but not insignificant interest in music during the decades of cultural ferment around the turn of the century. Essays on 'An Irish School of Music', 'Imitations of Palestrina',[61] 'The Musical Season in Ireland, 1899–1900', 'Church Music and Popular Taste', 'Irish Music in the Sixteenth-Century' and 'Haydn's Treatment of Melodies' support the suggestion that some degree of cultural engagement beyond the appropriation of music as a shibboleth of nationalism did take place. But nationalism would remain the ideology (however variously defined) against which *all* forms of music would necessarily be tested.

Brendan Rogers's essay on 'An Irish School of Music' countenances the essential obstacle to such a proposal, but only in passing:

> It may be argued that our long subjection to changes and modifications of all kinds, brought on by conquest, by immigration, by intermarriage, . . . has merged our individuality in that of surrounding races and deprived us of the claim to a separate artistic life. Nothing could be more groundless than such a contention.[62]

'Unity of national purpose' is the governing notion of cultural history to which Rogers appeals, in order to argue the validity of an Irish art music *within* the terms of progressive nationalism:

> It is difficult to understand upon what ground such a view can be maintained as that Irish music in particular should not be developed in any of the modern forms in which the musician    so delights. To accept such doctrine would be to condemn to barrenness and ultimately to death the most expressive monu-ment of our ancient national character and civilisation, to roll back the tide of progress in art, to stop inventiveness and originality in our artists; in short, it would be to condemn ourselves to a backwardness and stagnation which noth-ing in the past history of our country and nothing in the present condition of the art could excuse or palliate.[63]

Rogers made this argument in a cultural climate at worst indifferent, at best divided, on the question of an Irish art music. His advocacy of cross-fertilisa-tion between the ethnic and art traditions, between unity of national purpose and the resources of high art, reflects the wider ambitions of the revival itself. The argument that art music should find its rationale in the ethnic tradition was already implicit in Stanford; it now began to enjoy a wider currency. Although the appearance of music in the *New Ireland Review* and its sister journals would remain sporadic, the idea of an Irish art music gathered con-siderable momentum from within the folds of the Gaelic League and the National Literary Society. By 1897, some three years before the publication of Rogers's essay, a coherent response to the claims of art music in relation to the Celtic revival (and partly independent of it) was at last formulated. This response was the Irish music festival designated as the Feis Ceoil.[64]

The Feis was not *born* of dissent, but its origins can clearly be located in a movement towards the recognition of music in Irish cultural life which was itself divided. The initial impulse to organise a festival for the cultivation of 'Irish National Music' came from within the National Literary Society, some of whose members – pre-eminently Alfred Percival Graves and Annie Patterson – understood the preservation of folk melody to be the basis for a revival congruent with the rehabilitation and renewal of Irish literature. Annie Patterson's address to a meeting of the Gaelic League on 12 October 1894 moved for the founding of an 'Irish Musical and Literary Festival': subsequent overtures to other societies broadened the range of general support but quickly identified an essential conflict of interest between those who wanted to reanimate the idea of Irish music as an exclusively nationalistic design (based in part on the Welsh Eisteddfod) and those who sought a wider increase of musical activity in general. As ever, the question of music was sharply polarised by the issue of cultural affinity. The Gaelic League withdrew its initial support for the proposed festival, the National Literary Society confined itself to deliberations on the history and practice of the ethnic repertory. Writing of the crucial assembly of interested parties by which the matter was ultimately decided, Joseph Ryan wryly observes that 'it was indeed one of those archetypal Irish situations where the split was the first motion on the agenda',[65] a division of commitment which produced not one but two festivals, An tOireachtas (the Assembly) and the Feis, both of which were inaugurated in 1897, the former on 17 May, the latter on the day following.

This division was not necessarily hostile, and both festivals initially benefited from a co-operative exchange of personnel. But it is significant that the reception of music by the Gaelic League was to be determined by an assembly which not only confined its interests to the traditional repertory but regarded that repertory as a secondary manifestation of the Irish language itself. An tOireachtas was exclusive in its concentration on native cultural traditions, but this very confinement presupposed not the cultivation of a music festival *per se* but an assembly devoted to the broader concerns of Irish language and literature:

> The programme [of An tOireachtas] is of a diversified character. Competing essays, songs, poems and stories in the Irish language offered in competition will be read. A prize Rallying Song, which has been set to music by Dr Annie Patterson, will be sung by a choir of trained voices, Dr Patterson conducting.[66]

Such inclusiveness might appear innocuous in other contexts, but the promotion of music thus copperfastened the perception of the indigenous tradition as adjunct to an essentially verbal culture. Music was thereby doomed to remain on the periphery of debate because it enjoyed no special claim as an independent mode of artistic expression. On the contrary, it permanently laboured as symbol of the revival itself.

The Feis Ceoil provided a means by which music might be emancipated from the cultural duress of this symbolism; it advanced the notion of Irish music as an independent mode of artistic endeavour, and it examined afresh the possibilities of reconciliation between the ethnic repertory and the European aesthetic:

> This festival marks an epoch in the history of Irish music. It is intended to be a gathering of Irish musicians assembled to do honour to those world-famous musicians, dead and living, whom Ireland can claim as her own. It will be this; but it is meant to be more than this. The idea which has animated and inspired the promoters of the Feis is nothing less than the initiation of a musical renaissance in Ireland.[67]

In its emancipation from the constraints of cultural nationalism, the Feis created a mental (and physical) space for the cultivation (as against preservation) of music in Ireland. It provided an opportunity for public performance across the spectrum of musical endeavour, and it acted as a stimulus to composition. In these respects it filled a void in Irish cultural discourse: it transcended the nationalist symbolism of Irish music as a subset of the Gaelic League and it consolidated the movement towards music as a cultural preoccupation which might reduce the polarisation of native and colonial traditions. If the Feis undoubtedly accommodated these traditions, it did so in a manner congenial to the development of music as a permanent resource in Irish culture. Within the first ten years of its existence, it had established itself as the primary focus of a broader constituency of musical interest than that inhabited by the Gaelic League and the 'children of respectable Irish parents'; its annual competitions offered an unprecedented opportunity for assessment at both national and international levels which secured the continuity of performance standards manifestly required for the growth of music as a public art.[68]

The extent to which the Feis Ceoil responded to the literary revival as a whole is difficult to judge, but it certainly fostered a cautious rapport between formal composition and Celticism in its early competitions. The large-scale choral and orchestral works which these competitions attracted are the best evidence we possess of such a response, and some of them vividly illustrate the aesthetic problems which circumscribed the idea of an Irish music at once sensitive to the myths and materials of the revival and yet committed to the language and syntax of European romanticism. It is perhaps indicative of this problem that, whereas the Feis continued to sustain the performance of art music in Ireland after 1910, these competitions for original composition eventually lapsed.[69]

The first of them in 1897 produced a work which typifies a difficulty that was to endure. Michele Esposito's *Deirdre*, to a text by T.W. Rolleston, marks a major encounter between music and the literary revival.[70] *Deirdre* is a romantic cantata for soprano, tenor, baritone, chorus and orchestra. The poem by Rolleston is narrative in voice (enclosing passages of direct speech) and its account of the legend of the slaying of the Sons of Usna stems directly

from the world of the Celtic Twilight. As a late nineteenth-century gloss on
Irish legend, it effectively translates the materials of folklore into the voice and
gesture of Yeats's early poetry:

> A blind hand sowed the seed of Fate
> The black earth bred it,
> The kind rain fed it.
> And branch on branch and leaf on leaf
> It flourished and waxed great
> Glory the fruit it bore, and Love and Grief.[71]

Esposito avoids the re-creation of an 'Irish note' in his response to this text;
the broad strokes of choral writing which dominate the setting draw directly
upon the stylistic precedents of Schumann and Mendelssohn without any
reference to the musical correlatives of Irish folklore. And given the exalted
syntax of Rolleston's diction, this compositional strategy appears to be justified. To rehouse the sentiments and narrative structure of Gaelic literature in
the context of late English romanticism is a process which is absolute in the
(verbal) text: the music likewise absorbs the tragedy into a (comparatively)
recent expressive medium.[72] Esposito was an accomplished if not especially
original composer whose piano music in particular comprises an authoritative meditation on the vocabulary and structures of a late nineteenth-century European tradition. That tradition speaks in *Deirdre*, but it does not
speak to Ireland in any special way. It is Synge's *Deirdre*, and not Rolleston's,
which we acknowledge as a prime re-creation of Irish myth within the
revival. Neither the language nor the music in the Rolleston–Esposito version seriously rivals it as a work which extends the Irish imagination. And
yet in its very emancipation from the burden of folksong quotation and/or
arrangement, Esposito's setting inherently argues the key question in Irish
music at the turn of the century: whether or not an imaginative musical
response to the myths of the revival could survive the ideological weight of
the ethnic tradition.

Esposito's own reply to this query may well have been determined by the
Feis Ceoil itself. The festival in subsequent years deliberately encouraged the
submission of works which were to be based on traditional airs, and the symphonies written by Esposito and his pupil Herbert Hamilton Harty accord-
ingly met this incentive in a manner which gave new life to the advocation of
cultural nationalism in Irish art music. But were these not Stanford's terms:
the composition of symphonic (or orchestral) structures which depended not
obliquely but utterly on the re-presentation of ethnic melody? Now that the
Feis Ceoil had adopted this strategy for the composition of Irish art music, the
response of composers such as Esposito and Harty enjoyed virtually a
national degree of cultural consensus: the future of Irish art music was seen
to lie in recourse to the ethnic past.

However attractive this formula seems in abstract terms, its application was less than satisfactory in practice. In the early years of the twentieth century, Esposito's musical style stringently discriminated between 'Irish' compositions and works in direct emulation of European classical and romantic repertory. This act of stylistic discrimination centred upon the reliance on folksong: the song cycle *Roseen Dhu* (1901) sets a sequence of poems by Alfred Perceval Graves which recovers the nationalist image of Ireland as the Dark Rosaleen of Mangan's verse. The blatant symbolism owes as much, indeed, to Young Ireland as it does to the literary revival, and Graves's poetic reads as a curious (and inferior) reanimation of the spirit of Thomas Moore:

> O! Sorrowful dream of the past
> That dissolved in the morn's magic ray,
> Why again is the grey shadow cast,
> Like a false, fairy mist oe'r my way?[73]

In this instance, Esposito's response likewise evokes a comparison with Sir John Stevenson's settings of the *Melodies*. The Irish air which forms the basis of each setting is identified beneath Graves's title, and the rubric 'arr. by M. Esposito' explicitly indicates the composer's secondary (even tertiary) role in the process of artistic production: first the text, then the pre-existent Irish air, then the arrangement by Esposito (complete with figurative preludes and postludes which reinforce the comparison with Stevenson). Once again the arrangement of ethnic melody had come to seem like a *sine qua non* in Irish art music. More than a badge of identity, it functioned as a shibboleth of cultural nationalism which curtailed the central process of composition itself.

If this judgement seems too severe, it is a conviction nevertheless upheld by the subsequent history of music in Ireland. The reliance on folksong would become the issue on which the whole question of Irish art music was to turn. In Esposito's case, the requirements of the Feis Ceoil excluded the possibility of overcoming a division in his own works which effectively contained his sense of Irish music as a separate entity defined by the arrangement of traditional Irish airs. The encounter between the European aesthetic and the ideological pull of the ethnic tradition which his work manifests is one which was destined to become central as Irish composers struggled to find a voice in the new century. The oppressive claims of ethnicity would complicate every significant development but one in Irish art music throughout the 1920s and 1930s. For many composers, notably those who followed Esposito as his students or professional colleagues, the implacable existence of the Irish air would largely delimit the range of expression and technique available within the wider compass of vocal and orchestral music. With the foundation of the new state in 1922, the corpus of traditional melody itself enjoyed an even stronger symbolic status than before, and was often pressed into fresh service as an agent of cultural nationalism. 'Folk Song' would become *the*

music of Ireland, and the yardstick by which tenuous exercises in the concert
repertoire might be assessed.

Raymond Warren's observations on the orchestral music of Hamilton
Harty touch on this difficulty, albeit indirectly:

> For a country with no full-time professional orchestra was hardly the place for an
> aspiring young conductor and no doubt this lack was one of the factors militat-
> ing against the establishment earlier in the [twentieth] century of an Irish national
> school of composition, a surprising loss to music in view of the wealth of national
> feeling in Ireland, which produced such fruits in poetry and drama. But the fact
> was that, like Stanford before him, Harty was bound to leave Ireland to pursue a
> musical career to his own standards. Like Stanford, too, Harty's musical nation-
> alism was a matter of interpreting an Irish experience within the terms of the
> Anglo-European musical language as he then understood it – the approach of
> Smetana and Rimsky Korsakov rather than of Bartók or Vaughan Williams.[74]

There is some irony in these wise discriminations. It seems logical to suggest,
as Warren does, that the lack of a professional orchestra in Ireland contributed to the failure to develop a significant body of original art music
answerable to the claims of the literary revival. But Harty's motivation in writing the *Irish Symphony* was chiefly the opportunity of having the work performed in Dublin during the Feis Ceoil in 1904.[75] Undoubtedly the lack of a
permanent professional resource inhibited the response of composers to the
surge of literary discourse which characterised the 'wealth of national feeling'
in Ireland at the turn of the century. Alongside the impoverished condition of
musical infrastructures stood another, less tangible difficulty: the polarised
condition of music itself. Between Yeats and Hyde, as it were, the idea of
music throughout this formative period of Irish cultural history could function only as a symbol of imaginative (linguistic) aspiration. Other than that,
it served to reinforce the claims of an ethnic reinvigoration (as it did in the
Gaelic League). The sheer pressure of the moment was overwhelmingly linguistic, not musical. And for the composer who sought to alleviate such pressure, the cultural prestige of the ethnic collections loomed as an inhibition to
creative musical discourse. Those who remained in Ireland all too evidently
experienced this inhibition.

Harty's first major essay in Irish music, the 1904 *Irish Symphony*, closely
followed the model established by his teacher, Esposito, in the production of
a work explicitly based on traditional airs. But his enforced professional exile
(notwithstanding frequent visits to Ireland as an accompanist) liberated him
from this obligation in two later works which drew him more closely to the
*inherent* cultivation of a national style (as in Bartók's case). The orchestral tone
poems *With the Wild Geese* (1910) and *The Children of Lir* (1938) are recognisably Irish works released from the imaginative constraint of folksong quotation. In this respect they represent a significant compositional advance on
the *Irish Symphony*, a work which emulates the exotic nationalism cultivated

by Stanford and Esposito. The tone poems escape the obligations of this nationalism (the traditional air as conduit of authentic feeling) and instead absorb both poetic and mythic programmes of extra-musical significance by means of melodic and harmonic structures which express an affinity with the modal contour of the ethnic tradition. *With the Wild Geese* reifies thus the poetry of Emily Lawless, in which the narrative descriptions of war and its aftermath govern the family of thematic materials mustered by Harty in the service of sheer programme music. The crucial distinction between *With the Wild Geese* and the *Irish Symphony* is thereby one which exists between arrangement and original composition. And it is that distinction which makes Harty's tone poem 'a seminal work in the history of Irish music'.[76]

Harty's affinity with (as against slavish dependence upon) the ethnic tradition remained virtually constant throughout a long if occasional career in composition. In many works, that affinity reverted to the introduction of folk-like melodic structures, but in *The Children of Lir*, his last major *opus* for orchestra (and vocalising soprano), he once again addressed the issue of an Irish composition emancipated from the claims of direct or near-direct quotation.

As with its predecessor, *The Children of Lir* reconciles an explicitly Irish programme with the musical language of late romanticism. Its narrative and descriptive gestures (candidly rehearsed in Harty's own note for the first performance) are altogether disengaged from the concept of orchestrated folk-song, although the sectional integrity of 'Finola's Lament' late in the piece does allude to the ethnic tradition in its unmistakably Irish structure and decoration. But the distance between allusion and reproduction is significant of Harty's achievement. *The Children of Lir* imbues the genre of symphonic poem with an essentially Irish (and highly personal) cast of mind in which Harty's own distance from the Celtic revival is crucial. The work is absolutely free of that anxiety of influence which plagued the efforts of those who remained at home: it flies past the tense encounter of cultural debate and most especially the controversies over authenticity and style which remained irrelevant to Harty for the greater part of his professional career. If the work attracted international criticism it was not on account of its Irish subject matter. If Harty's romantic vocabulary seemed dated by 1939, how much more dated was the widespread failure in Ireland to respond musically in any enduring way to a literary movement which was by then itself part of the cultural past?[77]

\*     \*     \*     \*     \*

> The two abstractions – Ireland and the Irishman – regarded one another irreconcilably across a gulf in my thought – the one a serene and delicate loveliness inviolate and holy, her ancient wounds purged and healed and forgotten on such days of clear wind and sun as this, a lovely and darling dream of God, the other baffling and baffled, tossing in a feverish trance between an aged and benumbed national consciousness and the glamour of a tawdry and alien civilisation only half understood and never to be assimilated.[78]

The short story 'Ancient Dominions' appeared in a collection published as *Children of the Hills: Tales and Sketches of Western Ireland in the Old Time and the Present Day*, in 1913. It was written by the composer Arnold Bax (1883–1953) under his favourite pseudonym 'Dermot O'Byrne'. Scholars have long recognised Bax's engagement with Ireland as central to his development as a composer, but the passage cited here from 'Ancient Dominions' asks us to reconsider that engagement in the light of Irish cultural history and Bax's understanding of it. Given his condemnation of Stanford and Harty, given his claim to have been 'the first to translate the hidden Ireland into musical terms', and above all, given his explicit sense of debt to the poetry of Yeats, Bax would seem to occupy a crucial position in the cultural history of music in Ireland in the early decades of the twentieth century. No other composer sought to encounter the literary revival as directly as he; no other composer so completely disavowed the ethnic tradition as a cul-de-sac of creative endeavour, and no other composer perceived so acutely the essentially linguistic turn (from Irish to English) as the primary constituent of the revival. That Bax was imbued with the influence of Ireland is an issue which scarcely requires much elaboration given the scrutiny which his work has recently enjoyed; that Bax exemplifies the problem of an Irish art music overshadowed – overtaken – by the literary revival does call for comment.

From his first visit to Ireland in 1903 Bax immersed himself in the Irish language and 'steeped [himself] in history and saga, folk-tale and fairy-lore'.[79] Although his permanent residence there was a matter of less than three years (he lived in the Dublin suburb of Rathgar from 1911 to 1914), his visits to the west and northwest of the country were constant: 'The village of Glencolumcille was soon discovered in West Donegal, and was to be Arnold's spiritual haven for the next thirty years [i.e. from 1903] and the fountainhead of much of his music.'[80] Later still he found in Cork and Dublin new friends, amongst whom he was to die in 1953.

Bax's experience of Ireland can be distinguished on two levels. He was a 'spiritual tourist' in his discovery of rural Ireland, to borrow Seamus Deane's somewhat disdainful description of Synge, but his exposure to Ireland was also conditioned by his reading of Yeats. He found in Yeats's early poetry, above all in *The Wanderings of Oisin* (1889), 'a lifelong vision which never failed him'.[81] He thus encountered Ireland under the aegis of a Celticism which lent coherence to an otherwise commonplace journey of discovery. Bax's awareness of Yeats, of the artistic precedence of his poetry, allowed him to reconcile his infatuation with Ireland and his aspirations as 'the British composer, Arnold Bax'.[82]

Four phases in Bax's relationship with Ireland determined his development as a composer, and each of them addresses the question of music and the literary revival. The cluster of early tone poems which begins with *Cathaleen-ni-Hoolihan* (1905) and continues with *Into the Twilight* (1908), *In the Faery Hills* (1909) and *Roscatha* (1910) comprises a body of work directly influenced not only by Yeats but by the search for a compositional voice which preoccupied Bax in the years immediately following his departure from the Royal Academy of Music (1905). The second phase of development represents his most sustained encounter with the literary revival under the pseudonym 'Dermot O'Byrne': Bax did not abandon composition during this period (1911–13), but he devoted substantial time to his reputation as poet and writer of short stories (and plays) which in turn drew him to the political and cultural milieu of the revival itself. The third phase was an attempt to respond to the Easter Rising of 1916 first as a poet, then as a composer (in the immediate aftermath of the Rising). The final phase shows Bax's reintegration of his Irish experience within the boundaries of his professional commitment as a composer of orchestral works in the tradition of late romanticism. *The Garden of Fand*, scored in 1916 and first performed in 1920, crystallises this moment of transition from one commitment (Ireland) to another (British music).

However vulnerable to contradiction, this fourfold reading of Bax and Ireland is clearly supported by the music which he wrote between 1905 and 1916. Ireland did not disappear thereafter from his scores (on the contrary), but that central engagement with her cultural evolution no longer endured.[83] *Farewell, My Youth*, Bax's volume of autobiography, ends in this way:

> For a day or so later I crossed over to England, not to revisit Ireland for over four years, and with the exception of 'AE' never again to see one of my Dublin friends in the land of Ireland.
>
> The golden age was past! . . .
>
> If I return now I am an utter stranger in that city [Dublin] of my young manhood, knowing amongst the indifferent population not one soul . . . that was intimate with mine when for too short a time I was an adopted – and, I like to believe, not unloved – child of Eire.
>
> Farewell, my youth![84]

It is the remarkable sense of Dublin (and Ireland) providing the formative influence on Bax's musical imagination which is of special interest here. Bax's experience – unencumbered by the deprivation and polarisation of Irish musical culture – sharply clarifies the relationship between music and literature in Ireland as one which could scarcely survive the linguocentric preoccupations of the revival itself.

The early tone poems establish the paradox of Bax's preoccupation with Yeats: *Cathaleen-ni-Hoolihan* is headed by a quotation from 'To Ireland in the Coming Times' (1893) which advertises artistic communion, identification, the prospect of belonging to a tradition:

> Know, that I would accounted be
> True brother of a company
> That sang, to sweeten Ireland's wrong,
> Ballad and story, rann and song.

Whether or not the genesis of *Cathaleen* included any reference to Yeats's *Cathleen* we do not know, but Bax's work stands as a declaration of intent: to emulate the literary revival in music. Bax sought and found in Yeats the conduit of his response to Ireland, but his own creative reflex he knew and believed to be novel. It was not merely that Ireland could provide the stimulus necessary for the development of a musical imagination already conditioned by professional training and sociocultural commitment to the European aesthetic. It was that Bax regarded his discovery of Ireland as a form of cultural revivalism which was strikingly comparable to that of Yeats:

> As burningly as any half-starved peasant poet of seventeenth- or eighteenth-century Munster I adored my beloved in all her symbolic presentments – as Eire, Foghla, Banba – as Cathleen ni Hoolihan . . . In imagination I fought in her wars of old and dreamt cloudily of new and less material conflicts . . . to be fought out perhaps in the fields of art and intellect – that final victorious contest which should restore Ireland to her leadership of western spirituality.[85]

A paradox lies between this commitment and the indifference which circumscribed it. *Cathaleen-ni-Hoolihan* remained unheard until 1970; the other early tone poems fared likewise (*Roscatha*) or were heard in London under Thomas Beecham and Henry Wood. In Dublin, Bax's early achievement went for nothing. There was no means to receive such a body of orchestral work which bypassed the wearisome debates on folk music in favour of a direct, narrative engagement with the myths of the revival.

Unencumbered by the burdens of ideology and tradition (made explicit once again in the pompous argument and counter-argument which surrounded the Feis Ceoil[86]), Bax's music, as with *In the Faery Hills*, explores the Celticism of Yeats's early verse. It does so in a language which was all but impossible to articulate in Dublin (or anywhere else in Ireland) for want of a musical infrastructure equal to the score. Bax could propose this exploration of the 'inmost deeps of the hollow hills of Ireland' as he pleased, but sooner or later the want of affirmation would recondition his professional impulses. It did just that by the end of the First World War.

Bax's early Irish projects are imbued with the spirit of the revival. His reliance on Yeats, his attempts to re-create the Yeatsian poetic in music, his identification publicly and privately with the romantic programme of Celticism cumulatively eclipse the piecemeal cultivation of art music by composers permanently resident in Ireland. But as he drew nearer to the literary sources of the revival, Bax began to see for himself how matters stood with regard to music. He began to understand the revival as a cultural phenomenon which depended so narrowly on the passing of discourse from one language to another that perforce it would remain largely indifferent, as Yeats himself indisputably was, to the possibilities of a further transition, from language to music. The horn-call which opens *In the Faery Hills* becomes in this reading symbolic of the lost cause of art music as an independent force in the Irish mind. To 'sing' in the usage of the revival was exclusively a question of metaphor.[87]

The 'second personality' which Bax developed as 'Dermot O'Byrne' is also symbolic of this recognition. Bax's years in Rathgar, his intimacy with AE, with Padraic and Molly Colum and his social access to the future leaders of political rebellion (including Pearse) were informed and enabled by his progress as a writer: 'My allegiance in those years was divided between literature and music.'[88] Lewis Foreman tells us that Bax began to write passages of Yeatsian verse almost as soon as he went to Ireland; his command of Irish led to collaboration on a partial translation of Synge's The Shadow of the Glen, and in all he produced some four collections of verse, three of which were published in his lifetime. He wrote four plays (one of which, Deirdre, was written over his real name in 1907) and three volumes of short stories, which were published between 1912 and 1918. Foreman observes that the appearance of Children of the Hills 'cemented Bax's growing literary reputation' in Dublin, and it was this collection in particular which earned him generous assessment in the first edition of Ernest Boyd's pioneering study, Ireland's Literary Renaissance (1916):

> The novel, as such, continues to lack support, and our fiction still affects the form of the sketch and short story. Of the latter, Dermot O'Byrne's Children of the Hills (1913) showed unusual qualities, and announced a new writer from whom good work may be reasonably expected. The author is steeped in Gaelic lore, and the old language and history are an essential part of his art. His realism is the realism of Synge, with whom he has many points in common.[89]

If, as Foreman observes, 'there can never have been any doubt that his primary allegiance was as composer',[90] the question of Bax's degree of literary commitment during his years in Dublin is nevertheless germane to our understanding of his music in the cultural history of the period. Put plainly, the literary revival could (and did) respond to Dermot O'Byrne, but not to Arnold Bax. Although Bax's music was in theory receptive to themes of the revival, it could not in turn be received in a cultural climate which relegated music to the unpremeditated recreation of the peasant. Yeats's famous observations on the wider relevance of the Irish Literary Theatre and the National Theatre Society, for example, convey the cultural assumptions which fostered just such an exclusion:

> This movement [to establish a national theatre] should be important to those who are not especially interested in the Theatre, for it may be a morning cockcrow to that impartial meditation about character and destiny we call the artistic life in a country where everybody, if we leave out the peasant who has his folk-songs and his music, has thought the arts useless unless they have helped some kind of political action, and has, therefore, lacked the pure joy that comes out of things that have never been indentured to any cause. [my italics][91]

It is a safe bet that Yeats did not have music in mind as an exemplar of art released from the immediacy of political motivation. Given this assumption, together with the impoverished provision for music in Dublin, it is not hard to understand why Bax for a time developed his response to the revival in language rather than music. Having come to Ireland as a composer, he found that 'there was no talk of music whatever';[92] having decided to remain (if temporarily), he found it best to follow suit and remain silent on the subject himself. It is not that Bax abandoned composition, but rather that he perceived its irrelevance to the programme of cultural reanimation so brilliantly sponsored by Yeats and his associates.

Bax's own contribution to that programme, however transient, was of sufficient interest to attract the admiration of central figures in the revival (including AE and the Colums), and for a time, as Foreman cautiously observes, 'he may have been more successful in encapsulating mood and atmosphere in words rather than notes'.[93] His reputation as an admittedly minor participant in the literary renaissance was not by chance: his encounters with Yeats, Hyde (in correspondence) and the Colums, together with his more constant association with AE and the inhabitants of Glencolumcille, collectively demonstrate the extent of a preoccupation with Ireland which underlay his fiction, plays and poetry.

This preoccupation culminated in Bax's volume of poetry entitled A Dublin Ballad, together with a number of musical works which were written in the immediate aftermath of the Easter Rebellion in 1916. 'The trauma of 1916 acted as a catalyst on Bax's creative imagination.'[94] His one meeting with Patrick Pearse endured for long afterwards in his memory, and the heady admixture of idealism and romantic mysticism which he discerned in the Rising itself came to seem continuous with the Celticism which drew him to Ireland in the first place:

> It was still late eighteenth century in County Dublin, as in many parts even of the city itself. And now it was all too old and sleepy to awaken again in the ordinary course of human affairs. Only a cataclysm could ever disturb its drowsy retrospective dream of bewigged and embroidered violence and lechery, of priest-baiting and faction-fighting, of a starved, unlettered peasantry, shrewd and metaphorical of speech, of the flaming follies and heroisms of scatterbrained yet noble revolt against alien tyranny.[95]

In this passage, as in 'Ancient Dominions' and his Rebellion poem 'Shells at Oranmore' (partly published in 1966 by the Irish Department of External Affairs in celebration of the fiftieth anniversary of the Rising), Bax's literary persona eclipses the composer, just as the revival itself eclipsed the possibility of an Irish art music. In 'Ancient Dominions', Bax was prepared to voice just that degree of cultural polarisation between 'national consciousness' and 'a tawdry and alien civilisation' which Yeats's writings sought to transcend. It is clear that for Bax, disdainful of 'Carlow or Cavan rhapsodies', art music could scarcely find its métier amidst this turbulent poetic.

The tone poem *In Memoriam Padraig Pearse*, which is deposited in University College, Dublin, underlines this reading. Dated 9 August 1916, and existing only in short score, it elegises the patriot (with a melody pragmatically reused in Bax's music for the film *Oliver Twist*) in tones of high lyricism far removed from the Celtic Twilight. Its technique – its very medium of expression – lies beyond the range of cultural reference which it addressed in Ireland, and its *raison d'être* was to exclude it from English patronage. It has consequently remained in the limbo of Bax's manuscript, incomplete and unperformed. Related settings for voice and piano on the same subject went the same way. Lewis Foreman lists three such (with texts by AE) as 'lost', although one of these, *A Leader*, is also in the library of University College, Dublin.[96] If, as Foreman suggests, the symphonic variations for piano and orchestra also commemorate Pearse, this motivation was not apparent when the work was first given in London on 23 November 1920.

Is it safe to conclude that Bax's compositional response to the Rising lacked the kind of cultural environment which accommodated his poetry? Can it be that these meditations remained (for the most part) private and uncirculated because they were voiced in a music that was neither wanted nor understood? It is at least valid to pose such questions. The mere condition of a London performance as the ordinary destination of Bax's music is not as innocuous as it might appear, given the state of the art in Ireland. Music so inherently stimulated by Irish political and cultural history (in the making) could nevertheless find no place there.

Bax's imaginative withdrawal from Ireland after the intensity of these 1916 settings (he had physically withdrawn in 1914) signifies a recovery of his perspective as a composer. Ireland would continue to figure in his imaginative landscape, but he had run the course of his existence as a predominantly Irish artist. *The Garden of Fand*, composed in 1913 but not scored until 1916, re-integrates the idea of Ireland into the fabric of British music. The romance of Celticism which first attracted Bax usurps the more problematic engagement of the Rebellion-inspired works, for which there had proved to be no cultural breathing space. Although 'it was all given to me by Ireland',[97] the score of *The Garden of Fand* declares by mood, technique and above all by orchestral texture its primary commitment to impressionism. The mental journey which Bax had undertaken from his reading of *The Wanderings of Oisin* to his commemoration of Pearse recedes. It becomes finally irrelevant to this more hospitable conception of Ireland as a trope of pastoral remembrance and myth. It would be ungracious to add that the pathway to knighthood was now clear. But if Bax's claim to have been the first 'to translate the hidden Ireland into musical terms' has any significance for Irish cultural history, we must acknowledge the element of betrayal that all good translations necessarily entail. Had Bax remained in Ireland, his temporary exchange of music for literature might well have become permanent. There is no doubt that his music would have suffered as a consequence and that a different, more personal betrayal would have ensued. As late as 1952, in the foreword to *Music in Ireland*, he could write of his 'desire for the country's musical awakening'[98] as a phenomenon which even then lay in the future. The duality of his own response to Ireland, apostrophised by the existence of Dermot O'Byrne and Arnold Bax, reinforces the argument that the art music which he explicitly attributed to the existence of Yeats endured in a cultural vacuum. It would be absurd to censure Bax for having escaped that vacuum, for having recovered a sense of Ireland amenable to his progress as a composer. It was only his linguistic prowess that could hope for recognition in Ireland.

The limits of this recognition ironise the exclusion of Bax's music from the cultural ferment of the revival. Boyd compares him favourably to Synge (as above) in style and subject matter, but insists on Bax's originality as a writer nevertheless. This commendation is doubly ironic: firstly in the musical quality habitually attributed to Yeats and Synge and now extended to Bax by an early historian of the renaissance; secondly in the decision which Synge took to abandon music in favour of the theatre. But Synge's turn towards language signifies a wider turn from the polarised condition of music in Ireland towards the musical condition of literary discourse. This reorientation of music in the Irish literary imagination is the subject of the closing chapter of this study. Bax knew all about the Irish literary imagination, and profited honestly by it. But the music which he wrote in Ireland under its stimulus could not find a place there.

This failure of accommodation unquestionably belongs to Irish cultural history.

# SEÁN Ó RIADA AND THE CRISIS OF MODERNISM IN IRISH MUSIC

You are quite right, of course. I am cut off here. There is no music. None whatever. One feels its absence.[1]

The real cause of the failure to appreciate good music in Dublin is that the people have never been taught to do so: that is the reason for their sheer apathy and their impoverished taste.[2]

Irish folk music, unlike that of nations whose music followed a normal course of development, has never been properly assimilated into a broader tradition of art music, due to the chasm – political, social and religious – which existed for centuries between the spontaneous song in the vernacular which was the natural expression of the Irish people, and the purely English tradition of music-making in the towns . . . Due chiefly to the country's chequered history, the general organisation of music in Ireland is much behind that of other countries.[3]

It is all very charming of the late Sir Arnold Bax to write that 'of all the countries in the world Ireland possesses the most varied and beautiful folk music' . . . but there is an even more insistent truth in the view that folk-music does not answer any of the problems of a composer.[4]

Seán Ó Riada (1931–71) bids fair to become the crucial figure in Irish music of the twentieth century. His work and, to an extent, his life are expressive of those problems of voice, style and cultural tradition which circumscribe and define the condition of music in modern Ireland. He embraced the prevailing difficulty of reconciling the burden of an ethnic tradition with the aspirations of an emancipated art music, and he entered a decisive claim for the composer as an artist of independent significance in the cultural fabric of Ireland in the 1960s. Ó Riada's unsettling progress from one form of music to the next, in addition to his comprehensive (if sporadic) exploration of music in the theatre, in the cinema, in the recording studio, in the concert hall, in church, and not least in a host of domestic and social settings, speak of a compelling, restless address. His work connotes a startling degree of failure and success: at once the only composer to have been wholly received into the cultural matrix of Ireland's preponderantly linguistic sense of itself, and at the same time a figure of tragic indirection and unresolved insight. He brought into sharp focus the plight of the composer in Ireland, dependent upon a con-

125

fused aesthetic and an impoverished infrastructure. He sought to endorse and absorb the structures of European art music even as he immersed himself in the idiom of his indigenous musical past. He made the journey, as it were, from serialism to *sean nós* and stumbled upon their anguished irreconcilability. The curve of Ó Riada's musical imagination led downwards.

If this assessment has any merit, it is that the works themselves so persuasively advance it. In his symphonic essays, in his music for film and in his cultivation of an original deportment for the traditional repertory, Ó Riada explicitly meditated upon the question of voice and style in Irish music to the extent that each successive phase of his compositional development undermined its predecessor. On occasion, these meditations were histrionic and naïve; on occasion (as in the film music), they were inexorably wedded to a wider reappraisal of cultural history in which the question of nationalist self-determination was uneasily posed alongside questions of artistic maturity in the aftermath of the Celtic revival and political independence.

For Ó Riada, these questions were complicated by the disintegration of musical consensus in Europe. He knew that art music could not function as a homogeneous concept in the wake of the Second Viennese School and its repudiation of tonality. He also knew that the predominant perception of an 'Irish' art music depended upon an undernourished and overworked representation of the corpus of ethnic melody which led again and again to the same hopeless cul-de-sac of arrangement and variation. Painfully conscious of the dislocated condition of music in Ireland, Ó Riada countenanced new dislocations elsewhere. In his efforts to invent a stable mode of compositional technique which might be answerable to the immediate context of modern Ireland, he repeatedly espoused and then abandoned the cultivation of a European aesthetic independent of the native repertory. The very premise of 'original composition' strained under the duress of Ó Riada's brilliant recourse to folk melody, particularly because the latter was understood by his (non-musical) contemporaries to be an essential prerequisite for Irish music of any meaningful kind. His film scores, written 'in the idiom of an Irish symphonic period that had never happened',[5] facilitated an expressive (and emotive) alignment of orchestral representation and (for the most part) nationalistic imagery which sustained the traditional aesthetic assumptions that continued to underlie the reception of Irish music, new or old. Which is to say: Ó Riada's recourse to music as the intelligencer of film established a satisfying continuity with the hitherto prevailing perception of Irish music as the intelligencer of verbal art forms. A widespread complacency thereby attended the acclaim which this music enjoyed: Ó Riada was to be regarded for a time as having solved the difficult equation of contemporary music in a specifically Irish context.

But this complacency most certainly did not attach to Ó Riada himself. It is almost pitiful to contemplate the conflicting duality of his composition before he finally retreated into novel (and immensely influential) representations of the native repertory. The early orchestral works, especially *Hercules*

*Dux Ferrariae* (1957), signal a degree of authenticity and flair which few of his later compositions would surpass. The score of *Hercules* stands apart from ethnic Irish music: its forbears are European rather than Irish, and its technical strategies and textures summon Bartók and Stravinsky (notwithstanding its relaxed deployment of serial techniques).[6] His major essay in art music, *Nomos no. 2* for baritone, chorus and orchestra (1965), brings to an extreme pitch Ó Riada's preoccupation with the European aesthetic, even if it also represents an abnegation of that aesthetic in retrospect: a point of view which the composer himself was to evince with increasing defensiveness in the six remaining years of his life.[7] *Nomos no. 2* (the vaguely generic description itself betokens indirection[8]) functions as a watershed in Ó Riada's spectacular but disturbing progress as a composer. Its compositional voice is set scrupulously apart from the trilogy of film scores which overlap its five-year period of gestation: *Mise Éire* (I am Ireland) (1959), *Saoirse?* (Freedom?) (1960) and *An Tine Bheo* (The Living Fire) (1966).

These film scores made Ó Riada famous: a trite accomplishment, perhaps, save for the fact that the cultural context from which they emerged was so defiantly at odds with music as an independent art form. Against a background of indifference and ignorance, Ó Riada claimed for Irish art music a distinctive role in the cultural emancipation of the 1960s. But it was a role that could scarcely be sustained. If Ó Riada vigorously renewed the plausibility of an accessible mode of Irish art music, he just as vigorously came to undermine and then to repudiate it. The acclaim which greeted the film scores came to seem increasingly impertinent to his own aesthetic quest for a tenable vocabulary in Irish music. The romantic orchestration of folk melodies bestowed on Ó Riada a cultural élan that was at the last spurious and effete: the composer rapidly exhausted this vein of musical utterance because it offered nothing more than a glamorously effective postscript to the whole tradition of folk-music arrangement. But neither could he sustain the compositional integrity of *Nomos no. 2*. This, too, he abandoned. How and why Ó Riada thereafter relapsed into an intensive regeneration of the ethnic repertory is the principal concern of this chapter.

Ó Riada's significance in the cultural history of music in Ireland is curiously prone to exaggeration. The very fame he attained has tended to eclipse that difficult continuity of artistic endeavour with which many of his immediate forbears and contemporaries were engaged through the middle decades of the twentieth century. It would be wholly irresponsible to that endeavour to suggest that Ó Riada's widespread reception in the 1960s somehow diminished the *inherently* musical significance of other figures.[9] But, in terms of cultural history, it is nevertheless important to recognise Ó Riada's career as the seminal encounter between the musical imagination and its context in modern Ireland. The way in which Ó Riada was received and understood, and the way in which he responded in turn, are both prescriptive, to the extent that the immediate reception of his music was fundamental to the development of music in Irish cultural history from 1970 onwards; the negotiations, moreover, which Ó Riada advanced, as between his own compositional impulse and the cultural expectations which he partly helped to nourish, largely determined the perception of original composition in late twentieth-century Ireland. It was Ó Riada, rather than any other Irish musician, who forced the abiding difficulty of art music in Ireland to its crisis. No other artist so stringently tested its currency, no other figure so wilfully influenced its cultural afterlife. If the concept of 'art music' entered the cultural matrix of modern Ireland largely through his influence, it was Ó Riada's subsequent repudiation of this concept which likewise fomented a damaging redundancy with regard to any music other than the traditional repertory. But this repudiation did not come lightly. It derived from a painful scrutiny of Ó Riada's own understanding both of Irish music and of the function of a contemporary composer within that comprehension. The results of that scrutiny produced in Ó Riada a crisis of such magnitude that it destroyed not only his own belief in the concept of original composition, but also the means by which this concept might be integrated within the synapses of the Irish mind.

To understand this crisis, three issues need some degree of explication. There is firstly the background from which Ó Riada emerged: those apparently fallow and yet preoccupied decades between 1920 and 1950, in which the condition of Irish music (particularly as to education, performance and composition) was repeatedly assessed and largely deplored. It is this period which provides the backdrop to Ó Riada's encounter with modernism in European music, in addition to his uniquely tense engagement with the creative demise of Irish art music as a stultifying idea, contained by the pressures of aesthetic rationalisation. Secondly, there is the question of Ó Riada's biography as an expression of fundamental, musical need. The remarkable transformation from 'John Reidy' to 'Seán Ó Riada' embraces a singular sense of quest which is articulated in a host of related phenomena: the exchange of English for Irish, of Dublin for Cúl Aodh, of the symphony orchestra for Ceoltóirí Cualann. These exchanges (overlaid by the purely contingent and sometimes chaotic plurality of his activities as a musician) appear to signify Ó Riada's pursuit of a musical *modus vivendi* answerable to his own restless aesthetic. Finally, there are the works themselves as an expression (indeed a partial outgrowth) of cultural revivalism in the 1960s. The manner in which these works became for Ó Riada an inexorable rejection of the European *status quo* is self-evidently central to this expression. The mental journey from *Hercules Dux Ferrariae* to *Ó Riada sa Gaiety* (an evening of traditional Irish music given in the Gaiety Theatre, Dublin, in 1969) was Ó Riada's own, but it attained to symbolic status insofar as the reception of music in Ireland was (and is) concerned. Ó Riada had found a voice that gave to traditional Irish music a cultural centrality which it had never before enjoyed. That it was also a voice which silenced the claims of art music did not, with one sovereign exception, appear to provoke much concern.

The atrophied condition of music in Ireland in the immediate aftermath of the foundation of the Irish Free State in 1922 invites gloomy comparison with the prevailing inertia of the 1880s and 1890s. Political emancipation complicated rather than resolved the cultural status of music. The aggressive programme of officially sponsored language revival naturally drew music in its wake, and in the process confirmed the role of music as a vital exponent of 'Irish Ireland' philosophy. In such a climate, the cultural chauvinism of Douglas Hyde's 'de-anglicisation' enjoyed vigorous renewal. In particular, the ideology of cultural separatism espoused by writers such as Daniel Corkery and D. P. Moran (among many) necessarily repudiated the development of music except as an adjunct of nationalistic expression. Even in this regard, however, the new state showed little evidence of commitment: the drive to rehabilitate the Irish language did not particularly ameliorate an awareness of the oral tradition in music, notwithstanding the continued activities of the Gaelic League and the Irish Folk Song Society. [10]

If the state remained impassive, individual musicians did not. The baleful tone of deploration which characterises so much periodical literature on music in the period 1920–50 is virtually unrelieved: a long complaint of neglect was entered on behalf of music which overarched the less tangible (but no less consequential) preoccupation with the ethnic tradition and its implications for an Irish art idiom. It may appear singularly ironic that as musical infrastructures gradually improved in the aftermath of this sustained attrition, the central aesthetic impasse between Irish and European impulses hardened. It is worth suggesting that this development to some extent reflected the productive divergence between the state's projected image of itself and the bleaker version of Ireland offered by certain contemporary writers. Terence Brown's incisive remark that 'The Irish short story of the 1930s and forties registered a social reality that flew in the face of nationalistic self-congratulation' adumbrates a less productive conflict between the complacent understanding of music as nationalistic expression and music as an international art.[11] It was precisely this conflict, reformulated in terms of an 'either/or' crisis of identity and purpose, which Seán Ó Riada so drastically confronted in the 1960s. There can be little doubt that the wholesale appropriation of the ethnic tradition (as with the language) in the cause of the 'new nationalism' exacerbated this conflict.

The articulation of musical discontent in the 1920s and 1930s clearly gained momentum from the general reappraisal of Irish ideas in the wake of political independence. The disengagement from romantic nationalism so vividly espoused by writers including Sean O'Faolain, Frank O'Connor and Brian O'Nolan found a correlative in musical discourse: O'Faolain's arresting repudiation of Ireland as a Gaelic Eden, an Ireland shrouded by snow in which 'life was lying broken and hardly breathing',[12] stands behind the straitened pessimism of the musical debate:

Irish folk-song and the bardic music of the seventeenth and eighteenth centuries seems to have fixed itself on the popular imagination, lending to this
country a reputation for musical culture which it does not yet possess. Nicely-
turned phrases, such as 'our music-loving people' and 'our heritage of music'
have made this legend a household word. Nobody likes to hear that *this* is the
land without music, a land that is literally music-starved.[13]

Thus Aloys Fleischmann,[14] newly appointed professor of music at University
College, Cork, writing in *Ireland Today* in 1936. Together with John Larchet,[15]
Frederick May,[16] Eamonn Ó Gallochobair[17] and Brian Boydell,[18] Fleischmann
was to prove central to the reanimation of Irish musical ideas in the mid-
twentieth century. Such figures did not register disaffection from afar; on the
contrary, they were intimately involved with the development of a host of
musical infrastructures – in education, in musical performance, in the emergent potential of sound radio – which conditioned their individual aspirations
for Irish music. These aspirations centred upon musical composition itself,
but the designation 'composer' appears inadequate as a description of their
individual status (with the possible exception of May), given their influential
commitment as ideologues of music in Ireland.

This commitment was not uniform. Larchet, the senior figure in this
group, was to find his principal *métier* in education. As with Fleischmann
after him, he entered a public 'plea for music' two years after his appointment
to the chair of music at University College, Dublin, in 1921:

A dispassionate analysis of the present position of music in Dublin is rather dis-
couraging. It possesses no concert hall, good or bad, and no permanent orchestra which could be called a symphony orchestra . . . most of the people have
no knowledge of Strauss, Brahms, and the great volume of modern orchestral
music. Few are acquainted with any important works of later date than Wagner's 'Ring of the Nibelungen'.

Little interest is taken in chamber music or choral music; a large percentage
of music lovers in Dublin have never heard a string quartet . . . In such circumstances, it is inevitable that Dublin should contribute nothing to the support or progress of music.[19]

One might with fairness suggest that Larchet subordinated his own compositional (and scholarly) inclinations to the redress of this appalling impoverishment. 'A Plea for Music' reads almost as a personal credo from which Larchet
was to derive his unfailing adherence to the primary requisites of musical literacy and education:

The real cause of the failure to appreciate good music in Dublin is that the people have never been taught to do so: that is the reason for their apathy and their
impoverished taste. Our system of musical education is not merely wrong, it is
fundamentally unsound.[20]

This act of identification preoccupied Larchet throughout his career. Personally and professionally he espoused a supreme tact in his negotiation through the mire of musical indifference which he patiently attempted to redeem. As an educator, Larchet was engaged at virtually every level of what musical life there was: if anything, he disavowed the frequently wearisome polemics of aesthetic debate in favour of a pragmatic and multifarious encounter with the materials of music itself. As professor in University College, Dublin, and in the Royal Irish Academy of Music, his ideological convictions were expressed in a form of musical education which enlisted the European model of compositional technique as a means of musical awareness. This is not to gainsay Larchet's immense reputation as a teacher of composition *per se*, but Larchet's abiding concern was to instil a sense of craft, and thereby an understanding of the European aesthetic by which Irish musicians might respond to art music as a strictly germane consideration in the development of original music in Ireland. His preoccupation with modal counterpoint is evidence of this conviction.[21]

Larchet's own compositional voice, nevertheless, implicitly recognised the pervasive difficulty of reconciling two traditions. His whole career as an educator depended to some extent upon his pragmatic cognisance of Ireland's verbally dominated cultural matrix. As director of music at the Abbey Theatre from 1908 to 1934, his contribution was necessarily incidental to verbal art forms, and his (literal) proximity to Yeats, Lady Gregory and Lennox Robinson afforded him a particularly immediate exemplar of this creative subservience. Once again, this is not to gainsay the impact of his widely admired and consummately skilful arrangement of Irish airs for the pit of the Abbey Theatre, but Larchet's position in the theatre is plainly symbolic of the secondary role of music as a creative force within the artistic milieu of the new state. He rationalised that position in two ways. Firstly, he maintained an extraordinarily diverse range of teaching duties which addressed the overwhelming need for musical education (and above all for musical awareness) in Ireland. Secondly, he took from his work at the Abbey Theatre a compositional model – the representation of the ethnic repertory in impeccably fastidious arrangements – which might provide the basis for a liberal reinterpretation of the whole question of Irish art music. Joseph Ryan remarks that Larchet by precept and example set out 'consciously to foster a national expression largely based on folksong'.[22] This, inevitably, was to prove a vain hope, but it was not unique to Larchet. In his case, certainly, this ambition was constantly modified by an overriding concern with the degree and quality of Irish musical awareness which so strikingly affected Larchet's whole career. His own music in fact betrays this purposeful absorption of the prior claims of education. Larchet's modest and well-made rehabilitation of Irish folk music depends not on the ethnic tradition but on the precedent of European musical nationalism. He sought and found in Grieg, in Smetana, in Dvořák, a European model of musical thought consonant with his own perception of music in Ireland. That this was a model destined to fail does not detract from Larchet's significance in the cultural history of Irish music. On the contrary, it is precisely because Larchet so steadily countenanced the fundamental requirements of education that his own compositions belong to Irish cultural history not as mediocre gestures of colonial appropriation: instead, they mark an encounter between Irish music and the European tradition which continued to preoccupy his contemporaries in their quest for an authentic and durable compositional voice.[23]

This quest, of course, was contained by the normally fractious contemplation of the ethnic repertory. Aloys Fleischmann's extended rebuke in *Ireland Today* (November 1936) of a compositional mode circumscribed by the cult of folk music bluntly concluded that the 'propagation of one [folk music] does not lead to the development of the other [art music]'.[24] Earlier that year (July), the young composer Frederick May, then in his middle twenties, had joined the debate with an extended appraisal of 'Music and the Nation':

> Anyone who reflects on the present state of music in Ireland is bound to be filled with the most profound depression. We might have hoped that the quickening of life which began in the eighties of the last century with the inception of the literary revival, and which later imparted fierce energy to our politics, would have aroused our musical consciousness to some slight activity; that the wave which bore forward a great literary and political movement would not have left music quite untouched. But the wave was broken and receded, leaving us as we were before, in a state of almost complete stagnation.[25]

Thus three central acts of recognition attended the perception of music in Ireland: that the cultural prestige of folk music did not entail a healthy complexion in terms of the actual condition of music; that the burden of this very tradition inhibited access to and cultivation of original art music; that the literary revival did little or nothing for the development of music *per se*. These themes, together with the general cry of cultural stagnation, were to be sounded again and again in Irish periodical literature over the next twenty years. Notwithstanding the claims and counterclaims voiced in the acrimonious debate over the significance of the ethnic repertory (a debate which simply confirmed the polarisation of art versus folk music, and which did not find compelling resolution in composition itself), there was general agreement among Irish musicians as to the impoverished condition of the art in Ireland.

There was also significant development. The Dublin Philharmonic Society, established in 1927 by the recently appointed director of the Army School of Music, Fritz Brase, not only restored to the capital some semblance of regular orchestral playing (and in Terence Brown's phrase 'saved the city from complete mediocrity in musical matters'), but also sponsored – albeit to a limited degree – the performance of works by Irish composers, including Stanford, Harty and Harold White (Dermot Macmurrough). The decisive advance in this respect, however, came with the foundation in 1926 of a 'station orchestra' as part of the Irish radio broadcasting service, 2RN. Its steady growth from four to forty musicians (in 1942) was accompanied by an increase in public concerts which by the mid-1940s created a regular audience for the orchestral repertoire for the first time in independent Ireland. Radio Éireann was to prove seminal in the cultivation of music: it provided a stable platform for new composition, it ensured that the European repertoire became audible after years of silence, and it fomented a revival of interest in the collection and performance of the ethnic repertoire. The cluster of ensembles and regular programmes which grew around the principal orchestra consolidated the station's position as the foremost disseminator of music in Ireland, a role which it was to maintain throughout the 1950s and beyond. Radio Éireann would henceforward prove indispensable to the well-being of Irish music, and thereby vulnerable to the criticism which such a central role inevitably attracts.[26]

Criticism endured. The pages of Seán O'Faoláin's journal, The Bell, which cultural historians have been inclined to recognise as exceptional in its liberal scepticism and freedom from the doctrinaire piety so embarrassingly abundant in postwar Ireland, proved hospitable to musical discussion. In the late 1940s and early 1950s, a small number of regular contributors, including Fleischmann, John Beckett, Walter Beckett and Brian Boydell, established a presence for music in terms largely unencumbered by the aesthetic debate.[27] Instead, the preoccupation with music as an issue in Irish culture found expression in more practical concerns. Many of these anxieties had been voiced a generation earlier by Larchet and his contemporaries, and it is depressing to come upon them thirty years afterwards, and still unresolved. Brian Boydell's essay on 'The Future of Music in Ireland', published in The Bell in January 1951, is a case in point: despite the existence of the radio orchestras, despite the manifest improvement in a host of musical infrastructures which had taken place since the mid-1920s, Boydell famously urged that 'music in Ireland . . . is in a shocking state'.[28]

Boydell's condemnations were impassioned, but they were not irrational. He tackled five areas of particular deficiency, four of which echoed the concerns (again, with depressing exactitude) of Larchet's 1923 'Plea for Music'. First and foremost among these was the question of education. Boydell recognised the deplorable neglect of music as an element of formal school education, but, as Larchet had done almost thirty years before, he also advocated a pragmatic and persuasive distinction between education *about* music and formal musical training. This distinction – between the reception and understanding of music on one side and the acquirement of professional skills on the other – is one which seems scarcely to have registered in the minds of his contemporaries. The notion of cultivating an audience for music, of developing a serious interest in music as against the mediocre command of an instrument, failed to take in Ireland, with the result that a diminished audience for music stood in ironic relationship to the recent improvement in musical infra-structures.[29]

Boydell's censure of Radio Éireann is different in kind. He asserted that 'By far the greatest power in the field of professional music is the broadcasting service, which holds a large share of the responsibility for the future of Irish music',[30] but indicted the station because of its less than generous and largely unsympathetic treatment of orchestral musicians. Boydell sensed that the reception of musicians (composers as well as performers) on terms adequate to their professional skills was likely to remain indifferent within Ireland gen-erally unless it was first improved in state organisations such as Radio Éire-ann. Likewise his insistence that the building of a concert hall (partly in order to house a national symphony orchestra) was 'an urgent necessity': such developments (or the lack thereof) could be taken to indicate the real extent of Ireland's commitment to music.[31]

This commitment came under greatest scrutiny with the publication in 1952 of *Music in Ireland*, a symposium edited by Fleischmann, with a fore-word by Arnold Bax.[32] No other document has so comprehensively addressed the *status quo* of Irish musical life in any period, although the principal focus of *Music in Ireland* was the (then) present. Organised in three large sections ('Music and the Institutions'; 'The Profession of Music'; 'Music and the Pub-lic') and prefaced with an historical survey, *Music in Ireland* surveyed the plural condition of music to one end: to establish that 'the general organisa-tion of music in Ireland is much behind that of other countries'.[33] Fleisch-mann's strategy in this endeavour was novel: rather than magnify the general complaint of generations, he determined to list and describe every conceiv-able dimension of public music making in Ireland. In this way, each subdivi-sion of musical activity (education, professional organisation, professional training, performance, composition, broadcasting, festivals, church music, the development of individual genres, the presence of music in major urban centres, musical societies, recital series, library sources and music libraries, registers of music teachers, dealers and instrument makers) was subjected to individual scrutiny, with the result that broad conclusions were substantiated by detailed evidence. Fleischmann's own assessment of 'The Organisation of the Profession' was thereby an authoritative reading, explicitly dependent on the information amassed in the book itself.

This assessment was inevitably pessimistic:

> As it is, the Irish country towns and villages are starved of music, and the inhabitants of the vast majority of them have never seen an orchestra nor a chamber music ensemble . . . In some of the cities the position is little better.[34]

Fleischmann and his contributors repeatedly draw attention to the poor qual-ity of infrastructures, the corrosive want of general (music) education and the low level of remuneration which continued to afflict the development of music in the 1950s. Each of these deficiencies was to be addressed in some measure after the publication of *Music in Ireland,* but progress was slow: three problems repeatedly raised in the book, namely the lack of a national concert hall, the dearth of widespread music education in schools and the need for a conservatory, continued to exercise Irish musicians for decades afterwards. Of these three, only the first has to date been resolved.

*Music in Ireland* spoke to a country absorbed by economic depression, mass emigration and cultural stagnation. If the book has a slightly aggrieved tone, it does not whinge: the varied rhetoric of its individual contributors lends colour to the presentation of one prevailing concern, but the volume never lapses into self-pity or vapid fulmination.[35] It draws together the thinking of virtually every major participant in Irish music of the 1930s and 1940s, and it sponsors a uniquely detailed account of a *status quo* urgently in need of development. It also clarifies the context from which Seán Ó Riada was to emerge, within a few years of its publication.

Two contributors to *Music in Ireland* provide a different kind of context for Ó Riada, in that they typify the extremes of compositional voice which the polarised condition of music in Ireland continued to nurture. We have already glossed Frederick May's bleak assessment of the literary revival and its failure to stimulate a corresponding movement in music. As a student of composition, May reached beyond Ireland (after a period of study with Larchet) and brought his technique to maturity under Gordon Jacob and Vaughan Williams in London. A travelling studentship enabled him to study with Berg in Vienna, but Berg's death took place just prior to his arrival there. May nonetheless remained in Austria (as a student of Egon Wellesz) and consolidated his position as a composer wholly versed in contemporary idioms of European musical discourse.

This achievement was to prove burdensome for May. Afflicted with a cruel condition which produced constant noise in his head (oto-sclerosis), May's impulse for composition was weakened in any case by his financial insecurity and the grim realisation that the talent he possessed must remain largely irrelevant even to the small nucleus of those committed to art music in Ireland. The combination of these difficulties was to result in a career largely abandoned in his early thirties, although May lived into his seventy-fourth year. His uneven record of employment (including a spell at the Abbey Theatre in succession to Larchet), his unapologetic insistence on the validity of composition as a permanent (rather than part-time) occupation and his tragically diminished store of creative music eerily foreshadow certain aspects of Ó Riada's career.[36] May's string quartet in C minor – written prior to his studentship in Vienna but unperformed until 1948 – and his *Songs from Prison,* a setting of poems by Ernst Toller for baritone and orchestra composed in 1941, explicitly provide impeccable precedents for Ó Riada's art music, in particular the first and second *nomoi,* the second of which is also for baritone, orchestra (and chorus). To hear the string quartet – by repute one of the most significant and accomplished works of original Irish music in the twentieth century – is to recognise an original voice emancipated from the constraints of the ethnic tradition.[37] If there are elements of that tradition within May's score (certain lyric passages have an unmistakably Irish intonation), these are wholly absorbed into the texture, so that May's voice is his own. That he should have accomplished this degree of emancipation in an early work and yet failed to exploit it fully is expressive of personal incapacity to be sure, but also of the paralysing indifference with which such work was received in Ireland.[38]

*Songs from Prison* is preoccupied with a condition which neighbours indifference. It is not too much to suggest that Toller's anti-fascist symbolism operates for May at a personal level: the creative torpor, the dead weight of tradition, imprisons the compositional spirit in Ireland.[39] *Songs from Prison* may not be a self-conscious adieu to composition in the face of this oppression (the text offers a final hope for spring), but its mood and construction unquestionably relate the work to Ó Riada's second *nomos*. The syllabic insistence upon text, the motivic and textual recurrences and the sheer expressionism of both works link one to the other. May, in short, technically and spiritually establishes an antecedent for Ó Riada's art music.

The force of precedent is also present in the works (compositional and otherwise) of Eamonn Ó Gallochobair. In a somewhat ambiguous contribution to *Music in Ireland*, 'The Cultural Value of Festival and Feis',[40] Ó Gallochobair tried to distinguish between competitions devoted to the ethnic tradition and competitions largely taken up with 'cosmopolitan music', in terms that might reflect the Gaelic origins of one and the English antecedents of the other. While he conceded that the former had indeed borrowed the element of competition from the British prototype, Ó Gallochobair discerned cultural tension in such discrete forms of competition: 'So is the battle joined between Festival and Feis: it is the old political battle fought ideologically.'[41]

As a frequent commentator on music in Ireland from the mid-1930s onwards, Ó Gallochobair found himself in trenchant opposition to precisely that degree of emancipation so ardently commended by Fleischmann and May. His atavistic sense of Irish music was combined with an increasingly defensive attitude towards formal education and indeed towards the aesthetic of art music itself. In 1936, he bluntly formulated these attitudes as an outgrowth of 'the Irish mind':

> The sensitive mind in Ireland to-day is still influenced by the same things and in the same way as was the sensitive mind in Ireland long ago . . . I am trying to say that for the Irishman, the Irish idiom expresses deep things that have not been expressed by Beethoven, Bach, Brahms, Elgar or Sibelius – by any of the great composers – and that where the vehicle used for the presentation of the Irish idiom is the vehicle of any of these men or their schools – then the Irishman is conscious of a clash of values, a struggle for mastery and he rejects the presentation as 'wrong'.[42]

Some twenty-two years later, in a radio broadcast transmitted in 1958, the same argument was presented from a new premise, namely that 'the Gael belongs to the Mediterranean and not to the North-German tradition' and that in consequence the composer in Ireland is alone: 'there are no textbooks for him'.[43] This effort at musical realignment (from Europe to the Mediterranean) established an interesting precedent for Ó Riada's similar claims put forward in the series of broadcasts transmitted four years afterwards and entitled *Our Musical Heritage*.

Ó Gallochobair's achievement as a composer was prodigious by Irish standards: five operas (of which three are substantial in length), eleven ballet scores, four masses, about fifty vocal settings, in addition to a variety of small-scale orchestral and chamber works. His appointment as director of music at the Abbey (he followed May) and his subsequent appointment as first conductor of the Radio Éireann Light Orchestra (established in 1948) gave him considerable opportunity to implement his compositional ideals, and whereas his entire *œuvre* still awaits comprehensive scrutiny (as does that of his contemporaries) it would appear reasonable to agree with the suggestion that 'his impact as a critic and commentator was not matched by his achievement as a composer'.[44] Nevertheless, there is continuity in this achievement, which effectively sustained the tradition of modest arrangement of the ethnic repertory as a preferable substitute for the bolder integration with the European aesthetic so compellingly advanced by May. In this respect, too, Ó Riada's increasing preoccupation with traditional music as a resource less and less hospitable to European transformation finds precedent. As an ideologue and as a composer wholly indebted to the ethnic tradition, Eamonn Ó Gallochobair must be regarded as a decisive precursor of Ó Riada.

Educated by Fleischmann, appointed to the Abbey Theatre in succession to Ó Gallochobair, drawn like May to the vocabulary of European modernism and like Ó Gallochobair to the cultural pre-eminence of traditional melody, appointed to Radio Éireann (as assistant director of music), Seán Ó Riada can thus be advanced as the crucial recipient of Ireland's musical progress in the decades immediately prior to his emergence as a composer. Virtually every aspect of his professional career finds its source in these decades, and the process of slow amelioration which this period witnessed likewise prefigures the rapid progress which he made through the infrastructures and conflicting ideologies of music in Ireland. Without these developments, Ó Riada's journey of discovery would have been impossible; without them, too, his apprehension and resolution of artistic crisis could not have taken place.

\*   \*   \*   \*   \*

> The first thing to note, obviously enough, is that Irish music is not European.[45]

The relationship between biography and art could scarcely be more intimate than is the case in Seán Ó Riada's short life. His rapid assimilation and exhaustion of those modes of employment available to the composer in Ireland seem to embody his own insistent search for a durable aesthetic, and his progress from career to career clearly mirrors his quest for an authentic compositional voice. More ebullient than May, more sensitive than Ó Gallochobair, Ó Riada followed them into Radio Éireann and the Abbey Theatre, just as he was to follow his professor, Fleischmann, into University College, Cork. On one level the spread of his career simply rehearsed in rapid motion the slow assemblage of posts by which the composer in Ireland might earn a living: Frederick May's principal complaint. From this point of view, Ó Riada appears an impulsive, charmed and reckless author of his own misfortune, moving restlessly through one institution after the next. On closer inspection this reading proves transparently false. For all his self-indulgence, Ó Riada showed considerable enterprise and a permanent sense of professionalism in the pursuit of his career. Its apparently provisional nature – administrator, broadcaster, theatre musician, performer, entrepreneur, university lecturer, as well as composer – belied a constant preoccupation with music in Ireland, and specifically with the discovery of an authentic mode of Irish composition. If anything, Ó Riada's life attained to the cyclic motion which he discerned in Irish music as its pre-eminent quality: 'the serpent with its tail in its mouth'.[46] From Cork, to Dublin, to Paris, back to Dublin and finally to Cork, his physical journey, interleaved with this constant preoccupation, spells out Ó Riada's self-conscious quest for a degree of musical experience which would authenticate his own abilities as a creative artist.

This quest can also be read as a series of transformations or conversions. Although his earliest intimation of musical awareness concerned traditional music, the striking feature of Ó Riada's life and works is the extent to which he first absorbed and then rejected the European aesthetic. It is this motion above all others which characterises his achievement; the gesture of transformation itself being paradigmatic of Ó Riada's musical thought. This gesture was anything but modish: it extended to virtually every dimension of his life, artistic and otherwise. In brief, the movement from European to ethnic music was in close keeping with other movements, from 'John Reidy' to 'Seán Ó Riada', from the English to the Irish language (in everyday life), from Dublin to the West Cork Gaeltacht in Cúl Aodh, from the medium of Western art music (principally the symphony orchestra) to the medium of traditional Irish music (principally an ensemble presentation of the repertory which he himself in large measure devised).

Writing about Ó Riada in 1967 as a possible candidate for 'the great Irish composer whom we are all awaiting', Charles Acton, then music critic of *The Irish Times*, sketched the composer's aesthetic understanding as he received it from Ó Riada himself:

> Coming from West Cork, he regards the Irish language as his mother tongue, at least to the same extent as English: and his musical environment was the remnant

of Irish traditional music in its various genres. He claims that the genius of this is
a cyclic repetition with a succession of small variations, rather than the dramatic
pattern of sonata form or fugue developed by European art music as a final inheritance from classical Greece. He sees the contrast as between the Eurocentric,
Hellenic tradition and the older tradition of the Indo-European peripheral lands
back from Ireland, through *cante jondo* and Arab tradition, to Indian ragas.
Hence, he claims, when he began studying music at University College, Cork, in
1948 . . . he found the standard forms of art music inherently unsatisfying.[47]

Midway through this assessment Acton adds a rider to this sketch: 'I think
that the enormous success of his new band plus the great popular response to
it and his various film-music commissions have combined to retard the true
development of his vision.'[48] We shall return to that critique as a singular and
vital expression of concern.

The first perspective, then, from which to understand the significance of
Ó Riada's musical development comes from his own sense of history and the
career which this so manifestly informed. Ó Riada told Acton that his great-
grandfather had translated Homer's *Odyssey* into Irish, 'though the MS (alas,
never published) was burnt in Seán's own sight, page by page, by an alcoholic
grandson'.[49] There is a pre-ordained symbolism in this anecdote which is so
germane to Ó Riada's occasionally histrionic sense of artistry as to reek of fabrication. But the story serves its purpose: the drunken destruction of a cor-
nerstone of Western literature *translated into Irish* has an appositeness to Ó
Riada's creative struggle which is worthy of Faust. Such a translation could
not be allowed to take place, or at least to endure. And where the composer
himself attempted to address both traditions simultaneously, the European
and the Irish, that effort must also end in redundancy or failure. This was Ó
Riada's own compulsive understanding, but it was an insight which attained
on occasion to conventional wisdom: Aloys Fleischmann's remark after the
composer's death that both traditions were 'irreconcilable' in Ó Riada's music
had long been countenanced by Ó Riada himself.[50]

What factors hardened Ó Riada's conviction that his future as an Irish
composer specifically entailed a rejection of the art tradition? The shrill tone
of defensiveness which he brought to this question in the last years of his life
betrays a degree of indecision:

> Now the rational side of me can, therefore, cope with European music. The
> instinctive side of me is involved in traditional music because I am first and
> foremost, more than most Irish composers, involved in traditional music. But
> there is a third side and that is, no matter what I say to you now today, I do not
> know what my instinct is going to make me do next week, or even tomorrow,
> and I can't prophesy to you.[51]

Such disavowal of any kind of rational basis for the rejection of European
music was completely at odds with Ó Riada's gradual but deliberate renun-

ciation of the modernist aesthetic in the course of his compositional career. But pressures there must have been: on the day that the score of *Hercules Dux Ferrariae* was published in 1969, he calmly announced that he had decided to disband Ceoltóirí Cualann, the ensemble which he had founded in 1961.[52] It was through Ceoltóirí Cualann that he most effectively articulated his rehabilitation of traditional music by means of a radical revision of the *céili* band. This allowed Ó Riada an opportunity of incorporating the elaboration of Irish melodies performed in ensemble. The fundamental difference between Ó Riada's ensemble and its *céili* band prototype was that the former combined the textural range of individual instruments (uileann pipes, flute and whistle, fiddles, bodhrán, and, in emulation of the traditional harp, a harpsichord), whereas the latter blatantly (and popularly) espoused a mix of traditional and contemporary timbres, including the piano and modern percussion instruments. Beyond instrumentation, Ceoltóirí Cualann evinced a palpably novel approach to the traditional repertory, an approach conditioned by Ó Riada's inventive exploitation of traditional styles and techniques hitherto contained by individual (solo) performance. By rationalising the virtuoso elements of such performance, in which ensemble (and unison) versions of the melody were interleaved with bravura displays of technical and expressive variation, Ó Riada achieved a remarkable fusion of stylistic integrity and original deportment. It was this fusion that gave Ceoltóirí Cualann its distinctive sound, which was yet contained by processes of variation inherent in the tradition itself. In simplest terms, it was a formula that projected the integrity of tradition in a manner which would allow the tradition itself to develop.[53]

Ceoltóirí Cualann did not wholly entail the demise of Ó Riada's career as a composer in the European tradition, but his formal compositions thereafter were largely restricted to occasional pieces: the Hölderlin songs, music for film scores, the two settings of the mass ordinary.[54] The chronology of public performance might suggest otherwise, but in fact the greater part of his work as a composer of original music was complete by the early 1960s.[55] Moreover, it seems clear that Ó Riada wished for a time to adapt the performance conventions of European art music to his Ceoltóirí Cualann concerts: quite literally the presentation of traditional music in evening clothes, as in the 1969 concert recorded as *Ó Riada sa Gaiety*. This may have been a form of inverted snobbery, but it may also have represented an attempt to establish such performances as the proper mode of Irish art music.

A more pervasively didactic and prescriptive motivation attended his lecture series on traditional music, broadcast in 1962 as *Our Musical Heritage*. In these lectures, illustrated by excerpts from Ceoltóirí Cualann and other musicians, Ó Riada attempted to underwrite his espousal of the ethnic repertory with a blend of admonitory sentiment, aesthetic commentary and stringent repudiation of Europe:

Irish music is not merely not European, it is quite remote from it. It is, indeed, closer to some forms of Oriental music. The first thing we must do, if we are to understand it, is to forget about European music. Its standards are not Irish standards; its style is not Irish style; its forms are not Irish forms.[56]

The tone of *Our Musical Heritage*, the very rhetoric it employs, could come straight from Eamonn Ó Gallochobair and the worst traditions of defensive, jingoistic insularity.[57] Ó Riada does argue persuasively for a committed standard of traditional performance, and his range of musical references within the tradition enhances its depth and breadth of expression. But the ideology which stands behind *Our Musical Heritage* is a virulent strain of nationalism which sanctifies a degree of musical stasis ('our innate conservatism') worthy of Thomas Davis. Why Ó Riada should have had recourse to such overheated propaganda can only be explained paradoxically by his own achievement as a European composer, an achievement which argues against the very premise of *Our Musical Heritage*. In these lectures, the rejection of John Reidy for Seán Ó Riada is so brutally emphatic that the author gives every appearance of protesting too much. Some great hurt lies beneath.

Nearer the surface, perhaps, two implications arise from the success of Ceoltóirí Cualann, the prestige of the film scores and the rhetoric of *Our Musical Heritage*. One is that Ó Riada discovered in traditional music not simply a strongly congenial mode of artistic discourse, but a coherent language continuous with the past and amenable to the modifications of the present. The other is that by contrast with the plural complexity and disengaged aesthetic of European modernism, Irish music offered to Ó Riada a sense of identity – culturally and musically – by which his own voice might be distinctive and audible. He had already registered a distinctive voice in *Nomos no. 2*, but one which spoke of alienation rather than fluent absorption. In the ethnic repertory, by contrast, he discovered a tradition in which the voice was unbroken and untroubled by aesthetic or expressive crisis. This discovery drew him nearer and nearer to the rigid template of traditional art (sometimes explicitly nationalistic), a process that would not have been of much consequence in a lesser musician. In Ó Riada's case, however, consequences loomed large.

The second perspective from which to understand Ó Riada's career is that of Ireland's cultural history in the 1960s. Terence Brown concludes that in this period (and in the following decades):

> . . . it became less and less possible for writers and artists to celebrate such things as 'indigenous Irish life' without evasion or sentimentality. Rather the new Irish reality was ambiguous, transitional, increasingly urban or suburban, disturbingly at variance with the cultural aspirations of the revolutionaries who had given birth to the state. And if the new Ireland made a naïve, conventional folk-art impossible it also put paid to the artist as cultural hero.[58]

These conclusions self-evidently are at variance with Ó Riada's conception of Irish music as it developed in the same period. In a remarkable essay on 'Seán Ó Riada and the Ireland of the Sixties', Louis Marcus redeems for the composer precisely those qualities of cultural heroism and conventional folk-art ('the outstanding artistic figure in the Ireland of the sixties') which Brown shows to have been largely abandoned by the end of the decade.[59] Marcus does not damn Ó Riada with faint praise, rather he acknowledges that two major obstacles hindered his art: a 'Gaelic renascence that flowered in the sixties after half-a-century of stagnation *only to fade again* in the venality and doubts of the seventies' and the fact that whereas Ó Riada 'had abundant sensitivity and an imperative need to create . . . He lacked only one thing – a language.'[60]

The first of these obstacles provides a clue to Ó Riada's difficult position in Irish cultural history. Whereas his rehabilitation of the ethnic tradition earned him widespread acclaim in the white heat of this 'Gaelic renascence', Ó Riada himself clearly regarded his film scores and the evolution of Ceoltóirí Cualann as respective phases in the search for a comprehensive and durable compositional mode or 'language', as Marcus has it.[61] And because the arts in Ireland grew away from an ethnically homogeneous (and nationalist) *mentalité* in the late 1960s – in the theatre, in poetry, in fiction and in the visual arts – towards a more plural and distinctively European mode of discourse, Ó Riada's retreat in the opposite direction came to seem more and more isolated.[62] Notwithstanding the success of Ceoltóirí Cualann, Ó Riada's disillusion with the ensemble and his 'rediscovery of Carolan' attest to further uncertainty and indecision.[63]

The second obstacle – the lack of a coherent musical language – is more difficult to place culturally. Louis Marcus is worth quoting at length on this point:

> Ó Riada was born in a country that had missed two centuries of European musical development, and into a time when that development had itself collapsed in confusion. Unlike an artist in a stable framework which he can both rely on and refine, Ó Riada found a world in which there was chaos between the incongruous poles of serialism and Gaelic *sean nós*. I always felt that in his efforts . . . to rehabilitate the 18th century harpist Carolan as a composer there was, along with a genuine musical regard, a longing to touch the hand of the last Irishman for whom the Gaelic and European traditions of music were not irreconcilable.
>
> Of course, the problem was not purely a musical one. Art does not exist in a social or historical vacuum. Both serialism and *sean nós* are responses to types of human experience. But these experiences, like their musical counterparts, were worlds apart, for Ireland had long been isolated . . . from the upheavals of Western culture. Ó Riada was an exception. More than anyone working in the early sixties (perhaps more than any Irish artist since Joyce), the aged mind of Europe and its current *Zeitgeist* were to Seán matters of urgent reality rather than intellectual curiosity.[64]

There is much that is astray in this reading: it exaggerates Ó Riada's European sensibilities even by comparison with his composer-contemporaries in Ireland (Boydell, Bodley, Victory, Potter, Kinsella), to say nothing of such sovereign exemplars of an Irish art directly based in Europe as Samuel Beckett and Louis le Brocquy. Secondly, as I have tried to argue in this book, Carolan's status as an Irish composer was profoundly problematic in relation to the music of his European contemporaries. Thirdly, the bald statement that Ireland had 'missed two centuries of European musical development' tends to eclipse the existence of two musical traditions in the country – one ethnic, the other colonial – which mutually impinged on Irish cultural history at least from the 1770s onwards. Nevertheless, Marcus does advert to one crucial problem which all but hopelessly complicated Ó Riada's enterprise as a composer. That problem was the loss of a unifying aesthetic in Europe itself.

That this loss conventionally defines a central feature of musical modernism is not difficult to absorb. What is complex, however, is the extent to which it inhibited Ó Riada's development as a specifically Irish composer. Between 1955 and 1965, he had had recourse to essentially two kinds of European idiom – that of late nineteenth-century romantic nationalism (as in the film scores), and that of a tonally directed serialism (as in the first and second *nomoi*). The first of these was a logical extension (however brilliantly accomplished) of that long tradition of folk music arrangement which so stringently contained the concept of original composition in Ireland until the second half of the twentieth century. The second was an encounter with modernist techniques vitiated by tonal and structural continuities (counterpoint, melodic and rhythmic coherence, the textural palette of romantic expressionism) long employed in central Europe (Stravinsky, Bartók, Prokofiev) as a creative emancipation from the implications of total serialism. The 'Byzantine chess games' of total serialism were for Ó Riada an even darker cul-de-sac than the conventional orchestration of folk melodies. Neither idiom, however, provided a satisfactory conduit for Ó Riada's acutely self-conscious musical imagination, particularly in respect of his absorption of and preoccupation with the ethnic tradition itself. If the 'aged mind of Europe' and its 'current *Zeitgeist*' were matters of special urgency to Ó Riada, this was because he discovered therein the irrelevance of traditional Irish music to the aesthetic of art music. The disappearance of a unifying aesthetic in Europe confirmed this irrelevance. To redeem Irish music, one had to assert that it was not European, that it did not address the canons of high art, that it lay remote from the historicism of four centuries of Western musical culture.

This act of redemption would appear central to Ó Riada's commitment to the ethnic tradition. Unlike his central European contemporaries and forbears for whom folk music was an abiding preoccupation (Bartók and Kodály are obvious examples), Ó Riada lived in a country where the notion of art music specifically did not enjoy the analogous relationship with painting, sculpture, architecture which characterised its status for centuries in Europe. No great building, portrait or statuary summoned a musical correlative. Doomed as a gesture of colonial pastiche, art music simply could not survive independently of the cultural claims of the ethnic tradition. And this tradition, poised in Ó Riada's lifetime for widespread revival, began to enjoy precisely that degree of cultural consensus in Ireland which art music had so conspicuously lacked. When Ó Riada orchestrated *Róisín Dubh* in *Mise Éire*, when he brilliantly redeployed traditional Irish melodies in the ensemble arrangements of Ceoltóirí Cualann, he found immediate echo and approval. No such acclaim (beyond the smallest circle of cognoscenti) awaited original music which dispensed with (or simply moved beyond) the tradition.

It would be wholly unjust to conclude, however, that Ó Riada's abnegation of art music was a facile exchange of one tradition for another. The need was there to force the moment to its crisis, to confront the relationship between the ethnic repertory and a long-denied assimilation of the European aesthetic. When Ó Riada discovered that this relationship was hopelessly overcast by the tide of modernism, he posed an audacious alternative which was to prove immensely popular and influential. Instead of trying to reconcile two traditions, Ó Riada gave himself to the substitution of one for the other, down to the smallest detail: traditional music, literally, in evening dress. Ó Riada's career from 1962 until shortly before his death proclaims the representation of the traditional repertory as the proper, culturally alert business of the contemporary Irish composer. But the music itself discloses a constant unease. With every exchange (linguistic, domestic, musical) that marks Ó Riada's brief career, the claim of an Irish art music is gradually silenced.

\*   \*   \*   \*   \*

> What have I learned? Very broadly, that there are in this small Island two nations: the Irish (or Gaelic) nation, and the Pale. The Irish nation, tiny as it is at the moment, has a long, professional literary and musical tradition. The Pale, on the other hand, has a tradition of amateurishness. . . Three hundred years of this Pale amateurishness, are, however, ultimately boring. It has about the same relevance for the Irish nation as would a column about bee-keeping in a tricyclists' monthly journal.

> Seán Ó Riada to Charles Acton, 27 July 1971[65]

> Your analysis of our state suggests to me a difference of opinion between us analogous to the difference between the Westernisers and the Panslavophiles in nineteenth-century Russia. And I am avowedly, in that context, a Westerniser. I do not accept that 'Hercules' is foreign, I do not accept that Ireland should be the one country of Europe whose composers cannot contribute to the art of the Western world without being deracinated . . . If Ireland was artistically part of Europe in the Middle Ages, why would you cut her off now?

> Charles Acton to Seán Ó Riada, 2 August 1971[66]

The works of Seán Ó Riada's first maturity as a composer harbour the crises of style which were to affect his whole career. The first two *nomoi* (*Hercules Dux Ferrariae* and the work for baritone, orchestra and chorus) advance a technical command which builds on the achievement of Frederick May: if the latter's string quartet and *Songs from Prison* evince an Irish composer's intelligent encounter with the techniques of central European modernism, Ó Riada's *nomoi* confirm that encounter with a striking originality and assurance. *Hercules* in particular is a work of enormous promise (an observation so frequently made during Ó Riada's lifetime that the work came to plague him in later years) which signifies a commitment to the European aesthetic at once untroubled and resourcefully aware. The blend of tonally directed serialism, a *soggetto cavato* derived from the name of the patron of Josquin des Prez, and a systematic alternation of formal counterpoint and homophonic sonorities ensures the expressive and lyric address of *Hercules* as a significant contribution to the chamber-orchestral repertory.

Ó Riada's musical imagination, however, ranged almost immediately beyond the confines of *Hercules*: the work could not contain his impatient exploration of voice; nor could it satisfy his increasing sense of himself as an emphatically Irish composer. Without pretence to comparison in terms of significance or achievement, there is an instructive parallel to be drawn between his resolute abdication of stylistic continuity and that of Schoenberg in the second part of the *Gurrelieder*. With Ó Riada, too, there are the 'bonds of a bygone aesthetic' in *Hercules* which thereafter are broken in *Nomos no. 2*: the work is certainly bombastic, naïve, pretentious and overly ambitious in scope, but it also stands as an anguished and monumental lament for the composer's loss of innocence. It is a modernist work *par excellence*. The texts from Sophocles, the structural organisation and self quotation of material, and the ironic juxtaposition of Mozart, Beethoven and Brahms with Ó Riada's inventive strain of rhythmic motifs do not amount to much in terms of absolute originality (the precedent of Stravinsky in particular is never very far away). Nevertheless, *Nomos no. 2* is significant in two respects: it attests to Ó Riada's crisis of identity as a composer trained in the European tradition and it does so by means of an heroic pastiche which at the least is a courageous step beyond the *bien fait* tradition of *Hercules*. Courage on this scale was a rare commodity in Irish music of the early 1960s, and *Nomos no. 2* still endures as a vital text in the history of that music. The sheer expressive impact which Ó Riada achieved (to judge by the single recorded performance of the work) has rarely been equalled.[67] Once again, a work of huge promise was brought into being.

Other works in the short series of *nomoi* initiated by Ó Riada in the mid-1950s also espoused promise, but none of these attained to the significance of the first two.[68] Thus Charles Acton could make the arresting but factually correct statement in 1967 that 'much of Ó Riada's most significant work was composed, or at least had its origins, in a period round 1956–57'. It was Acton, too, who identified the second *nomos* as the composer's 'farewell' to the musical tradition of his European training (an observation apparently autho-rised by Ó Riada himself).[69] That arrival and departure should come so close together might well have signalled to Ó Riada's contemporaries that some-thing was seriously amiss, were it not for the prestige which his film scores enjoyed. It was precisely these works, and the evolution of Ceoltóirí Cualann, however, that concerned Acton, as we have seen above. Acton's worry was that these preoccupations distracted the composer from the realisation of his creative potential: a point of view that sat oddly with the cultural and popu-lar acclaim which Ó Riada began to enjoy in the immediate aftermath of his association with Gael Linn and the release of the films *Mise Éire*, *Saoirse?* and *An Tine Bheo* in particular. [70]

Ó Riada's film scores cannot wholly be regarded as a distraction from his work as an original composer. They represent in part a late-romantic response to that idealistic revival of Gaelic culture which disappeared in the face of sterner realities, particularly the Northern crisis, which erupted in the late 1960s. George Morrison's film *Mise Éire* projected images of the Easter Rising which Ó Riada's music explicitly romanticised: this was precisely its function. The cyclical treatment of the ethnic melody *Róisín Dubh* and in particular its brilliantly evocative orchestration potently expressed that high degree of naïve optimism which *Mise Éire* evoked.[71] Ó Riada drew directly upon the native repertory in order to meditate on the birth of a nation. This was a strategy inexorably wedded to the medium of film itself and notably distinct (although not discontinuous) from that tradition of 'folk-music arrangement' to which he contributed as musical director at the Abbey Theatre. Instead, the scores of *Mise Éire* and its sequel, *Saoirse?*, addressed that vital association between music and text by which music in Ireland had achieved intelligibility and sig-nificance for almost two centuries. Ó Riada's music gave meaning to visual rather than verbal images, but the result was the same: the meaning of the music (and thus of Irish music in general) was conditioned by its immediate context.

There are modifications in the score of *Saoirse?* which bear out this read-ing: whereas the music of *Mise Éire* is confined to projections and rhapsodic variations of the ethnic corpus of melody, the more politically aware tenor of *Saoirse?* (apostrophised in the question mark of the title) draws exclusively upon the ballad tradition. In the second film, Ó Riada's arrangements aban-don the heady romanticism of *Mise Éire* (notwithstanding similarities in scor-ing[72]) in favour of more deliberate character pieces. Thus the militaristic demeanour of 'Step Together' and the programmatic scoring of 'Joybells' (strongly reminiscent of Prokofiev) in *Saoirse?* border nervously on parody. This tendency is accentuated in the 1966 film, also made in celebration of the Easter Rising, *An Tine Bheo*. By then, Ó Riada had felt that his mind was 'already overexposed to 1916 before I started'.[73]

The difficulty in dismissing these scores, however, is that they articulate so successfully the cultural ideology which gave rise to the films in the first place. For Ó Riada, it was an ideology which at its most extreme divorced him from any kind of sustained cultivation of art music: therein lay its principal musical consequence. Although he continued to respond to commissions to write incidental music for a number of films, television and radio programmes, there is not much to suggest that beyond *An Tine Bheo* Ó Riada was particularly concerned to pursue film music as a means of attaining or developing a compositional voice. This, too, he effectively abandoned.

To have written music with such outstanding success in two utterly distinct compositional idioms and to have attenuated both in rapid succession undoubtedly speaks of a crisis of imagination. The film music and the original scores overlap in conception, but not at all in style or vocabulary. Ó Riada's resolution of that crisis was the formation of Ceoltóirí Cualann.

I have already argued that Ceoltóirí Cualann provided Ó Riada with the means of rehabilitating the traditional repertory as a substitute for creative composition. From its inception in 1961, this ensemble focused the composer's absorption with the ethnic repertory and dominated his thinking about Irish music. Ceoltóirí Cualann became, in effect, Ó Riada's mouth piece: a group of traditional virtuosi governed by the composer's projection of Irish melody as a structural chain of variations in which the juxtaposition of individual and sectional textures with the impact of the whole ensemble (largely in unison) sustained the inherent musical interest. Ceoltóirí Cualann may have had its origins in the *céili* band, but a more useful analogy ironically exists with art music: having exchanged the European aesthetic for the traditional repertory, Ó Riada exchanged one kind of orchestra for another. This exchange was both brilliant and novel: the musicians whom Ó Riada gathered round him were the finest executants available, and in the aftermath of Ceoltóirí Cualann's dispersal, many of them regrouped under Paddy Moloney as The Chieftains. The unbroken series of recordings, concerts and radio broadcasts given by Ceoltóirí Cualann from 1960 until 1969 testifies to Ó Riada's successful 'experiment' with Irish music, in which he renovated the traditional repertory and placed it at the centre of the Irish cultural matrix.

Louis Marcus has crucially observed of Ceoltóirí Cualann, however, that it had 'early become yet another cul-de-sac in his [Ó Riada's] restless search for a language'.[74] There is substance to this remark, although one might modify it by suggesting that in this third phase of his career the search had become less restless and more subdued than before. In addition, Ó Riada's increasingly antagonistic relationship with music other than the ethnic repertory made of Ceoltóirí Cualann a slightly pompous form of national, official entertainment. The formal demeanour of their 1969 concert in the Gaiety Theatre, Dublin, given in the presence of Eamon de Valera (President of Ireland), conferred an uneasy status on the music itself: it was as if Ó Riada wished to appropriate the decorum of public performance in respect of one tradition, while supplanting one kind of music with another.

Of considerably more significance than the evening clothes, however, was Ó Riada's inclusion of the harpsichord (his own instrument within the ensemble) as the pre-eminent voice in Ceoltóirí Cualann. Advanced by Ó Riada as an approximation of the sound of the Irish harp, the use which he made of this instrument to cohere and control his projection of musical structure is the most striking feature of the recordings which he made with Ceoltóirí Cualann throughout the 1960s. It is the harpsichord which undoubtedly signifies Ó Riada's lingering ambiguity about the traditional repertory, particularly because of its alternating 'continuo–concertino'-like deployment in Ó Riada's arrangements. The harpsichord (and other keyboard instruments, although to a much lesser extent) points beyond the ethnicity of Ceoltóirí Cualann towards some dimly intuited rapport between two traditions. And it is perhaps significant that Ó Riada's last recordings, made after the dissolution of Ceoltóirí Cualann, should attempt to realise on that instrument 'the true spirit of the Irish harp composers'.[75] To listen to the composer's lonely harpsichord meanderings on *Ó Riada's Farewell*, over which the spirit of Carolan hovers, is to countenance one dislocated soul informing the other.

\* \* \* \* \*

The crisis which I have sought to describe here was for the most part occluded by the acclaim which greeted Ó Riada during his brief lifetime. Expressions of genuine dissent were rare. This is what makes Charles Acton's abiding note of concern throughout Ó Riada's career so remarkable: as someone who had witnessed and reviewed the première of virtually every significant original composition by Ó Riada, he was better placed than most to observe the downward curve towards self-indulgence and silence which ended with the composer's death in October 1971. The famous exchange of open letters conducted between Ó Riada and Acton, occasioned by the latter's scathing notice of a 'one-man show' given by the composer in July of that year, sharply apostrophises the conflict of interests which ultimately paralysed Ó Riada's movement as an artist.[76] On one side of this exchange, Acton (clearly unaware of Ó Riada's illness) urged that he recover the discipline necessary to the realisation of his great promise as a composer of international significance. On the other side, Ó Riada defensively repudiated this ambition: it belonged to the Pale, from which he had defiantly exiled himself.[77] Death cut short this debate, and Acton's obituary concluded that, although Ó Riada had shown the promise to be 'our first great composer',

> The width of his activity, his zest for actual life threatened the realisation of this promise, a continued anxiety to many of his friends. As a result, and of his life being so tragically cut short in his prime, this promise cannot now be fulfilled.[78]

Such plain speaking appears in retrospect more courageous than the grandiloquent laments with which Irish literati greeted Ó Riada's decease, laments which ranked his achievement alongside that of Yeats and Joyce and which simultaneously projected him as a martyr to the cause of high culture in Ireland.[79] These exaggerations tend to overshadow the truth of Acton's assessment, namely that Ó Riada both possessed and failed to realise the potential of definitive and memorable musical achievement, by which Irish art music for the first time might rank in comparison with Irish literature.

But a second, more fundamental truth clearly attends Ó Riada's life and work. However tantalising the prospect of a 'great Irish composer', it was one which for Ó Riada was doomed to remain a mirage in the desert. The more nearly he encountered the ethnic tradition, the more difficult it became – his career makes this self-evident – to integrate that tradition within the language of the European aesthetic. With the exception of the late mass settings – in which composition becomes a vestigial activity – Ó Riada eschewed precisely this combination of ethnic repertory and international vocabulary in his original works. It is difficult not to conclude that such a combination would have represented an act of 'colonial' (mis-)appropriation absolutely inimical to his instincts as a composer. The political condition of being Irish, when added to the then unstable notion of a 'great composer', produced an aesthetic complexity which proved untenable. To take on the loss of a unifying aesthetic in Europe *and* the polarised condition of music in Ireland was simply too much to bear. Having forced the recognition of this crisis, Ó Riada took refuge instead in fertile, culturally apposite representations of a very small stock of traditional melody.

These representations, together with the film scores, earned for Ó Riada a degree of cultural recognition never afforded before or since to an Irish composer. His influence was such that the perception of music in Ireland as an original art form was almost wholly contained by his work with Ceoltóirí Cualann in particular. It was a perception which endured in the virtuoso finesse and bravura of The Chieftains and more recently in the reanimation of Ó Riada's productive cult of musical personality so effectively espoused by Mícheál Ó Súilleabháin. In both cases, the concept of original composition is virtually indistinguishable from more or less successful adaptations of the Ó Riada model; which is to say that 'original composition' is a meaningless term, other than to describe the variation and novel deportment of the traditional repertory itself. Those composers who meanwhile engage with Irish music other than the tradition are remaindered, in Raymond Deane's memorable phrase, to 'the honour of non-existence'.

The significance of Ó Riada, then, is not that he was the 'greatest Irish composer of the twentieth century' but that he silenced the claim of original art music as a tenable voice in the Irish cultural matrix: he silenced it too in its address upon the Irish mind. In its stead, he advanced the claim not of original composition but of the ethnic repertory itself. The eager reception of this claim in a country dominated by verbal art forms is itself part of the cultural history of music in Ireland. So too is the indifference to European music

– with certain notable exceptions – which has proved pervasive in Ireland almost to the end of the twentieth century. It would be absurd to lay this indifference at Ó Riada's door, but neither can one ignore the pivotal role which his endorsement of the ethnic repertory has played in the general reception of music in Ireland in the twenty-five years since his death. Ó Riada's huge gifts forced a degree of recognition and repudiation which profoundly affected not only his own ability (and inability) to compose, but the understanding of music in the cultural fabric of modern Ireland.

Other composers, no less committed to authenticity of voice and style, exercised minimal influence on the reception of music in Ireland as an *essential mode of artistic and cultural discourse*.[80] Ó Riada, for better and for worse, was to determine the significance of music in Irish culture to a degree unprecedented in two centuries. The crisis enacted in his own life and works, together with its resolution, defined the terms of that discourse in the 1970s and beyond.

# EPILOGUE
## Music and the Irish
## Literary Imagination[1]

In this book, I have tried to understand the formation of a recurring problem with regard to music in Ireland by placing it in the context of the history of Irish ideas from the end of the eighteenth century until about 1970, and I have found it useful to think about music in Ireland under the aegis of certain prevailing concepts in that period, notably antiquarianism, romanticism, political history, the language question and (religious) devotional reform. Throughout, the recurring trope of cultural polarisation between ethnic and colonial ideologies of culture – the problem itself – has intruded like a magisterial *cantus fermus* upon the history of musical ideas in Ireland, and it is this question of polarisation, first and last, which has been the one most difficult to interpret and contain.

The impact of music on the Irish literary imagination is advanced here as belonging to that history of ideas, if only as an epilogue or afterword, because the relationship between music and text has always been so prominent in the cultural history of modern Ireland.

The projection of music as an agent of cultural discourse in Irish literary history, moreover, is a phenomenon which infers a significant attitude of mind with regard to the perception of music in Ireland. When literature is so conditioned by implicit or explicit reference to music, the chances are that some consideration of it will prove useful in any exercise in cultural history which has music as its principal focus. In simplest terms, literature can mean 'writing about music' (as in periodical literature), and such writing in Ireland, as I have argued, has itself proved to be endemic to the formation of modern Irish literature. I have also argued that the concept of an independent mode of Irish music which emerged in the nineteenth century was imbued with such strength of extra-musical and specifically political feeling that the relationship between music and literature showed itself to be intimate, vexed and formative. In this epilogue, I shall want to press home the implications of that argument. In particular, I shall want to show that the *idea* of music accumulated such a powerful condition of political and cultural significance in Ireland through the nineteenth century that the projection of this idea superseded the will to develop ideologies and infrastructures necessary to the cross-fertilisation of ethnic and European musical resources (themselves polarised by the associative properties of music in Ireland).

My thesis throughout chapters three and five of this study has been that narrative, poetic and dramatic modes of literary discourse reanimated the idea of 'Irish music' throughout the nineteenth century, so that the metaphorical power of music imaginatively eclipsed any real concern with the cultivation of music *per se*. That music endured as an agent of cultural discourse is naturally not in question here. What I do want to query in this epilogue, however, is the manner in which this discourse was modified and inhibited by non-musical processes, and by literature in particular. The cultural mutation of the ethnic repertory, by which its rehabilitation was transformed to the extent that music became an agent of sectarian civilisation, is one such process. The consolidation of 'Irish music' as as symbol of cultural and then political aspiration and as a function of something other than itself in Irish literature is another. Both of these admittedly complex processes bear upon our understanding of music as a resource in terms of the Irish literary imagination. The second of these processes is not vague: 'Irish music' as an idea enters the literary imagination as a function of the imaginative process itself. This is plainly evident in Yeats, but it is also prominent in Synge and Joyce. This epilogue examines my reading of music in Ireland in the light of that process.

*   *   *   *   *

Seamus Deane has this to say about the proximate condition of music and literature in Ireland during the nineteenth century:

> With the founding of *The Nation* newspaper, and the subsequent separate publication of the volume *The Spirit of the Nation* (1843), comprising what is called 'Political Songs and Ballads', poetry finally achieved popularity by allying itself with music and disengaging itself from any serious attempt to deal with Irish experience outside the conventions imposed by the powerful, if callow, demands of the Young Ireland movement. Thus, three kinds of music influenced the development of poetry through the century. Moore's *Irish Melodies* provided nationalist sentiment with a degree of respectability that was guaranteed by the possession of a drawing room and a pianoforte. When the sentiment prevailed over the nationalist feeling, these melodies, which were for their audience in Ireland like arias from an extended national operetta, had to compete with songs from three genuine operettas that became such an integral part of Dublin musical life by the turn of the century: The *Bohemian Girl* (1843) by Michael Balfe (1803–70) [*recte* 1808–70], *The Lily of Killarney* (1862) by Julius Benedict (1804–85) and *Maritana* (1845) by William Vincent Wallace (1814–65). Balfe's 'I dreamt I dwelt in marble halls', 'Benedict's 'The Moon has raised her lamp above' and Wallace's 'Yes, let me like a soldier fall' and 'There is a flower that bloometh', became, with Moore's songs, part of the standard repertoire of those ubiquitous tenors including James Joyce's father, Joyce himself and John McCormack . . .
>
> On the other hand, *The Nation's* poets used many old Irish airs and some of their own making to further the militant tradition of rebellion against the English, or as they put it 'Saxon' rule and oppression.

These songs, often execrable as poetry, had an enormous appeal to all of a national cast of mind, but few of them were deemed to be as 'respectable' as the melodies and arias of Moore and the operettas.

Finally, the translators and collectors, from James Hardiman and George Petrie to John O'Daly, D.F. MacCarthy, Edward Walsh and Douglas Hyde, were anxious to preserve in English as much as possible of the original spirit of the Irish songs and poems they translated, seeking thereby some ultimate reconciliation between the English language and that essential spirit . . . This more scholarly tradition, was, oddly, closer to the mass of popular songs that had remained in the common possession of the people at least since the eighteenth century and often from a much earlier period. In all these instances, there was a mobilisation of poetry to the national purpose of re-awakening and recovering the sense of Ireland's uniquely tragic and heroic history. As a result, poetry and popular song became an important weapon in the long war against colonialism . . . It was assumed, therefore, that when the old Irish music was put to new English lyrics, the native spirit would hibernicise the English language rather than be anglicised by it.[2]

If Deane's reading of Irish literature in English during the mid-nineteenth century is correct, the implications for this alliance between music and poetry in particular are vitally germane to this study. It is not merely that Deane identifies demotic musical culture as the mobiliser of nationalist feeling, as the spark which ignites the weapon of anti-colonial warfare; it is that he acknowledges the prevailing condition of music in nineteenth-century Ireland: music as intelligencer of the text. My own attempt to identify a sense of music in Ireland as the outgrowth of antiquarian research on one hand and as the expression of a politically coherent ideology on the other during the first half of the nineteenth century is obviously consonant with this reading, but in the second half of the century I would discern a development beyond these complementary positions, namely the use of music as the prepotent symbol of renascent culture (notwithstanding the Irish language itself).

The outgrowth of these ideas in the collections of Bunting and Petrie, in the songs of Moore and in Davis's appropriation of the street ballad, together with Hardiman's *Irish Minstrelsy*, signifies a degree of cultural self-awareness with regard to music which is unmistakable. In each phase of this development, the original dialectic between antiquarianism and romanticism (as between Bunting's impulse to preserve Irish music and Moore's explicitly political intention of reanimating it) informed the understanding of 'Irish music' either as an icon of the past (carefully transmitted) or as an image of the present (ideologically transformed). Thus even within the boundaries of scholarly debate, as in Ferguson's review of Hardiman, the inherent aesthetics of Irish music were superseded by Hardiman's own reading of the lyric as an expression of political aggrievement and by Ferguson's counter-reading in which the textual quality of Hardiman's translations excluded any concern with the music itself.

I do not mean here to suggest that this preoccupation with text implies an indifference to music but rather an appropriation of music in the service of certain political and cultural claims, and ultimately the claim of a coherent Celticism. Moore's commitment to a history of Irish outrage and degradation,[3] Davis's romantic nationalism and his prescriptive zeal for a music which would nourish the propaganda of Young Ireland, and Petrie's stark motivation for his scholarly address upon the preservation of music (the ravages of the Famine) were predicated upon two factors in particular. One was the understanding of music as an indispensable intelligencer of verbal feeling; the other was a powerful assumption that Irish music by its nature belonged to the past. Mangan's restoration of political allegory to Gaelic song in his version of *Róisín Dhubh* would apostrophise for Yeats and his generation the decisive blend of fundamentally musical symbolism and radical translation which enabled the new Irish literature in English. In this admirable synthesis, by which the arguments for cultural separatism were resolved, music could function not literally, but figuratively. It would always retain its symbolic status with regard to the culture of the Gael, but it could now serve too as a metaphor of the imaginative process itself.

That it did so in Yeats, in Synge and in Joyce is beyond question. But this very prominence entailed a curious disregard for the thing itself in the history of Irish ideas. On one side there was 'Irish music', an indiscriminate object of cultural stasis (the folk tradition, the romantic ballad, the handful of well-remembered arias); on the other, there was the burgeoning condition of Irish literature in English at an imaginative rate unprecedented in three centuries. Between these two new polarities, the condition of art music lapsed into mediocrity or silence. New music in the art tradition would remain strictly incidental to the Irish mind (as in the theatre) or as a subject of bewilderment and indifference to those preoccupied by the rich harvest of poetry and drama which was yielded between 1880 and 1920.

That Irish music should be lodged permanently within the imaginative terms of a Gaelic past was the cultural ideal almost casually evinced from within the literary revival ('the peasant who has his folk-songs and his music', in Yeats's phrase). It is this assumption which underlies Yeats's virtually constant sense of lyric redress, notwithstanding his own disdain for music *per se*. Music for Yeats is Song, and the notion of verse as texted music appears to permeate his writing, even if his references to Irish music are rarely explicit. His identification, moreover, with Young Ireland and with Davis, Mangan and Ferguson in 'To Ireland in the Coming Times' (1893) is voiced in terms of the poet as lyricist, and we may ruefully note that this sense of literary history confirms the reception of music as an idea in Yeats's work which is absolutely contingent on the communication of textual meaning. Even in the plays, most especially in *The Countess Cathleen* (1899), music enters the text in essentially two ways: first, as an incidental support for the songs which the old woman recites, and second, as a metaphor for the transcendent power of the imagination. The 'sensual music' of which Yeats writes in 'Sailing to Byzantium' (1927) is actually set *against* the process of poetry itself ('monuments of unaging intellect'); 'Easter 1916' (1921) sustains the normal convention in Yeats, by which poetry *is* song.

My purpose here in culling what are random examples is not to redeem Yeats's hostility to music; it is to suggest that the pressure and appeal of Irish literature as an essentially lyric mode are reflected in Yeats's poetic voice to the extent that music itself all but disappears. What endures is the symbolism of music, together with its connotations of form, order, allusion. The progress is so simple that it escapes attention: Yeats takes from Irish music (that complex of verbally dominated elements identified here by Seamus Deane) its narrative and symbolic resonances and thereby completes the passage of translation from one culture to the other. The expedient having failed as between two musical traditions, it now brilliantly succeeds in literature. Literature in Ireland – expressly in terms of the Celtic revival – comes to appropriate the music of Gaelic culture. However impoverished the translation from one musical culture to the other, however poor the transition from one mode of Irish music to the next, literature provides a continuity which music does not. And as Irish literature gathers pace and inestimable imaginative strength (not least from its explicit address upon music), the prospect of an Irish art music of commensurate integrity withers away. In Yeats, as in Synge, certain modes of Irish literature begin to function as substitutes for a tradition of art music. In the case of James Joyce, the pressure of such a suggestion reaches breaking point.

Far more than Yeats, Synge struggled to rationalise what he knew of music with his evolution of a poetic mode (answerable in his case to the dramatic vision of Aran and Wicklow). In a remarkable exposition of Synge's musical background, Ann Saddlemyer has recently established not only the provenance of Synge's musical studies at the Royal Irish Academy of Music but also his determination to compose music, an ambition which was prior to his first efforts as a writer. Saddlemyer indeed imputes to this preoccupation with music a formative influence on Synge's dramatic prose style, and she cites an amusing letter from his mother to his older brother by way of evidence of this absolute commitment:

> Johnnie is so bewitched with music that I fear he will not give it up. I never knew till lately that he was thinking of making his living by it seriously; he spares no pains or trouble and practises from morning till night, if he can. Harry [her son-in-law] had a talk with him the other day, advising him very strongly not to think of making it a profession. Harry told him that all men who do take to drink. And they are not the nicest of men either, but I don't think his advice has had the least effect . . . the sound of the fiddle makes me quite sad now.[4]

Synge did not repine, and spent a year in Germany as a student of violin and piano. Nevertheless, he did abandon music, and his avowed reason for having done so gives one pause for thought: 'I saw that the Germans were so much more innately gifted with the musical faculties than I was that I decided to give up music and take to literature instead.'[5] None of this would be of much moment were it not for the implications it has for our understanding of the place of music in Synge's literary imagination and by extension in the Irish literary imagination as a whole. Synge's plays are shot through with a language that is conventionally described as intensely musical, but the real issue is his awareness of music as a paradigmatic force in the evolution of his own literary structures. The *caoine* and ballad poetry, he argued, were 'form without ulterior ideas', music, architecture and painting were 'form with ideas', higher poetry and drama, 'ideas with form'. He would aspire to the last of these. Ann Saddlemyer argues that Synge's realisation of this aspiration was so closely patterned on his understanding of musical structure and his passionate belief that music and dramatic poetry were close kindred, that the plays are best understood as a species of literature controlled by the technical processes of music.[6] Her comment that Vaughan Williams's adaptation of *Riders to the Sea* barely adds a single line and takes the text otherwise as it stands betokens the (perhaps) unique implementation of musical structure and articulation which characterises so much of Synge's dramatic writing. Even in *The Playboy of the Western World*, speeches function as arias and plot is suspended thereby to facilitate the outpouring of feeling, as Katharine Worth has lucidly and famously demonstrated of *Riders to the Sea*.[7]

Two issues in Irish cultural history may thus be read from Synge's use of music. One is that his wider musical awareness is an exception which proves the general rule of silence with regard to music of the European art tradition. Synge was attracted to far more than the *idea* of music, he was imbued rather with the experience itself. His explanation for having turned from music to literature deserves a moment's speculation in light of this preoccupation. He must have recognised in Germany a centrality of musical vision, of musical infrastructure and of musical idea in the German mind that was simply without parallel in Ireland. By transferring his attention to the centrality of language in the Irish context, Synge could harmonise his own creative musical impulses with the linguistic cultural matrix in which he found himself. There is evidence that to the end of his life he preferred music to the theatre, but his will to creative expression overcame this preference in favour of language.

The second issue leads us from Synge to Joyce, where the preoccupation with music is no less intense. This preoccupation is pervasive with regard to its metaphorical condition and seminal (if occasional) with regard to structural paradigm. I would like to suggest that in Joyce the use of music as an expressive resource is itself expressive of the condition of music in Irish cultural history and in the widest possible terms. The amorphous clutter of Joyce's imagination can overpower the will to think through its taxonomic processes. But those processes are contained at least in part by his obsessively exact interest in the contours of Irish cultural life at the turn of the

century. This is especially true of his interest in music. The secondary literature on Joyce is legion, and the extent of his musical allusions forms a considerable part of it.[8] What would appear to emerge from this research is that
Joyce drew upon that vast culture of song which characterised middle-class
life (in Dublin especially) so that the categories identified by Seamus Deane
above – balladry, Moore's *Melodies*, operatic arias – together with a host of
popular songs and theatrical numbers are woven into an immense fabric of
musical metaphor, by which music is enlisted as a means of imagining the
past and modifying the present. If Joyce's imagination proves the contin-
gency of music in Ireland more thoroughly than any other writer, it is
because his works convert the raw material of this music into metaphor. This
act of conversion is various: in 'The Dead', for example, the succession of
musical events is an accumulation of distinct types (opera, salon music,
musical anecdotage) which gradually narrows to the prepotent impact of *The
Lass of Aughrim*, a ballad which crucially encodes the central concern of
Joyce's fiction in this instance.[9] In the 'Sirens' episode of *Ulysses*, the attempt
to emulate the somewhat rarefied structure of a *fuga per canonem* in language
signifies an experiment in prose which is formally controlled by Joyce's conception of thematic counterpoint. But Joyce's musical imagination, at the
last, is primarily lyric, and in this respect wholly typical of the cultural milieu
which nourished it. In addition to Moore, for example, *Finnegans Wake* contains something in the order of a thousand songs; in *Ulysses*, there are at least
four hundred, many of which recur at points of obvious structural or emotional significance.

If we do speak here of an essentially lyric imagination, and one moreover
which is biblically comprehensive in its range of address, it seems reasonable
to suggest that Joyce's encounter with music as an imaginative resource tends
to redefine the perception of music in Ireland through the agency of language
which is itself definitive of modernism. In *Ulysses*, for example, the steady
stream of musical allusions which pervades so much of the structure aspires
to the condition of a meta-language, in which fragments of popular musical
culture attain to thematic status. This conversion of music into language
clearly affects the stature of Joyce's prose: *Finnegans Wake* merely represents its
most extreme condition. *Ulysses* more easily affords a platform of insight into
Joyce's language as 'meta-music', a development which originates in his
importation of Irish musical consciousness (song by song, as it were) into fiction.[10] Once again, the process is so transparent it is scarcely perceivable:
Joyce's dependence on the nominative, associative and symbolic properties of
music is so exhaustive that it defines his fiction. The shards and fragments of
a dislocated musical culture, hopelessly polarised by language and long political usage, are now diligently harvested by literature. To suggest that music is
an intelligencer of verbal feeling in Joyce is drastically to understate the case.
Music – the felt life of music in Ireland – conditions Joyce's fiction so completely that it thereby achieves an aesthetic and artistic significance otherwise

unavailable to it. Joyce's transformation of the materials of Irish musical culture in *fiction* itself signifies the condition of *music* in Ireland.[11]

\*     \*     \*     \*     \*

Douglas Dunn has remarked that he can hear a 'disinterested, lyric note' in Seamus Heaney's poetry. Dunn says that it is 'woodnote, chalumeau, reedy and Irish'. It seems to him that it is with that 'frustrated relationship between lyricism and politics' that much of Heaney's poetry is engaged.[12]

This encounter between lyricism and idea, between the 'music of what happens' (in Heaney's own phrase) and a sense of language which is at perfect pitch, would seem to distinguish Heaney's voice in contemporary poetry. His ideas are mediated, conditioned, qualified by a poetic voice which is so apparently musical that to comment upon it entails the risk of redundancy. Except in one respect. If there is a conjunction between lyricism and history in Heaney's poetry, it echoes that long tradition of verse which passes from Irish (Gaelic) into English in the nineteenth century via Moore, Ferguson, Mangan and the Celtic revival. Writers establish their own forebears. In Heaney's case the precedent of bardic impulse to be found in the traditions of high Gaelic culture and more immediately in the poetry of Yeats is lyric, musical and declamatory. When we speak of the music in Heaney's poetry we do so more than conventionally; an entirely new register of sound and sensibility informs it. I am prepared nevertheless to risk the suggestion that in Heaney one finds intact not merely that long tradition of music as intelligencer of the text, but additionally an imaginative emancipation from music which his poetry enacts. To trace in Heaney a line of descent from the music and verse of Moore through the reanimated lyric conventions of the Celtic revival is to trace in effect the dislocated condition of music in Ireland. In Heaney, language has so completely absorbed music that music itself becomes superfluous.

Any one of the ten Glanmore sonnets from *Field Work* (1979), for example, is so intensely musical in its preoccupation with the sound of language that language itself becomes a substitute for music. In that progression there are implications for the condition of music in Ireland. It is not only that in Heaney (as in Yeats before him) music is Song in the nominative case. It is also that his poetry achieves structures of sound, sense and imagery engineered with a degree of originality which so far eclipses the condition of Irish art music that no useful comparison between the two is tenable. Given this poetry and the brilliant tradition of Irish letters to which it belongs, what need of Irish music? What claim attaches to the prospect of an Irish music in the European tradition?

Heaney intuits the despair of this query in his poem 'In Memoriam Sean O'Riada', also from *Field Work*. The poem tries to reconcile Ó Riada's creativity with the wellsprings of the soil ('He conducted the Ulster Orchestra/like a drover with an ashplant/herding them south').[13] But Heaney for once does not manage to negotiate terms to sustain this arresting image and the poem instead wavers between reminiscence, inventive natural cameos and the essentially uncoordinated enterprise of Ó Riada's art. It is as if the poem duplicates just that aesthetic dilemma which plagued Ó Riada himself. At the conclusion, it retreats into a suspended lyricism at once intense and inconclusive: 'O gannet smacking through scales!/Minnow of light./Wader of assonance.'

Just once the poem addresses itself squarely to Ó Riada's cruel predicament as the most gifted composer by far in Ireland:

> As he stepped and stooped to the keyboard
> he was our jacobite,
> he was our young pretender
> who marched along the deep
>
> plumed in slow airs and grace notes.

Heaney is right: the hopes of an Irish art music lay with Ó Riada, whose characterisation here as the failed redeemer recalls Mangan (specifically, 'My Dark Rosaleen'), the Irish ballad and the doomed promise of political (and hence artistic) emancipation: our Young Pretender, our musician versed in the European aesthetic of high art whose heart and musical mind were set on Ireland. The projection of Ó Riada as the figure who might have emancipated Irish art music from its cultural thralldom represents an acute insight into the condition of music in Irish cultural history. As with the fated Pretender, so too with Ó Riada, caparisoned in high art but unable to achieve the promised deliverance. Heaney's alignment of Irish music and politics is not original except perhaps in its gentle rhetoric of artistic disintegration. The allusion to 'My Dark Rosaleen', given especially Ó Riada's permanent association with the Irish melody of that designation in *Mise Éire*, confirms an association of ideas between political and artistic emancipation as these apply to the state of Irish music.

The function of music in Irish literature as symbol, as political and cultural signifier and perhaps above all as metaphor of the imagination, has been considerable.[14] The paradigmatic force of the lyric (of verse made intelligent by music) in this literature has unquestionably determined the conventional understanding achieved between music and cultural separatism in the Gaelic tradition. In the new Irish literature in English, the idea of music, the 'supreme theme of Art and Song' in Yeats's phrase, proved itself so expressively fertile that the inherent cultivation of an art music was silently neglected. One might suggest that the predicaments of language and history crowded it out. But the relationship between music and Irish cultural history is often at its most intense between that intersection which Irish literature has repeatedly provided. In Irish poetry, drama and fiction, the very trace of music as a dislocated presence in Irish affairs is unmistakable.

# NOTES

## Introduction: Music and the Perception of Music in Ireland

1   Giraldus Cambrensis, *Topographia Hiberniae* (c. 1187), trans. John J. O'Meara and reproduced in Seamus Deane (ed.), *The Field Day Anthology of Irish Writing* (Derry, 1991), Vol. 1, pp. 239–40.

2   F.S.L. Lyons, 'The Burden of Our History' (1978), in Deane (ed.), *The Field Day Anthology of Irish Writing*, Vol. 3, p. 582.

3   Richard Kearney, 'The Transitional Crisis of Modern Irish Culture', in *Irishness in a Changing Society*, ed. Princess Grace Irish Library (Gerrards Cross, 1988), p. 94.

4   It is difficult to find *any* consideration (other than passing mention) of music in Irish cultural criticism: it is ignored, for example, in F.S.L. Lyons's seminal *Culture and Anarchy in Ireland 1890–1939* (Oxford, 1979) and in Richard Kearney (ed.), *The Irish Mind: Exploring Intellectual Traditions* (Dublin, 1985); in Kearney's *Transitions: Narratives in Modern Irish Culture* (Dublin, 1988) the presence of music is confined to a critique of the rock band U2. The same absence is for the most part notable in journals such as *The Crane Bag* (1977–85) and *The Irish Review* (1986–), both of which are widely acknowledged as pre-eminent in the intellectual reanimation identified here. Terence Brown's *Ireland: A Social and Cultural History 1922–79* (London, 1981) contains a number of brief but extremely useful references to music in the development of the state and to the revival of traditional music in the 1970s. The appearance in 1994 of Mary Helen Thuente's excellent study of the United Irishmen and the rise of literary nationalism, *The Harp Re-strung* (Syracuse, 1994), has nevertheless done much to redress the general neglect of music in Irish cultural history noted in this introduction.
    Despite the existence of a long tradition of periodical literature on music in Ireland, this tradition has all but disappeared from the current reassessment of Irish ideas. This dearth is modestly redeemed by the presence of music in *The Field Day Anthology of Irish Writing*, which also includes a rare instance of extended commentary (by Seamus Deane) on Irish music, cited in the epilogue to this book. Brian Kennedy's *Dreams and Responsibilities* (Dublin, n.d.), a formal study of arts policy in Ireland, is itself an indispensable document in the cultural history of music from the founding of the state. Although a comprehensive history of Irish music has not appeared since Grattan Flood's *A History of Irish Music* (Dublin, 1905; repr. Shannon, 1970), the publication of Axel Klein's *Die Musik Irlands im 20. Jahrhundert* (Hildesheim, 1996) and Joseph Ryan's dissertation 'Nationalism and Music in Ireland' (PhD diss, National University of Ireland, 1991) have redeemed the neglect endured by Irish music in the nineteenth and twentieth centuries in particular.

5   John Blacking, 'Some Problems of Theory and Method in the Study of Musical Change', *Yearbook of the International Folk Music Council*, Vol. IX (1977), p. 19. For

a survey of art music in Ireland, see Harry White, 'Ireland: Art Music', in Stanley Sadie (ed.), *The New Grove Dictionary of Music and Musicians,* 7th edn (London, in preparation). Some of the arguments advanced in this introduction were previously rehearsed in Harry White, 'Music and the Perception of Music in Ireland', *Studies,* Vol. 79, No. 313 (1990), pp. 38–44. See also Rionach Uí Ógáin, 'Traditional Music and Irish Cultural History', in Gerard Gillen and Harry White (eds.), *Music and Irish Cultural History* (*Irish Musical Studies* 3) (Dublin, 1995), pp. 77–100, and Harry White, 'The Need for a Sociology of Irish Folk Music', *International Review of the Aesthetics and Sociology of Music,* Vol. 15, No. 1 (June 1984), pp. 3–13.

6   See Breandán Ó Buachalla, 'Poetry and Politics in Early Modern Ireland', *Eighteenth-Century Ireland,* Vol. 7 (1992), p. 152. Ó Buachalla cites two studies which inform the reading of Irish cultural history offered here: N.P. Canny, 'The Formation of the Irish Mind: Religion, Politics and Gaelic Irish Literature 1550–1750', *Past and Present,* Vol. 95 (1982), pp. 91–116, and Tom Dunne, 'The Gaelic Response to the Conquest: The Evidence of the Poetry', *Studia Hibernica,* Vol. 20 (1980), pp. 7–30. See especially Dunne, p. 30: 'Gaelic poetry as a whole, from the mid-sixteenth to the early eighteenth centuries, offers evidence less of a response to colonialism than of an inability to respond – as if the shock had been too traumatic, the change too radical and final for the learned classes, as it had been, for example, for the Northern Earls after Kinsale.'

7   See Roy Foster, *Modern Ireland 1600–1972* (Harmondsworth, 1988), especially chapters 8 and 9, 'The Ascendancy Mind' and 'Economy, Society and the "Hidden" Irelands', pp. 167–225. Notwithstanding my debt to Foster's clarification of two cultures in Ireland, it is Seamus Deane's reading of this question which has influenced my own interpretation of the role of music therein.

8   See Roy Foster, 'We Are All Revisionists Now', published in *The Irish Review* (1986) and reproduced in *The Field Day Anthology of Irish Writing,* Vol. 3, pp. 583–6. Foster concludes that 'to say "revisionist" should just be another way of saying "historian"' (p. 586) but his own reading of Irish historiography strongly diverges from some of his contemporaries, notably Seamus Deane and Desmond Fennell. See Ciaran Brady (ed.), *Interpreting Irish History: The Debate on Historical Revisionism 1938–1994* (Dublin, 1994) for a conspectus of views on revisionism which indicate widely divergent approaches (notably represented by Deane, Fennell, Brian Murphy, Oliver Mac Donagh, Steven Ellis and Foster). Ellis's essay, 'Writing Irish History: Revisionism, Colonialism, and the British Isles', *The Irish Review,* No. 19 (1995), pp. 1–21, argues for a more inclusive and comparative understanding of colonialism in Ireland which yet does not appear to me cognisant of the biculturalism which plainly informs much periodical literature in Ireland throughout the period 1770–1970.

9   For an illuminating conspectus of readings which are characterised by mutual disagreement as to the significance of political culture in the development of Irish literature, see the essays and excerpts by Conor Cruise O'Brien, Seamus Deane, Terence Brown, Richard Kearney, Declan Kiberd, Denis Donoghue and Edna Longley edited by Luke Gibbons in *The Field Day Anthology of Irish Writing,* Vol. 3, pp. 561–653. One conviction which abides throughout these readings is that political, religious and ideological spheres of engagement have constantly intersected in the development of Irish culture. Professor Seán Connolly has suggested to me that cultural revival in Ireland can also be regarded as a conservative political

strategy insofar as 'Irishness' might be separated from Catholicism. He points out that cultural leadership amongst the Ascendancy might be regarded as one means of reconstituting a vanished political and social authority. See David Cairns and Shaun Richards, *Writing Ireland: Colonialism, Nationalism and Culture* (Manchester, 1988), pp. 1–41.

10    Seamus Deane, 'Arnold, Burke and the Celts', in *Celtic Revivals* (London, 1985), p. 21. This insight enjoys axiomatic status in the contemporary cultural debate.

11    An insistence on cultural polarisation as between ethnic and colonial interests in Ireland seems to entail the neglect of other cultural paradigms which might clarify, for example, the function of Unionism within the gamut of Irish culture.

12    This is obviously the case, for example, with reference to religion: Tone, Davis and Parnell were all Protestants whose contribution to revolution and constitutional reform in Ireland undermines the alignment between politics, religion and culture indicated here. Nevertheless, the 'either/or' condition of Irish culture persists (as in Davis's cultural nationalism) in spite of such modifications. It is a singular fact of modern Irish cultural history that so many of its extreme ideologues emerged from the Protestant tradition.

13    Deane, 'Pearse: Writing and Chivalry', in *Celtic Revivals*, p. 66.

14    Deane, 'The Literary Myths of the Revival', in *Celtic Revivals*, pp. 28–37.

15    For an exposition of Irish cultural history to which this summary is wholly indebted, see Brown, *Ireland: A Social and Cultural History*, chapters 1–5.

16    Kearney, 'The Transitional Crisis of Modern Irish Culture', p. 82.

17    Joyce's modernism is distinguished by its reliance on that tradition of Irish history and myth which he repudiated and then reintegrated into fiction. His later works define the European avant-garde even as they are ineluctably Irish.

18    Kearney, 'The Transitional Crisis of Modern Irish Culture', pp. 83–4.

19    Richard Kearney, introduction to *Transitions: Narratives in Modern Irish Culture*, republished in *The Field Day Anthology of Irish Writing*, Vol. 3, p. 633.

20    Kearney, 'The Transitional Crisis of Modern Irish Culture', p. 79. Kearney is here writing of Irish literature of the 1970s and 1980s.

21    See especially chapters 3 and 5. I have preferred the terms 'ethnic repertory' and 'ethnic tradition' to 'folk music' in the course of this study, because the last of these designations is so value-laden.

22    This phrase is borrowed from Seamus Deane's Field Day pamphlet of the same name: *Civilians and Barbarians*, Field Day Pamphlet No. 3 (Derry, 1983).

23    Carl Dahlhaus, *Nineteenth-Century Music*, trans. by J.B. Robinson (Berkeley, 1989), p. 38.

24    For a survey of musicology in Ireland to 1988, see the present author's report in *Acta Musicologica*, Vol. 60 (1988), Fasc. III, pp. 290–305.

25    See 'Musicology, Positivism and the Case for an Encyclopedia of Music in Ireland', in Gerard Gillen and Harry White (eds.), *Musicology in Ireland* (*Irish Musical Studies* 1) (Dublin, 1990), pp. 295–300.

## Carolan, Handel and the Dislocation of Music in Eighteenth-Century Ireland

1    Joseph Cooper Walker, *Historical Memoirs of the Irish Bards* (Dublin, 1786; facsimile reprint, New York, 1971), p. 161. (Hereafter, *Irish Bards*.)

2    This distinction has been maintained, for example, in Roy Foster's reading of
     cultural history in the eighteenth century. See his *Modern Ireland 1600–1972*
     (London, 1988), 'The Ascendancy Mind' and 'Economy, Society and the "Hid-
     den" Irelands', pp. 167–225. Foster's use of both terms follows Daniel Corkery's
     *The Hidden Ireland* (London, 1924) which sternly insists on the recovery of a
     tradition of Gaelic culture repressed by the colonisation of Ireland. Foster
     dwells on the extraordinary architectural achievement of Ascendancy Dublin
     but characterises this as part of a 'culture of exaggeration': 'The Ascendancy
     built in order to convince themselves not only that they had arrived, but that
     they would remain. Insecurity and the England-complex would remain with
     them to the end' (*Modern Ireland*, p. 194). Although Foster acknowledges that
     the 'Hidden Ireland' concept of cultural history is currently under duress, he
     allows that 'Gaelic literature provides a perception of Ireland at this time [i.e.
     the eighteenth century] that cannot be derived from the observations of English
     travellers and Ascendancy memoirs, and often conflicts with them' (*Modern Ire-
     land*, p. 196).
          The term 'Protestant Ascendancy' itself has also been queried by W.J.
     McCormack in *Ascendancy and Tradition in Anglo-Irish Literary History from 1789
     to 1939* (Oxford, 1985), insofar as this term has conventionally been used to
     characterise the ruling class in Ireland from the Battle of the Boyne until the Act
     of Union. McCormack shows that the term only enjoyed general usage from the
     1790s onward, and he prefers the description 'Protestant Interest' as a more
     accurate designation of the sense of identity (political and otherwise) which the
     Anglican polity in Ireland undoubtedly maintained. This issue is further
     debated by McCormack in 'Vision and Revision in the Study of Eighteenth-Cen-
     tury Irish Parliamentary Rhetoric', *Eighteenth-Century Ireland*, Vol. 2 (1987), pp.
     7–36 and in Gerard O'Brien, 'Illusion and Reality in Late Eighteenth-Century
     Politics', *Eighteenth-Century Ireland*, Vol. 3 (1988), pp. 149–56. Finally, see
     James Kelly's attempt to rationalise the somewhat polarised arguments of
     McCormack and O'Brien in 'Eighteenth-Century Ascendancy: A Commentary',
     *Eighteenth-Century Ireland*, Vol. 5 (1990), pp. 173–88.
          Notwithstanding these arguments for and against the term, I have retained
     it here, although I have also had recourse to 'Protestant Interest' as a more gen-
     eral designation on occasion. The phrase 'Ascendancy mind' seems to me the
     most useful of such terms for the purposes of cultural history, and I have used
     it accordingly.
3    For a reading of cultural history firmly committed to the idea of two traditions
     of triumphant Ascendancy and dispossessed Gaelic civilisation, see Seamus
     Deane, 'Arnold, Burke and the Celts', in *Celtic Revivals* (London, 1985), pp.
     17–27. Deane's understanding of Edmund Burke as the greatest of Irish political
     thinkers is consonant with the liberal humanism implicit in some aspects of
     Ascendancy musical thought, although as with Burke's writings, the impact of
     this thought was to be dissipated in the enduring polemics of the two cultures
     throughout the late eighteenth and early nineteenth centuries. See also Deane's
     essay, 'Swift and the Anglo-Irish Intellect', *Eighteenth-Century Ireland*, *Vol.* 1
     (1986), pp. 9–22. The idea of a sharp division between Ascendancy and dispos-
     sessed Catholic is strongly reformulated (against the grain of revisionist readings)
     by Kevin Whelan in the opening chapter of his *The Tree of Liberty* (Cork, 1996).

4    A distinction is required here between the revision of accepted myths and the origins of such myths in eighteenth-century Ireland. To contrast, for example, Louis Cullen's penetrating argument that an Irish Catholic Interest not only existed but flourished during the period of the Penal Laws (c. 1700–60) with the cultural perception of native barbarism or vanished civilisation advanced by writers such as Thomas Campbell and Joseph Walker (see below) illustrates the difference between cultural and political history. Cullen's advocation of an exaggerated culture of Catholic survival is substantiated by his evidence of ownership, political activity and professional advancement among certain Catholic families in the south of Ireland. This evidence, however, does not gainsay the documented belief in cultural oppression which found expression in the same period. See Louis Cullen, 'Catholics under the Penal Laws', *Eighteenth-Century Ireland*, Vol. 1 (1986), pp. 23–36.

5    For a detailed survey of music in Dublin during this period, see Brian Boydell, 'Music, 1700–1850', in T.W. Moody and W.E. Vaughan (eds.), *A New History of Ireland, IV: Eighteenth-Century Ireland 1691–1800* (Oxford, 1986), pp. 568–629. Cf. Boydell, 'The Dublin Musical Scene 1749–50 and its Background', *Proceedings of the Royal Musical Association*, Vol. 105 (1979), pp. 77–89 and T.J. Walsh, *Opera in Dublin, 1705–1797* (Dublin, 1973), Appendix C, 'A list of the more important operas, masques and stage oratorios produced in Dublin between 1705 and 1797', pp. 325–31. Brian Boydell's *A Dublin Musical Calendar* (Dublin, 1988) supersedes and corrects some of the information found in these sources.

6    Although I attempt to explain this failure in terms of cultural dislocation, it is useful to acknowledge Brian Boydell's more pragmatic explanation in his introduction to *A Dublin Musical Calendar*:

> In the face of the distinguished contribution made to literature by Irish writers, whose number and quality is out of all proportion to the population of the country, the historian of Irish music is apt to be apologetic about the absence of a comparable contribution in the field of musical composition . . . the chief reasons for the very limited extent of Irish musical composition in the Georgian period are to be found in the small size and isolation of the musical public . . . the highly technical training of the composer depends to a great extent on experiencing the performance of a wide variety of music, which in turn depends upon the size and cosmopolitan nature of the community in which he lives. . .
>
> The only composer of Irish birth who was active during the first sixty years of the eighteenth century, and who attained any notable recognition abroad, was Thomas Roseingrave, and he worked mainly in London [pp. 22–3].

Given that Boydell is at pains to emphasise the rank and stature of Dublin by comparison with London (to which it was second in size of population) and given also the extraordinary range of musical events which the city enjoyed, this explanation requires further elaboration. I would argue that any satisfactory account of such widespread creative impoverishment must countenance the seminal difficulties of cultural, and thereby musical antagonism addressed in this present discussion. This is not to question the vital importance of Boydell's research, without which such an argument would be meaningless.

7    For an authoritative discussion on the proper form of Carolan's name see Donal O'Sullivan, *Carolan: The Life, Times and Music of an Irish Harper* (London, 1958),

Vol. 1, p. 37. O'Sullivan shows that the correct rendition of the composer's name is Carolan (and not O'Carolan). When Carolan brought his own name into his poems he used the form *Cearbhallán* (and not *Ó Cearbhallán*)

8      For information on Pilkington, a clergyman born in Dublin *c.* 1700 and husband of Laetitia, whose memoirs were published in 1748, see Walsh, *Opera in Dublin*, p. 18. Pilkington's son John was active as a singer in the Dublin theatre in the 1740s. Laurence Whyte published a collection of *Poems on Various Subjects, Serious and Diverting* (Dublin, 1740), in which the *Dissertation* appears. He also published a poem in praise of *Messiah* in Faulkner's *Dublin Journal* on 20 April 1742, one week after the first performance of the oratorio. (See O.E. Deutsch, *Handel: A Documentary Biography* [London, 1955], pp. 546–7.) The texts of these poems by Pilkington and Whyte are edited and annotated by Bryan Coleborne in Seamus Deane (ed.), *The Field Day Anthology of Irish Writing* (Derry, 1991), Vol. 1, pp. 409–14.

9      The full title reads: *A Philosophical Survey of the South of Ireland, in a series of letters to John Watkinson, MD.* Thomas Campbell (1733–95) was a native of Tyrone and chancellor of St Macartin's, Clogher.

10     Gráinne Yeats, 'Carolan, Turlough', in Stanley Sadie (ed.), *The New Grove Dictionary of Music and Musicians* (London, 1980), Vol. 3, p. 813.

11     For biographical information on Carolan's predecessors and contemporaries in this respect see O'Sullivan, *Carolan*, Vol. 1, pp. 17–19. Much of O'Sullivan's material is drawn from the collections of Edward Bunting and the information which the latter gathered at the Belfast Harp Festival in 1792. O'Sullivan's edited version of the memoirs of Arthur O'Neill (1734–1818), which were dictated to Bunting and are preserved in his manuscripts, is also a valuable source of information on the relationship between Catholic patronage and the music of the harpers. O'Neill, himself a peripatetic harper of renown, was elected as resident master of the short-lived Belfast Harp Society in 1808.

12     For a discussion of these influences see 'Carolan and the Italian Masters', in O'Sullivan, *Carolan*, Vol. 1, pp. 144–8. O'Sullivan here relies upon the correspondence of Charles O'Conor, son of Carolan's chief patron, and on the various 'anonymous correspondents' cited in Walker's *Irish Bards* to substantiate Carolan's preference for Italian music. O'Sullivan also examines a variety of sources beginning with Goldsmith's essay (published in *The British Magazine*, July 1760), in order to trace the composer's reputed meeting with Geminiani and his supposed trial of musical skill in which he gave evidence of an astonishing ability to replicate Italian music at one hearing.

       Whatever the accuracy of such reportage, the printed versions of Carolan's music published in the eighteenth century do suggest evidence of Italianate influence. The best known example of Carolan's music in the Italian style is the tune entitled 'Mrs Power or Carolan's Concerto' which appears as No. 154 in O'Sullivan, *Carolan*, Vol. 1, p. 245. O'Sullivan's notes to this air (Vol. 2, p. 97) show that it was first printed in John Lee, *A Favourite Collection of the so much admired old Irish Tunes, the original and genuine compositions of Carolan, the celebrated Irish Bard* ... (Dublin, 1780). In the preface to *A General Collection of the Ancient Irish Music* (London, 1796), Bunting remarks that the concerto manifests 'evident imitations of Corelli, in which the exuberant fancy of that admired composer is happily copied'.

In an important essay on 'Patronage, Style and Structure in the Music Attributed to Turlough Carolan', *Early Music*, Vol. 15 (1987), pp. 164–74, Joan Rimmer has discerned a variety of stylistic influences from French and Netherlandish sources, in addition to Italianate forms, which may to an extent be aligned with the various families whose patronage the composer enjoyed. Rimmer remarks that 'the most consistently assured pieces from his whole working life are, however, those with Irish roots: the Irish jigs, some of the instrumental elegies and the lyric songs' (p. 172).

13   See O'Sullivan, *Carolan*, Vol. 1, p. 84: '. . . there is a direct connection established between Swift and Carolan by what we know of the circumstances of the composition of "Pleáraca na Ruarcach". As mentioned in the notes to that air, the words were written by the poet Hugh McGauran, the tune was composed by Carolan, and the English verse translation was made by Swift.'

14   O'Sullivan, *Carolan*, Vol. 1, pp. 125ff, gives details of these publications, the earliest of which to survive wholly intact is John and William Neal, *A Collection of the Most Celebrated Irish Tunes* (1724) which has been reissued in a facsimile edition by the Folk Music Society of Ireland (1986). This edition contains a useful introduction by Nicholas Carolan. The collection includes a set of variations on 'Pleáraca na Ruarcach' by Lorenzo Bocchi, then resident intermittently in Edinburgh and perhaps also in Dublin (1724–9). He is given prominent mention in Pilkington's *The Progress of Music in Ireland* (see below). He is known to have set some of Pilkington's verse.

15   *The Progress of Music*, lines 63–6.

16   *The Progress of Music*, lines 13–16.

17   *The Progress of Music*, lines 101–4.

18   Although Bryan Coleborne and T.J. Walsh (as note 8 above) are in agreement that this 'Vagrant Bard' is indeed Carolan, one ought to register the possibility that Pilkington merely intends the figure in the poem to symbolise the natural potency of Irish music rather than to designate Carolan himself. The former interpretation does not interfere with the essential contrast Pilkington draws between the effects of bardic music and those of the newly imported European idiom.

19   *The Progress of Music*, lines 201–4; 213–14.

20   *The Progress of Music*, lines 215–20.

21   *A Dissertation*, lines 137–42. 'Pheraca' is a corruption of the Irish word 'Pleáraca', meaning 'Feast'. For a gloss on these lines, see Nicholas Carolan's introduction to *A Collection of the Most Celebrated Irish Tunes* (as note 14) and O'Sullivan, *Carolan*, Vol. 2, pp. 119–22.

22   *A Dissertation*, lines 153–7.

23   Reproduced in *The Field Day Anthology of Irish Writing*, Vol. 1, pp. 667–8.

24   See *The Field Day Anthology of Irish Writing*, Vol. 1, p. 667.

25   Roy Foster observes that Goldsmith 'left no proof that he had any conception' of an Irish nation (*Modern Ireland*, p. 180), but we might refine this observation by suggesting that 'Carolan: The Last Irish Bard' clearly admits of the conception of an Irish 'race' as a distinctive entity within the two kingdoms; moreover the phrase 'being in some measure retired from intercourse with other nations' reinforces this distinctiveness. In language which is politically oblique, Goldsmith projects Carolan's music as an emblem of this race. The point for Goldsmith (in

this essay) is that this race belongs to the past: it has no real bearing on the political reality of the present. I would argue that Goldsmith must have perceived how untenable this projection was in actuality.

26  See the Advertisement to the book: 'But the time seems to be approaching, when the value of Ireland will be better understood, and when the maxims on which it is now governed, will be found too narrow, if not illiberal. To hasten that period is the design of the following letters and the favourite political wish of the writer.'

27  *A Philosophical Survey*, Letter 44, p. 448.

28  *A Philosophical Survey*, Letter 44, pp. 449–50. The italicised terms in this extract are phonetic approximations (or corruptions) of Irish words and phrases. Thus *Kin-du-Deelas* is *Ceann dubh dílis* ('dear dark-headed one'). For similar approximations and their Irish originals, see Frank Llewelyn Harrison, 'Music, Poetry and Polity in the Age of Swift', *Eighteenth-Century Ireland*, Vol. 1, (1986), pp. 37–64, Appendix, p. 63.

29  See note 12 above. O'Sullivan, *Carolan*, Vol. 1, p. 146, quotes from Goldsmith's account which specifies 'the fifth concerto of Vivaldi' as the piece played by Geminiani and thereafter repeated flawlessly by Carolan.

30  *A Philosophical Survey*, Letter 44, pp. 450, 452.

31  Joseph Cooper Walker (1761–1810) was born in Dublin. He was a founding member of the Royal Irish Academy and an antiquarian whose range of interests included Irish and European music, theatre and military history. His work exemplifies the early Romantic tendency to prefer natural over 'artificial' manifestations in literature and music (and painting). In his *Historical Memoir on Italian Tragedy* (London, 1799), he is described on the title page as a member of the Arcadian Academy in Rome.

32  *Irish Bards*, pp. 65–6.

33  *Irish Bards*, p. 66.

34  *Irish Bards*, p. 134.

35  *Irish Bards*, p. 157–8.

36  *Irish Bards*, p. 156.

37  *Irish Bards*, Appendix VI, facing p. 67.

38  See Edmund Burke, *A Philosophical Inquiry into the Origin of our Ideas of the Sublime and the Beautiful* (London, 1757), ed. J.T. Boulton (London, 1958), p. 38: 'The passions which concern self preservation, turn mostly on pain and danger . . . and they are the most powerful of all the passions'. Although David Berman has argued that 'much of Irish philosophy was an indirect expression and justification of the Irish Anglican Ascendancy' (in 'The Culmination and Causation of Irish Philosophy', *Archiv für Geschichte der Philosophie* [1982], p. 267), Burke's subsequent rejection of the Ascendancy ideal allows us to reconsider his aesthetics at least in terms of music and society. If, as Seamus Deane has argued, 'Burke asserted that the Catholics of Ireland must be fully admitted to political and civic life if the country was ever to be stable and prosperous' (see 'Arnold, Burke and the Celts', p. 23), it is not unreasonable to equate Burke's advance of a radically reformed and integrated polity with Walker's similarly insistent formulation of Irish music as 'the voice of nature'. Walker deplores the rejection of Irish music (a natural outgrowth) by the Protestant Interest in terms which echo Burke's identification of a 'hidden' Ireland: 'there is an interior history of Ireland

*– the genuine voice of its records and monuments –* which speaks a very different
language from those histories from Temple and Clarendon'. See *The Works of the
Right Honourable Edmund Burke* (London, 1877), Vol. 6, p. 65, quoted in Deane,
'Arnold, Burke and the Celts', p. 25. [my italics]

39   For an assessment of these letters and their importance as a source of Carolan's
biography, see O'Sullivan, *Carolan*, Vol. 1, pp. 21–3. O'Sullivan also cites the
letters of O'Conor, some of which directly concern the publication of the *Irish
Bards* as a source of information independent of the correspondence actually
quoted by Walker in the book itself. For these letters see Catherine Coogan
Ward, Robert E. Ward and John F. Wrynn, SJ (eds.), *Letters of Charles O'Conor
of Belnagare* [sic]: *A Catholic Voice in Eighteenth-Century Ireland* (Washington,
D.C., 1988). This follows an earlier edition of the letters by Robert and Catherine Ward (1980) which is in fact more complete.

40   *Irish Bards*, Appendix VI, p. 95.

41   *Irish Bards*, Appendix VI, p. 95.

42   Walker notes that Carolan was 'never either affluent or indigent' (*Irish Bards*,
Appendix VI, p. 99).

43   *Irish Bards*, Appendix VI, pp. 98–100.

44   See *The Monthly Review*, Vol. 57 (December 1787), pp. 425–39. (Hereafter, 'Burney'.) Burney reviewed and contributed to this periodical from 1785 until
1802. See B.C. Nangle, *The Monthly Review, First Series, 1749–1789, Indexes of
Contributors and Articles* (Oxford, 1934), also Kerry S. Grant, *Dr Burney as Critic
and Historian of Music* (Ann Arbor, 1983), p. 363. It is interesting to note that,
according to Grant (p. 14), Burney complained to Edmond Malone that Walker
had been the bane of his existence for almost twenty years; and that Burney and
Walker had frequently corresponded on musical matters. These 'letters of infi-
nite politeness full of information about music' would appear to contrast
strongly with Burney's public regard for Walker's *Irish Bards*.

45   Burney, p. 425.

46   Burney, p. 427.

47   Burney, p. 428.

48   Burney, p. 433.

49   Burney, p. 433.

50   See Seamus Deane, *Civilians and Barbarians*, Field Day Pamphlet No. 3 (Derry,
1983), *passim*. It is useful to note that Deane's reading of Irish cultural history
as (in part) a ruinous distinction between civilised and criminal norms of
expression in the minds of English commentators advances Spenser's *View of the
Present State of Ireland* as a primary source of this distinction. Burney's reliance
on Spenser's condemnation of the Irish bard clearly perpetuates this distinction
specifically with regard to music.

51   Burney, p. 439.

52   Burney's commentary identifies two traditions, one dead, the other alive. His
attitude towards Carolan, however, does deserve to be distinguished from his
general rejection of music in Ireland (insofar as Walker describes it). As relics
of a past culture, the melodies of Carolan are of antiquarian and indeed aesthetic interest to Burney, although there is of course no suggestion that these
might be used to reanimate an indigenous mode of composition:

> The tunes of Carolan are regarded as genuine reliques of the national melody of Ireland, uncorrupted by Italian refinements, or the mongrel taste of England. The plaintive tunes of Ireland have so strong a resemblance to those of Scotland, that it would be extremely difficult for a stranger to distinguish one from the other. The lively tunes of Ireland seem, however, superior to those of their Caledonian neighbours; they excite a pleasanter and less obstreperous kind of mirth. [Burney, pp. 437–8]

53   Kevin Barry, 'James Usher (1720–72) and the Irish Enlightenment', *Eighteenth-Century Ireland*, Vol. 3 (1988), p. 121.

54   For an elucidation of Usher's musical aesthetics, see Kevin Barry's *Language, Music and the Sign* (Cambridge, 1987), pp. 55–67. There is to my knowledge no evidence of Usher having consciously aligned his 'philosophy of loss' with his defence of the Catholic position. We should be clear, however, that for Usher, 'Music then is a language directed to the passions, . . . let me add, also, that it awakens some passions that we perceive not, in ordinary life'. See the second edition of Usher's *Clio: or, a Discourse on Taste* (London, 1769; facsimile reprint, New York, 1970), pp. 150–1. The section on music is on pp. 149–55. Usher attacks the 'fantastic' dimensions of contemporary Italian music and insists upon the preservation of 'original, natural taste', in language which is notably consonant with Joseph Walker's reading of the 'voice of nature' versus Italian music, discussed here above.

55   See Boydell, *A Dublin Musical Calendar, passim.*

56   For example Roy Foster's remark in *Modern Ireland* that 'Ascendancy life in Dublin was not notably "cultured"; it was, for instance, largely undistinguished by musical achievements or serious patronage. Handel's celebrated première of Messiah on 13 April 1742 is, in fact, an outstanding exception to the general rule' (p. 185).

In general, music as a force in Irish cultural history has been more frequently ignored than commented upon. This situation has undoubtedly been aggravated by the apparent loss of much music which might otherwise have forced some assessment of Ascendancy patronage. With the paramount exception of Handel sources, plentifully extant elsewhere than in Dublin, works associated with the State Music in Ireland do not appear to have survived. Thus an apparently unavoidable lacuna in Brian Boydell's otherwise comprehensive research has been created by the absence of sources for seminal Dublin performances such as the birthday odes written by William Viner, J.S. Cousser and Matthew Dubourg over a period of some forty years (from 1707 onwards), oratorios such as *The Death of Abel* by Thomas Arne (a Metastasio setting premièred in Dublin in 1744) and major portions of the repertory of sacred music performed in St Patrick's Cathedral and Christ Church Cathedral. Whether or not this neglect of sources reflects a pervasive indifference to the preservation of music in official (often court) copies (the normal means of preserving occasional music in the early eighteenth century) must remain open to debate until this matter has been clarified by further research.

57   See note 28 above.

58   See Swift's poem 'The Dean to himself on St Cecilia's Day', quoted and discussed in Harrison, 'Music, Poetry and Polity', pp. 45–6. Although Harrison states that the poem does not show distaste for music, its clear alignment of 'players and

scrapers' with the dangers of popery argues against this mitigation. For further comment on Swift and music see below and also W.H. Eddy (ed.), *Satires and Personal Writings by Jonathan Swift* (London, 1967), pp. 264–7.

59    Harrison, 'Music, Poetry and Polity', p. 46.

60    See Harold Williams (ed.), *The Poems of Jonathan Swift* (Oxford, 1937), Vol. 3, pp. 956–61, in which the text of the *Cantata* is published. The musical setting by John Echlin (*d.* 1763) is partly reproduced in Harrison, 'Music, Poetry and Polity', p. 44.

61    Swift's objections are published in F.E. Ball (ed.), *The Correspondence of Jonathan Swift, DD* (London, 1910–14), Vol. 6, pp. 220ff. His communications to the sub-dean and chapter of St Patrick's Cathedral on this matter are reproduced in Deutsch, *Handel*, pp. 536–7, which also contains the conflicting minutes of Mercer's Hospital for 23 January 1742, recording Swift's original consent. The exact terms of Swift's withdrawal of permission leave no doubt as to his complete opposition to *Messiah* in particular and his contempt for concerted music in general.

62    See 'A Vindication of Mr Gay and the *Beggar's Opera*', published in the *Irish Intelligencer* in March 1728 and reproduced in Eddy (ed.), *Satires and Personal Writings*, pp. 264–7. Harrison in 'Music, Poetry and Polity' notes that '[Swift's] third and less creditable concern was his feeling that Gay's opera had exposed as "unnatural" the current taste for Italian music . . . He even went as far as to cite another's opinion that "the Practice of an unnatural Vice", for which many in London had been prosecuted some years before, had been "the Forerunner of Italian Operas and Singers".'

63    See W.H. Grindle, *Irish Cathedral Music* (Belfast, 1989), pp. 37–41, for an account of St Patrick's Cathedral Choir under Swift. Grindle quotes Swift in a letter to Alexander Pope in 1715: 'My amusements are defending my small dominions against the archbishop and endeavouring to reduce my rebellious choir' (p. 39).

64    See Boydell, *A Dublin Musical Calendar*, passim, for information on these composers and the performance of their music in Ireland. See also Harold Samuel, 'John Sigismund Cousser in London and Dublin', *Music and Letters*, Vol. 61 (1980), pp. 158–71 for useful information on the position of the visiting musician in Ascendancy Dublin.

65    See Boydell, *A Dublin Musical Calendar*, Appendix V (Index of Music Performed or Published in Dublin 1700–1760), pp. 295–307 and Appendix VI (Summary of Periods or Seasons), pp. 308–18. The latter appendix distinguishes between works given their first Irish performance and works actually premièred in Ireland.

66    Boydell, *A Dublin Musical Calendar*, p. 15. Boydell also remarks on the apparent omission of Cousser's instrumental music from Dublin concert programmes during his residence in the city. The information which follows here as to comparative frequency of performance (in respect of works by visiting musicians in Dublin) is wholly indebted to Boydell's research.

67    See note 62 above. For a discussion of ballad opera in Dublin, see Walsh, *Opera in Dublin*, pp. 33–91. For an elucidation of the ambiguous terminology of the genre and a discussion which places the performance of operatic works in the context of a largely spoken repertory, see John Greene, 'The Repertory of Dublin Theatres, 1720–45', *Eighteenth-Century Ireland*, Vol. 2 (1987), pp. 133–48.

68    In this connection it is interesting to note Frank Harrison's discussion of the
      version of *Plearáca na Ruarcach* which Charles Coffey used in *The Beggar's Wed-
      ding*. In this instance, Carolan's melody finds its way into a ballad opera, with a
      new version of Swift's translation made by Coffey. As *Plarakanororka, Plearáca
      na Ruarcach* occurs in a drinking scene in the opera and is performed by a char-
      acter who is pretending to be Irish. That a stage Irishman should sing one of
      Carolan's melodies is a fair indication of the cultural status of the ethnic reper-
      tory from within the Dublin theatre of the day. See Harrison, 'Music, Poetry and
      Polity', pp. 51–5.

69    According to Greene, 'The Repertory of Dublin Theatres', p. 139, *The Mock Doc-
      tor* was given as an afterpiece to various plays on twenty-four occasions between
      1720 and 1745.

70    See Boydell, *A Dublin Musical Calendar*, Appendix III (Societies and Charitable
      Bodies Connected with Music in Dublin), pp. 267–9. See the same author's
      *Rotunda Music in Eighteenth-Century Dublin* (Dublin, 1992) for a study of the
      concert seasons held there from 1749 until 1791.

71    See Winton Dean (with Anthony Hicks), *The New Grove Handel* (London,
      1982), pp. 113–14. Handel's theatrical genius, for example, remains almost
      wholly remote to those who advance *Messiah* as the true source of the com-
      poser's greatness. But one must distinguish between this exaggerated and blink-
      ered apotheosis of Handel as 'architect of the sublime' and the facts of the case
      as they presented themselves to a Dublin audience in the early 1740s. However
      limited the conception of Handel's achievement in Dublin (given the range of
      his musical imagination), his acclaim in Ireland as an architect of the sublime
      ought to be acknowledged as a fact of eighteenth-century cultural history and
      not condemned as a Victorian afterthought.

72    See, for instance, Deutsch, *Handel*, pp. 524–55, and Horatio Townsend, *An
      Account of the Visit of Handel to Dublin* (Dublin, 1852). For more recent research
      on the Dublin visit, see Donald Burrows, 'Handel's Dublin Performances', in
      Patrick F. Devine and Harry White (eds.), *The Maynooth International Musicolog-
      ical Conference 1995: Selected Proceedings, Part One* (Irish Musical Studies 4)
      (Dublin, 1996), pp. 46–70.

73    Deutsch, *Handel*, p. 529.

74    See the composer's letter to Charles Jennens dated 9 September 1742, pub-
      lished in Deutsch, *Handel*, pp. 554–5. It is herein that he refers to Ireland as
      'that polite and generous nation'.

75    Faulkner's *Dublin Journal,* 17 April 1742; in Deutsch, *Handel*, p. 546.

76    For details of the English reaction to *Messiah*, see Deutsch, *Handel*, pp. 563ff.
      and R.M. Myers, *Handel's Messiah: A Touchstone of Taste* (New York, 1948), pp.
      38ff.

77    *Irish Bards*, p. 159.

78    Goldsmith's essay was published in *The British Magazine* for February 1760. See
      also Charles Burney, *A General History of Music* (London, 1789; modern edition,
      1957), pp. 1005–6 and Burney, *An Account of the Musical Performances . . . in
      Commemoration of Handel* (London, 1785; reprinted, 1979).

79    See Dean, *The New Grove Handel*, p. 56: 'When, on 23 March [1743], Handel
      gave the first London performance of *Messiah*, he advertised it without title as
      "A New Sacred Oratorio", to avoid giving offence. The expedient failed . . . The

work fell flat, and never took with London audiences until Handel began to perform it for charity in the Foundling Hospital Chapel in 1750.'

80    These performance details are from Boydell, *A Dublin Musical Calendar*. The fact of this association is of singular interest not only for our understanding of the performance context in Dublin, but also with regard to the elevation of Handel as national figure and moral paragon immediately after his death. On this question see also Harry White, 'Handel in Dublin: A Note', *Eighteenth-Century Ireland*, Vol. 2 (1987), pp. 182–6.

81    A typical instance of private support is the performance of *Acis* on 7 February 1749, in Fishamble Street, which was advertised as a benefit for Mrs Arne (wife of the composer). The clearest indication of Handel's predominance in the repertory of Dublin societies and charities is to be found in Boydell, *A Dublin Musical Calendar*, pp. 309–18, where the continuous performance of his music is in marked contrast to the sporadic revival of works by Purcell and other composers.

82    Dean, *The New Grove Handel*, pp. 110–11.

83    See Deane, 'Swift and the Anglo-Irish Intellect', *passim*. Deane contrasts the benevolent philosophy of Francis Hutcheson with the pragmatic hedonism of Bernard Mandeville and shows that Swift's rejection of both was perpetuated by Burke's attack on the very foundations of Ascendancy thought.

84    It scarcely needs to be stated here that Handel's cultivation of oratorio in London on his return from Dublin was not primarily for the sake of charitable enterprise; on the contrary, his oratorios earned for him large sums of money and he died a wealthy man. See Dean, *The New Grove Handel*, pp. 57–71. In his last oratorio season, for example, he earned £1,952, and he left almost £20,000 in his estate.

85    *Irish Bards*, pp. 158–61.

86    For details of the increasing dependence of Dublin on London repertory, see Walsh, *Opera in Dublin*, pp. 150ff. and the same author's *Opera in Dublin 1790–1820* (Oxford, 1993) and Ita Hogan, *Anglo-Irish Music 1780–1830* (Cork, 1966), pp. 14–50, 123–36.

87    A misrepresentation which is prolonged by the enduring appeal of the oratorios and by comparative neglect of the greater part of the composer's operas, as Winton Dean has argued for over thirty years.

88    See O'Sullivan, *Carolan*, Vol. 1, p. 56. O'Sullivan's reading is in conflict with a perception of Carolan which originated not in the nineteenth century but in the immediate aftermath of his death. This projection of Carolan, however, is itself part of the cultural history of music in eighteenth-century Ireland and it enlightens our understanding of musical reception in Ireland during that period.

## History and Romanticism

1    Thomas Moore in a letter to (Sir) John Stevenson quoted in Hoover H. Jordan, *Bolt Upright: The Life of Thomas Moore* (Salzburg, 1975), Vol. 1, p. 145, from Wilfrid S. Dowden (ed.), *The Letters of Thomas Moore* (Oxford, 1964), Vol. 1, pp. 116–17. After the word 'collected' an asterisk in Dowden refers to the following: 'The author excepts Mr Bunting's valuable collection.'

2   Robert Chambers in *Chambers' Edinburgh Journal* (issue of 19 September 1840), quoted in Charlotte Milligan Fox, *Annals of the Irish Harpers* (London, 1911), p. 79.

3   The process by which the last of these three ideas overtook the other two is considered in chapter 3.

4   Seamus Deane, 'Arnold, Burke and the Celts', in *Celtic Revivals* (London, 1985), p. 21.

5   For a detailed account of the Harp Festival drawn from primary sources including *The Belfast News-Letter* and the publications of Edward Bunting, see Fox, *Annals*, pp. 97ff. More recent surveys include Janet Harbison, 'The Belfast Harper's Meeting, 1792: The Legacy', *Ulster Folklife*, Vol. 35 (1989), pp. 113–28, and Gráinne Yeats, *The Harp of Ireland, the Belfast Harpers' Festival 1792, and the Saving of Ireland's Harp Music by Edward Bunting* (Belfast, 1992).

6   From a circular issued in Belfast in December 1791 and reprinted by Edward Bunting in 1840. See Fox, *Annals*, pp. 97–8.

7   See Deane, 'Arnold Burke and the Celts', p. 24 and Chapter 1 of the present study.

8   From *The Belfast News-Letter* (13 July, 1792), quoted in Fox, *Annals*, p. 103. Although the festival rapidly acquired mythic status in the history of music in Ireland, the wide number of contemporary private and public sources which chronicle the event are agreed in detail as to its purpose, condition and outcome. In the memoirs of the harper Arthur O'Neill (1737–1816) and of Theobald Wolfe Tone, for example, the description of the festival published by Edward Bunting and successive antiquarians is corroborated. (See Fox, *Annals*, p. 103.) The correspondence of James MacDonnell (1762–1845) also bears out the extraordinary significance of the festival. As a member of the festival committee and afterwards of the short-lived Belfast Harp Society (1808–13), MacDonnell may be regarded as one of the prime movers of the revival of ethnic music in Ireland.

9   Edward Bunting, *A General Collection of the Ancient Irish Music . . .* (London, 1797), 'Preface', [p. i.] Bunting's account of the festival is concisely expressive of the motivation which brought it into being. It also is characterised by that blend of 'high antiquity' and pragmatism which was to distinguish so much of Edward Bunting's work for almost half a century afterwards.

10   Quoted in Fox, *Annals*, p. 99.

11   For biographical information on Bunting, see Eileen Dolan, 'The Musical Contributions and Historical Significance of Edward Bunting (1773–1843), A Pioneer in the Preservation of the Heritage of Irish Music' (diss., the Catholic University of America, 1977). It is useful to note here that Bunting was a professional musician and held organistships in Belfast and Dublin through the course of his career. Bunting issued a circular immediately prior to the publication of his 1840 volume which summarises the breadth of his ambitions: 'The hope of being enabled, by reviving the National Music, to place himself in the same rank with those worthy Irishmen whose labours have from time to time sustained the reputation of the country for a native literature, had, the Editor admits, no inconsiderable share in determining him on making the study and preservation of our Irish melodies the main business of his long life.' This avocation was also included by Bunting in the preface to the volume itself. (Quoted in Fox, *Annals*, p. 16.)

12    For a detailed bibliographical exposition of the Bunting collections, together
      with an account of their publication history and contents, see Dolan, 'Bunting',
      pp. 70–175. Ita Hogan, *Anglo-Irish Music 1780–1830* (Cork, 1966), lists some
      twenty publishers who issued collections of Irish airs between 1780 and 1830,
      including John Lee's *A Favourite Collection of the so much admired Irish Tunes, the
      original and genuine compositions of Carolan, the celebrated Irish Bard* (1780).
      What distinguishes Bunting's publications from many of these volumes is the
      more or less transparent condition of Bunting's sources, which range from
      melodies dictated to him at the Belfast festival to airs supplied by other con-
      temporary collectors. See Hogan, *Anglo-Irish Music*, pp. 91–100, and Dolan,
      'Bunting', pp. 70ff.
13    Andrew Carpenter and Seamus Deane, 'The Shifting Perspective (1690–1830)',
      *The Field Day Anthology of Irish Writing*, Vol. 1 (Derry, 1991), p. 962.
14    See *The Dublin Examiner*, August 1816, pp. 241–53. The extract cited here (p.
      251) is from a long review of Moore's *Irish Melodies* (Vols. 1–3), Bunting's first
      volume, Beethoven's arrangements of Irish airs (Edinburgh, n.d.), a volume of
      Irish airs arranged by Smollet Holden (Dublin, n.d.), and a selection of airs by
      Smith (no date or place of publication given). Although the review appeared
      anonymously, Aloys Fleischmann and other scholars are in agreement that its
      author was indisputably the young George Petrie. See Aloys Fleischmann,
      'Aspects of George Petrie. IV. Petrie's Contribution to Irish Music', *Proceedings of
      the Royal Irish Academy*, Vol. 72, Section C, No. 9, p. 198. For a definitive study
      of Beethoven's arrangements of Irish melodies, see Barry Cooper, *Beethoven's
      Folksong Settings: Chronology, Sources, Style* (Oxford, 1994) and the same author's
      'Beethoven's Folksong Settings as Sources of Irish Folk Music', in Patrick F.
      Devine and Harry White (eds.), *The Maynooth International Musicological Con-
      ference 1995: Selected Proceedings, Part Two (Irish Musical Studies, 5)* (Dublin,
      1996), pp. 65–81.
15    *The Dublin Examiner*, August 1816, p. 251. This censure notwithstanding,
      Petrie firmly acknowledged the seminal nature of Bunting's collection: 'Of all
      the persons who have been employed in the collecting or arranging of our
      music, Mr Bunting only was perfectly qualified for the task: he alone, under-
      stood its character or style and felt its peculiarities and beauties'. Petrie's objec-
      tion to Bunting's too-literal adaptation of harp style to the piano is part of the
      long history of dissatisfaction and disagreement which characterise the issue of
      performance practice in the traditional repertory to the present day.
16    Bunting, *A General Collection* (1797), 'Preface', [p. i].
17    Bunting, *A General Collection* (1797), 'Preface', [p. ii].
18    I prefer not to overwork this term: 'translations' is, at the last, a metaphor. But
      Bunting clearly hoped to persuade his readers that the airs naturally accommo-
      dated a tactful degree of harmonisation. In the sense that he wished to make
      them thereby intelligible, Bunting can be said to have translated what he heard
      (the authentic version) into what he wrote (the arranged version). See note 46
      below, where the same metaphor ('translations') is cited of the Moore–Steven-
      son arrangements of Irish airs.
19    A cheap Dublin edition of the collection appeared late in 1797 published by
      Hime. For a discussion of the various editions published during Bunting's life-
      time, see Seamus Ó Casaide, 'Bibliography of Bunting's Printed Collections',

*Journal of the Irish Folk Song Society*, Vol. 5 (orig. Vols. 22–5), 1927 (repr. London, 1967), pp. xxxv–xxxvii.

20   *The Dublin Examiner*, August 1816, p. 242.

21   'P.' [George Petrie], 'Our Portrait Gallery, No. 41. Edward Bunting', *The Dublin University Magazine*, January 1847, p. 69.

22   Fox, *Annals*, p. 23.

23   Petrie, 'Edward Bunting', p. 70.

24   See notes 12 and 19 above. The 'list of [Thomas] Moore's printed sources' cited by Veronica Ní Chinnéide in 'The Sources of Moore's Melodies', *Journal of the Royal Society of Antiquaries in Ireland*, 89, Part 2 (1959), pp. 109–34, includes (p. 117) volumes published by Holden, *Collection of Old-Established Irish Slow and Quick Tunes* (Dublin, 1806) and Sydney Owenson (Lady Morgan), *Twelve Original Hibernian Melodies* (London, 1805).

25   Roy Foster notes that Russell met Robert Emmet in Paris, where he was given the task of raising the rebellion in Ulster (*Modern Ireland* [Harmondsworth, 1988], p. 266). Bunting's aggrieved distress at Russell's betrayal by Lynch may well have called to mind the death in 1798 of his intimate friend Henry Joy McCracken, another United Irishman hanged for high treason. For an account of these events and their impact on Bunting, see Fox, *Annals*, pp. 34ff.

26   See Dolan, 'Bunting', pp. 140ff., for an explication of Bunting's decision to drop the Irish originals from the 1809 volume; also Donal O'Sullivan, 'A Short Account of Bunting as a Collector', *Journal of the Irish Folk Song Society*, Vol. 5 (orig. Vols. 22–5), 1927 (repr. London, 1967), p. xvi. Lynch himself was charged with high treason and released only on condition that he appear for the Crown against Russell.

27   The omission of the Irish originals from Bunting's 1809 collection made the latter appear more than ever an emulation of Moore's *Melodies*, the first volume of which had appeared in 1807. See Fox, *Annals*, pp. 45–7, for details of Bunting's efforts to take advantage of 'popularising the airs by turning them into drawing-room songs'. Bunting never again sought to do this.

28   See O'Sullivan, 'A Short Account of Bunting', p. xvi: 'Lynch had made fair copies, in a beautifully clear script, of most of the songs he had obtained, and these he had translated into English prose. No use, however, was made of the material thus prepared, and the only allusion to Lynch in the Preface is contained in the distant, if not contemptuous phrase, "a person versed in the Irish Language".'

29   Petrie, 'Edward Bunting', p. 70.

30   Petrie's contribution is in effect an exercise in organology and stands as a significant extension of the antiquarian tradition in which he was to succeed Bunting on the latter's death.

31   Quoted in Fox, *Annals*, p. 107. Immediately prior to this quotation, Fox observes: 'The second chapter of the 1840 volume opens with a remonstrance against the generally accepted idea of the characteristics of Irish music. What is there published in a condensed and toned-down form, we find a rough draft of, among the manuscripts. In this Bunting speaks his mind more vehemently than his literary coeditors sanctioned him to do in print. We think it well to reproduce the ragged and unedited phrases of Bunting himself' (p. 106).

32   Fox, *Annals*, p. 107.

33   Seamus Deane, 'Thomas Moore', *The Field Day Anthology of Irish Writing*, Vol. 1, p. 1053. For an assessment of Moore's *Melodies* and satires which is sympathetic to the reading offered here, see Mary Helen Thuente, *The Harp Re-strung: The United Irishmen and the Rise of Literary Nationalism* (Syracuse, 1994), pp. 171–92.

34   See Ní Chinnéide, 'The Sources of Moore's Melodies', pp. 109ff., for a detailed disclosure of Moore's reliance on Bunting and on other collections.

35   See the excerpt from Moore's memoirs cited in Fox, *Annals*, p. 32: 'It was in the year 1797, that, through the medium of Mr Bunting's book, I was first made acquainted with the beauties of our native music.'

36   I take my cue here from Oliver MacDonagh, *Ireland: The Union and its Aftermath* (London, 1977; 2nd impression, 1979), p. 14: 'In the modern sense of the words, nationalism and republicanism in Ireland date from the 1790s. They derived from and were to some extent determined by the French revolutionary experience.' One might want to add that these terms were also intimately related to the growth of romanticism in the same period.

37   A parliamentary bill in 1794 allowed the admission of Roman Catholics to Trinity College, although they were prevented from competing for scholarships, fellowships and other forms of remuneration and support. The consequence of this was that only a very small number of Catholics were admitted as students. For a cogent account of Moore's career in Trinity, including the United Irishmen background, see Jordan, *Bolt Upright*, Vol. 1, pp. 15–34.

38   Moore retained throughout his life a clear impression of the danger and sometimes fatal political awareness in which his college friends were immersed. His reminiscences in *The Life and Death of Lord Edward Fitzgerald* (1831) speak of 'that time of terror and torture'. For an account of the historical background to these episodes in Moore's life, see Foster, *Modern Ireland*, pp. 258–86.

39   A sentence from Moore's memoirs cited in Fox, *Annals*, p. 25.

40   See the editorial introduction to Emmet's 'Speech from the Dock', in *The Field Day Anthology of Irish Writing*, Vol. 1, p. 934.

41   From 'Mr Moore's Suppressed Preface to the IRISH MELODIES', dated 'Dublin, October, 1807' and published in *The Dublin Examiner*, June 1816, pp. 107–9.

42   From *Intolerance, A Satire*, quoted in Jordan, *Bolt Upright*, Vol. 1, p. 167.

43   Quoted in Jordan, *Bolt Upright*, Vol. 1, p. 167.

44   Quoted in Fox, *Annals*, pp. 28–9. Moore is specifically repudiating Bunting's criticism of Sir John Stevenson's arrangements of the melodies which appears on p. 6 of the introduction to the 1840 volume.

45   Moore, 'Letter on Music', quoted in *The Field Day Anthology of Irish Writing*, Vol. 1, p. 1055. Here Moore was anxious to align his romantic understanding of the ethnic repertory with his reading of Irish history. As Deane observes, Moore went to some lengths to explain how Irish music reproduced 'the features of our history and our character'; this was a matter of sincere belief and not of opportunistic apologetics.

46   Sir John Andrew Stevenson (1762–1833). Irish composer; Chorister and Vicar-Choral of Christ Church Cathedral and St Patrick's Cathedral; Honorary Mus. D. (Dublin, 1791); knighted in 1803. He composed music for several theatrical productions in Dublin and innumerable separate songs, duets, glees and catches. Best known for his 'symphonies and accompaniments' to Moore's

*Melodies*. Robert Chambers' reaction to these arrangements is characteristic of the generally poor opinion in which these were held: 'When we hear Sir John Stevenson's Irish Melodies played by a young lady on the pianoforte, or even on the pedal harp, we do not hear the same music which O'Cahan [*sic*] Carolan and Hempson played. It is as much altered as Homer in the translation of Pope.' (Robert Chambers in *Chambers' Edinburgh Journal* [as note 2], quoted in Fox, *Annals*, p. 79.) This contemporary understanding of Stevenson's work as *translation* is of some relevance to the argument advanced in this chapter. Stevenson and Moore were acquainted from 1799 and the former had set a number of Moore's verses, some of which were performed as glees by the Irish Harmonic Society. By 1807, Stevenson and Moore were firm friends. Moore defended Stevenson's 'symphonies' privately and publicly, as in his introduction to the third number of the *Melodies*, published in 1810. See John S. Bumpus, *Sir John Stevenson: A Biographical Sketch* (London, 1893), pp. 22–4.

47   *The Dublin Examiner* (August 1816), p. 250.
48   Sir Jonah Barrington, *Personal Sketches of His Own Time* (London, 1827), p. 166.
49   Cf. Bunting's preface to the third volume (1840), quoted in Dolan, 'Bunting', p. 86: '. . .but the Editor saw with pain, and still deplores the fact, that in these new Irish melodies, the work of the poet was accounted of so paramount an interest, that the proper order of song-writing was in many instances inverted, and instead of the words being adapted to the tune, the tune was too often adapted to the words, a solecism which could never have happened had the reputation of the writer not been so great. . .' It should be noted that Bunting was also prepared to admit that 'The beauty of Mr Moore's words, in a great degree atones for the violence done by the musical arranger to any of the airs which he has adopted.' This observation was made in reference to the second number of the *Melodies*.
50   Thomas Moore, *Irish Melodies [with] Symphonies and Accompaniments by Sir John Stevenson, Mus. Doc., and Sir Henry Bishop* (Dublin, 1879; repr. 1963), p. 62.
51   Moore's *Memoirs of Captain Rock, the Celebrated Irish Chieftain, with some Account of his Ancestors* was published in London in 1824. It is instructive to quote from the 'Suppressed Preface to the IRISH MELODIES' (as note 41 above) on the same sentiment: 'Our history, for many centuries past, is creditable neither to our neighbours nor ourselves . . . In truth, the poet who would embellish his song with allusions to Irish names and events, must be content to seek them in those early periods. And the only traits of heroism which he can venture, at this day, to commemorate, with safety to himself, or perhaps, with honor to the Country, are to be looked for in those times when the native monarchs of Ireland displayed and fostered virtues worthy of a better age' (p. 109). This strategy of allusion was Moore's principal means of admitting political commentary into the texts of his songs, but it is worth suggesting that the enormous popularity of the songs themselves eclipsed the force of Moore's satirical vein in his other writings, including *Captain Rock* and *Intolerance*.
52   See J.Th. Leerssen, 'How *The Wild Irish Girl* [1806] Made Ireland Romantic', in C.C. Barfoot and Theo D'haen (eds.), *The Clash of Ireland: Literary Contrasts and Connections* (Amsterdam and Atlanta, Ga., 1989), pp. 98–117. Leersen suggests that the hero and heroine of Lady Morgan's epistolary novel are possessed of a symbolic force by which they represent an avocation of England's knowledge and eventual love of Ireland.

53   Donal O'Sullivan, *Songs of the Irish* (Dublin, 1960), p. 7.

54   Moore, 'Suppressed Preface', p. 109.

55   This position was rapidly developed through the course of publication of the *Melodies:* Hoover Jordan observes that as early as October 1809 a writer in the *Leinster Journal* referred to Moore as 'that poet of the heart, who has done more by his poetic effusions than all the political writers who[m] Ireland has seen for a century'. By 1841, the *Dublin Review* was prepared to admit of Moore's political influence in surprisingly candid terms:

> We have somewhere seen it asserted that the influence (which all must admit) of the Irish Melodies in advancing the great cause of Catholic emancipation was exerted in the higher circles of English society, where the language of them and the sweet music to which it was wedded, excited a sympathy never before felt for the suffering country.

See Jordan, *Bolt Upright*, Vol. 1, p. 144. The notion of Moore as an advocate of Catholic emancipation expressly through the *Melodies* has also been eclipsed by their very popularity and by the overwhelming presence of O'Connell in Ireland. In chapter 3 of this study, Moore's better-known reputation as an agent of nationalistic self-determination (a reputation in large measure gained posthumously) is considered in the context of Young Ireland.

56   See, as an example, Hoover Jordan's remarks in *Bolt Upright*, Vol. 1, pp. 153ff.

57   The melody is from the 1797 collection and is discussed in Donal O'Sullivan, 'The Bunting Collection', *Journal of the Irish Folk Song Society*, Vol. 5 (orig. Vols. 22–5), 1927 (repr. London, 1967), pp. 24–5.

58   Quoted in Jordan, *Bolt Upright*, Vol. 1, p. 158. Such Tory sentiment in its way confirms the political significance of Moore's work and also by extension the close association between ethnic music and political agitation which had been formed in the minds of such commentators well before the appearance of the *Melodies*.

59   For a list of sources of journalistic criticism of the *Melodies*, see Thérèse Tessier, *La Poésie Lyrique de Thomas Moore (1779–1852)* (Paris, 1976), pp. 461–2.

60   See Petrie in *The Dublin Examiner* (August 1816), p. 244: 'We cannot agree with our bard [Moore] that the penal laws have any fair claim to all the honor which he is disposed to attribute to them; nor, as might be inferred from his words, that if national degradation and misfortunes be the greatest musical stimuli, we have not had an abundance of them from times remote.' Petrie was to endure in his criticism of Moore's recent provenance of the ethnic repertory for many years.

61   Charles Gavan Duffy, 'Thomas Moore' (1842), in *The Field Day Anthology of Irish Writing*, Vol. 1, p. 1251.

## Antiquarianism and Politics

1   The terms 'sectarian culture' and 'cultural sectarianism' employed in this chapter may require clarification, especially in view of Young Ireland's aspiration to transcend the divisions of class and creed which fortified the colonial–ethnic condition of Irish society in the nineteenth century. I use the term 'sect' here as in 'the followers of a particular school of thought in politics' (*Concise Oxford Dic-*

*tionary*, 8th edition), to denote the exclusive cultivation of a nationalist idea of culture which was central to Davis's writings in particular. The cultural values he espoused were sectarian insofar as they were wholly informed by the principles of nationalism. See Oliver MacDonagh's comments cited in note 7 below.

2   Thomas Davis, Preface to *The Spirit of the Nation* (Dublin, 1845), p. vi.

3   George Petrie, Introduction to *The Ancient Music of Ireland* (Dublin, 1855), p. xii.

4   George Steiner, *In Bluebeard's Castle* (London, 1971), p. 27.

5   This argument is pursued in chapter 5 of the present study.

6   Oliver MacDonagh, *Ireland: The Union and its Aftermath* (London, 1977; 2nd impression, 1979), p. 153.

7   For a brief account of the Young Ireland movement, see Roy Foster, *Modern Ireland 1600–1972* (Harmondsworth, 1988), pp. 310–17. It would appear to be a convention of modern Irish historiography to ascribe to Young Ireland precisely that programme of cultural regeneration analysed in respect of music in this chapter. Thus Oliver MacDonagh describes Young Ireland's deviation from the pragmatic politics of O'Connell as 'the nurturing – in some respects the invention – of a native culture. Its tone was one of total separation and self-assertion, perhaps more chauvinistic in the result than in the intention because of the inflation of its high-flown language and headlong romanticism' (*Ireland*, p. 59). The Young Ireland movement was notably isolated from the mainspring of European nationalism in one respect: it lacked a distinct linguistic identity. This is why Giuseppe Mazzini and *Giovine Italia* rejected the prospect of Young Ireland as a legitimate counterpart; this lack also explains the urgency which attended the revival of the Irish language not merely for its own sake but as an authentic marker of nationalism.
    Daniel O'Connell's famous indifference to the Irish language, his reluctance to break the connection with Britain (he envisaged two parliaments under one King) and his prevailing commitment to Catholic emancipation all provided grounds for serious dissent with Young Ireland. See also note 10 below.

8   See Foster, *Modern Ireland*, pp. 311ff.

9   Foster, *Modern Ireland*, p. 313.

10  My concern here is not with the political aftermath of Young Ireland but with the synthesis of political and cultural revival which it initially articulated (through *The Nation*) as a new force in Irish public life. It is in passing useful to note how O'Connell's pragmatism ('the blandishments, bullying and wheedling' of the Irish Bar, according to Foster) has been unfavourably compared to Young Ireland's purity of vision: this is no more cogently argued than in Arthur Griffith's edition of the writings of Thomas Davis. The preface to this volume stringently condemns the partisan advocations of Catholic emancipation insofar as these eclipsed the prior claim of national independence. Griffith puts the matter succinctly from the vantage of one wholly committed to sectarian culture: 'The width of the gulf that divided the minds of O'Connell and Davis is found by recalling that the former discouraged the national language and peculiar customs of his country and pointed the path of progress through assimilation, while the latter taught it was better for an Irishman to live in rags and dine on potatoes than to become anglicised. The men were at opposite poles in their outlook on Ireland, and if the object in which they were combined had been

achieved, O'Connell and Davis could not have been other than antagonists in the political arena, for the ideal Ireland of the one man was a smaller and happier England, while the ideal Ireland of the other conflicted with English civilisation at every point.' See Arthur Griffith (ed.), *Thomas Davis: The Thinker and the Teacher* (Dublin, 1916), p. xii. The distinction which Griffith makes here is fundamental to an accurate reading of Irish cultural history: the growth of a specifically sectarian culture as a counterpart to and fomentor of national independence must be distinguished from that long tradition of constitutional reform and local agitation which O'Connell mustered with such brilliance. It can be difficult to maintain the separate existence of ideas which so closely resemble one another, but I would argue that the distinction between Davis and O'Connell in political terms (i.e. Catholic emancipation vaguely aspiring towards repeal of the Union versus an imperative demand for national self-government) is one which obtains in the distinction between cultural assimilation (as in the literary revival) and cultural sectarianism (as in the Gaelic League). The development of musical thought in Ireland was unquestionably affected by the tension between these two notions. In politics, of course, it was the sectarian tradition which prevailed in the end, as with *The Nation* after Davis's death.

11   See Mary Helen Thuente, *The Harp Re-strung: The United Irishmen and the Rise of Literary Nationalism* (Syracuse, 1994), pp. 193–230, and David Cairns and Shaun Richards, *Writing Ireland: Colonialism, Nationalism and Culture* (Manchester, 1988), pp. 22–41, for readings of Young Ireland and its poetry and cultural politics.

12   Charles Gavan Duffy, *Thomas Davis: The Memoirs of an Irish Patriot 1840–46* (London, 1890), p. 89.

13   W.J. McCormack, 'The Intellectual Revival' in *The Field Day Anthology of Irish Writing*, Vol. 1, p. 1176.

14   See, as examples, the essays on Thomas Moore, on the novels of Lever and on 'Our Periodical Literature' reproduced in *The Field Day Anthology of Irish Writing*, Vol. 1, pp. 1248-60.

15   Foster, *Modern Ireland*, p. 313. Davis was born in Mallow, County Cork, and educated at Trinity College, Dublin. He was called to the Irish Bar in 1838 and joined the Repeal Association in 1840. He was co-founder of *The Nation* in 1842 along with Gavan Duffy, who was its first editor. Foster (*Modern Ireland*, p. 311) calls him the 'unofficial, but unchallenged leader of the Young Irelanders' between 1842 and his death in 1845. Aside from the popularity of his contributions to *The Nation* (essays, ballads, poetry), he is widely regarded as the most influential and disinterested 'patriot' of his generation. Foster adds that this reputation was in large measure due to his 'ceaseless labour on the committees of all the societies of which he was a member' (including the Royal Irish Academy).

16   Charles Gavan Duffy, *Short Life of Thomas Davis* (London and Dublin, 1896), p. 96.

17   Duffy, *Short Life of Thomas Davis*, p. 95.

18   For a representative collection of Davis's essays (including several pieces on Irish music, poetry, art, architecture, education, and antiquities, as well as on politics and history), see D.J. O'Donoghue (ed.), *Essays Literary and Historical by Thomas Davis* (Dundalk, 1914). (Hereafter, Davis, *Essays*). Many of these pieces

originally appeared in *The Nation.* Griffith, *Thomas Davis,* contains a number of songs and ballads by Davis (texts only) in addition to various pieces on these and other subjects.

19  Davis, *Essays,* p. 214.

20  Davis, *Essays,* pp. 160–3.

21  Davis, *Essays,* pp. 160–1. It is interesting to note that Davis deplores the performance of arrangements of Italian and English opera (Rossini and Balfe) by the temperance bands which formed an important element in the mass repeal meetings held by O'Connell after Catholic emancipation.

22  Davis, *Essays,* p. 162. Davis adverts to the design by Frederic Burton for the cover page of *The Spirit of the Nation,* a design which incorporates musical and political references explained in detail by Davis in an essay on 'Irish Art'. See Davis, *Essays,* pp. 164–6.

23  Davis, *Essays,* p. 241. The essay runs from p. 240 to p. 248. Notwithstanding Davis's reception of Irish music, what leaps from this passage is his incapacity to respond to the notion of music as an independent art: the suggestion that lyric forms and structures might 'injure' the required enunciation of text reinforces the exclusion of music except as a contingent intelligencer of verbal meaning.

24  Davis, *Essays,* pp. 264–78.

25  Davis, *Essays,* p. 269.

26  Davis, *Essays,* p. 271.

27  Davis, *Essays,* p. 273.

28  Davis, *Essays,* p. 274. To be fair, Davis adds that 'he will certainly gain much accuracy, and save much labour to others and himself by being so'. This qualification, however, does not take from Davis's strictly utilitarian concept of musical setting.

29  Davis, *Essays,* p. 278.

30  *The Nation,* 14 December 1844, quoted in Georges-Denis Zimmerman, *Songs of Irish Rebellion: Political Street Ballads and Rebel Songs 1780–1900* (Dublin, 1967), p. 81.

31  *The Nation,* 29 June 1844, quoted in Zimmerman, *Songs of Irish Rebellion,* p. 80. For a detailed history of *The Spirit of the Nation,* see pp. 75–86 of Zimmerman's study, 'Romantic patriotism and literary imitations of street balladry'. Zimmerman states that fifty editions were issued between 1845 and 1877 and that the fifty-ninth and last edition appeared in 1934.

32  *The Spirit of the Nation* (1845), 'Preface', p. vi.

33  Charles Gavan Duffy in *Young Ireland* (Dublin, 1884), p. 69, quoted in Zimmerman, *Songs of Irish Rebellion,* p. 80.

34  The review appeared in April, August, October and November of that year.

35  I am guided on Ferguson by Peter Denman, *Samuel Ferguson: The Literary Achievement* (Bucks., 1990). For a discussion of 'A Dialogue . . .', published in *The Dublin University Magazine* in 1833, see Denman, pp. 2–4. Ferguson (1810–86) was born in Belfast. Educated at Trinity College, Dublin, and called to the Irish Bar, Ferguson became an important contributor to *The Dublin University Magazine* and to other periodicals wherein he established a voice for a Unionist demeanour in Irish affairs that was yet nationalist. His poetry and criticism became important precedents for Yeats and the Celtic revival. President of

the Royal Irish Academy. Contributor to the third volume of Bunting's *Ancient Music of Ireland* (see chapter 2 above).

36  'Hardiman's Irish Minstrelsy', *The Dublin University Magazine*, Vol. 4 (July–December 1834), p. 153.

37  'Hardiman's Irish Minstrelsy', *The Dublin University Magazine*, Vol. 4 (July–December 1834), p. 153.

38  'Hardiman's Irish Minstrelsy', *The Dublin University Magazine*, Vol. 4 (July–December 1834), p. 464.

39  Denman, *Samuel Ferguson*, p. 34.

40  The difference between Ferguson and Davis with respect to Irish music is indicated by a comparison between Ferguson's censure of Moore's pro-Catholic agitations as these are expressed in the *Melodies*, and Davis's complaint that Moore is 'deficient in vehemence'. The striking similarity between them is that Davis and Ferguson both conceive of music as secondary to verbal nuance and meaning.

41  For biographical information on Petrie (1789–1866) see Dolan, 'The Musical Contributions and Historical Significance of Edward Bunting' (1773–1843), A Pioneer in the Preservation of the Heritage of Irish Music' (diss., Catholic University of America, 1977), pp. 187–203.

42  Aloys Fleischmann, 'Aspects of George Petrie: IV. Petrie's Contribution to Irish Music', *Proceedings of the Royal Irish Academy*, Vol. 72, Section C, No. 9, p. 202.

43  Petrie's earliest contribution to Irish studies was as a landscape painter; he subsequently became interested in the archaeology of Irish monuments, in which field he is widely regarded as a pioneer. From 1833 to 1839 he was active as a superintendent for antiquarian monuments in the Ordnance Survey, and, in addition to his prolific contributions to journals such as *The Dublin Examiner*, he founded the *Dublin Penny Journal* in 1832. For a useful overview of Petrie's achievement, see Alfred Perceval Graves, *Irish Literary and Musical Studies* (London, 1914; repr. New York, 1967), pp. 191–240. Although Petrie made much of his reluctance to take up the task of collecting and publishing the native repertory, it has to be understood that his interest in Irish music was lifelong. As stated in the introduction to *The Ancient Music of Ireland*, Petrie's primary motivation was to rescue a repertory of music endangered by the Famine. But he was also inspired to consolidate his interests in Irish music for scholarly reasons: in particular, he held strong views on the provenance of individual airs which openly clash with those of his predecessor, Bunting. (See the introduction, pp. xiv–xviii, where Petrie's divergences from Bunting are at their most explicit.)

44  The 1855 publication contains 147 airs, about half of which are supplied with texts. For a detailed scrutiny of the subsequent publication of the Petrie collections, see Marian Deasy, 'New Edition of the Airs and Dance Tunes From the Music Manuscripts of George Petrie LL.D., and a Survey of His Work as a Collector of Irish Folk Music' (PhD diss., National University of Ireland, 1982).

45  Petrie, Introduction to *The Ancient Music of Ireland*, p. xii.

46  Petrie, Introduction to *The Ancient Music of Ireland*, p. xii

47  See Seamus Deane, 'Arnold, Burke and the Celts', in *Celtic Revivals* (London, 1985), p. 25. In the introduction to *The Ancient Music of Ireland*, Petrie writes: 'I felt it was still possible . . . to gather from amongst the survivors of the old Celtic race, innumerable melodies that would soon pass away for ever; . . . For,

though I had no fear that this first swarm from the parent hive of the great Indo-Germanic race would perish in this their last western asylum; or that they would not again increase . . . yet I felt that the new generations, unlinked as they must be with those of the past, . . . will necessarily have lost very many of those peculiar characteristics which so long had given them a marked individuality; and, more particularly, that among the changes sure to follow, the total extinction of their ancient language would be, inevitably, accompanied by the loss of all that as yet unsaved portion of their ancient music which had been identified with it' (pp. xii–xiii).

48   See Fleischmann, 'Aspects of George Petrie', p. 195. Joyce was a disciple and colleague of Petrie's as Petrie was of Bunting's. Fleischmann, *The Sources of Irish Traditional Music, 1583–1855* (New York, 1998) culminates in the Petrie collections.

49   It is of course Petrie's *collections* (rather than Petrie himself) which attain to this cultural mutation. But Petrie's response to the Famine remains the decisive factor in this development. The preservation of Irish culture (including, as in Petrie's case, Irish music) in the post-Famine period became both a greater matter of urgency than heretofore and a symbol of distinctiveness with hitherto unfulfilled political implications.

50   This is not to deny that Petrie gave individual songs to Moore (and other arrangers of the ethnic repertory) in his early years: the point is that whereas Bunting's collections stimulated and enabled the dissemination of the ethnic repertory which Moore achieved in the *Melodies*, Petrie's work reinvigorated the collection of music in post-Famine Ireland and consolidated the perception of Irish music as a resource from the Gaelic past. This musical resource symbolised the intransigence of Gaelic culture in a climate of regeneration which insisted upon the integrity of sectarian modes of expression. The simplest instance of this sectarianism lies in the 'either/or' condition of the Irish language vis-à-vis the English language. Whereas the literary revival eclipsed this condition (much to the chagrin of the Gaelic League), the status of Irish music remained absolutely indentured to the ethnic repertory.

51   From an entry in Petrie's journals, cited in William Stokes, *The Life of George Petrie* (London, 1868), p. 317; see also Fleischmann, 'Aspects of George Petrie', p. 215.

52   As an example, see the introduction to Patrick Weston Joyce, *Ancient Irish Music* (Dublin, 1873).

53   It is useful here to advert to the work of the Academy in establishing for the first time modern editions and grammars of Irish language and literature, as well as to the wider circle of societies (such as the Gaelic Society, the Archaeological Society and the Celtic Society to which the 'Irish-Music' Society [Society for the Preservation of Irish Music] belonged). Petrie's own achievement as an antiquarian, together with that of his close contemporaries Eugene O'Curry and John O'Donovan, fortified the collection of Irish music as an act of scholarly preservation of comparable stature to the linguistic, topographical and archaeological rehabilitation of Gaelic culture.

54   For a summary of this censure, see Fleischmann, 'Aspects of George Petrie', p. 213.

55   Again, it is the influence of the collections themselves, rather than any self-conscious programme on Petrie's behalf, which validates this argument. In particular, three manifestations of that influence are: (1) the posthumous publication

of three further volumes of melodies collected by Petrie, including an edition by Charles Villiers Stanford between 1902 and 1905; (2) the tradition of similar collections by Joyce, Francis O'Neill and many others through the twentieth century; (3) the consolidation of the collected melodies as the *exclusive* projection of Irish music: this exclusivity was almost exactly analogous to the inherent exclusivity of one language (Gaelic/Irish) as against another (English).

56   Deane, 'The Literary Myths of the Revival', in *Celtic Revivals*, p. 34.

57   Deane, 'The Literary Myths of the Revival', p. 34.

58   This, in essence, is the argument pursued in chapter 5 of the present study.

59   By 'ideologues' I mean not the collectors themselves, but those commentators who wrote in their wake (as with Douglas Hyde, whose consideration of music is discussed here). Others include Michael Conrad (*The National Music of Ireland*, 1850), Alfred Perceval Graves (*Irish Literary and Musical Studies*, 1913), Carl Hardebeck (also a composer), Richard Henebry (*Handbook of Irish Music*, 1928) and Charlotte Milligan Fox (*Annals of the Irish Harpers*, 1911).

60   Hyde (1860–1949) was born in Frenchpark, Co. Roscommon, and educated in Dublin. He was co-founder of the Irish Literary Society in London, 1891, and president of the National Literary Society in Dublin, 1892. Co-founder and president of the Gaelic League, 1893. Playwright; professor of modern Irish at University College, Dublin, 1909–32. President of Ireland, 1938–45. *Love Songs of Connacht* was published in 1893 and *A Literary History of Ireland* in 1899.

61   Douglas Hyde, 'The Necessity for De-Anglicising Ireland' (1892) in Breandán Ó Conaire (ed.), *Douglas Hyde: Language, Lore and Lyrics* (Dublin, 1986), p. 153.

62   Hyde, 'The Necessity for De-Anglicising Ireland', p. 169. Hyde's impassioned display of cultural impoverishment is especially powerful in the matter of language: he cites scores of given names and surnames 'transmogrified' from Irish to English to demonstrate the loss of Irish from one generation to the next.

63   Hyde resigned in 1915 as president of the Gaelic League when it became politicised; for a discussion of the Gaelic League and its relationship with the Irish Republican Brotherhood which attempts to clarify Hyde's position as one of intellectual rather than political autonomy, see Foster, *Modern Ireland*, pp. 447–60.

64   Hyde, 'The Necessity for De-Anglicising Ireland', p. 167.

65   Until further research has been undertaken into the question of music within the Gaelic League, it is not possible to determine how widespread was Hyde's repudiation of the European aesthetic. But two issues can be safely advanced: firstly, that Hyde's antipathy to the art tradition in music *was* widely shared in nationalist periodical discourse, and secondly, that the Gaelic–Catholic synthesis which characterised Irish nationalism, particularly after the turn of the century, was to prove hospitable to this repudiation, even if Hyde himself disavowed the sectarian *political* turn of the Gaelic League. The association which ideologues of Gaelic culture drew between English colonialism and the traditions of art music endure in Ireland to the present day.

66   The phrase belongs to Denis Patrick Moran. The 'Irish Ireland' concept is the obverse of Hyde's 'West Britonism', one being an extreme rejection of the other. Moran reserved his most stringent commentary for movements which espoused some reconciliation between the two, as in the case of the literary revival. See also chapter 5 below.

67   Richard Henebry, *Irish Music* (Dublin, n.d. [1903?]), p. 14, cited in Joseph Ryan, 'Nationalism and Music in Ireland' (PhD diss., National University of Ireland, 1991), p. 132. Henebry was professor of old Irish at University College, Cork, from 1909 until his death in 1916 and vice-president of the Irish Folk Song Society. He is characterised by Joseph Ryan (as above) as being 'to music what ... D.P. Moran was to politics and literature: an Irish Irelander, disputatious, original and idiosyncratic, but with a commendable consistency and honesty' (p. 132).

68   Richard Henebry, *Handbook of Irish Music* (Cork, 1928), p. 55.

69   An epigraph drawn from Arthur Woulfe (1739–1803) and used in the first number of *The Nation* (Dublin, Saturday 15 October 1842).

70   Zimmerman, *Songs of Irish Rebellion*, p. 10.

71   Zimmerman (*Songs of Irish Rebellion*, pp. 46–7) adverts to the influence of the Young Ireland ballads on similar collections which appeared after the Famine, in particular on the ballads issued in the *United Irishman* (f. February 1848). In the several printed collections which appeared in the wake of *The Spirit of the Nation*, it is admittedly difficult to decide which publications directly reflected the influence of that volume and which merely sustained the wider tradition of ballad sheets. What can be advanced with certainty is that music throughout this tradition remained a secondary consideration.

72   N. Davies, *God's Playground: A History of Poland* (Oxford, 1981), Vol. 2, p. 8, cited in Jim Samson (ed.), *The Cambridge Companion to Chopin* (Cambridge, 1992), p. 149.

73   Zofia Chechlińska, 'Chopin Reception in Nineteenth-Century Poland', in *The Cambridge Companion to Chopin*, p. 208.

74   See Eoin MacWhite, 'Thomas Moore and Poland', *Proceedings of the Royal Irish Academy*, Vol. 72, Section C, pp. 49–62.

75   See Chechlińska, 'Chopin Reception', pp. 208–10: 'Already before 1830 Polish writers had defined those characteristics of Chopin's playing and music that would later be valued by the emergent Romantic era and highlighted in nine-teenth-century European criticism: its national character, its poetic and emotional qualities ("the expression of the heart", "the voice of the soul"), its originality and its melancholy and delicacy. Unsurprisingly, it was the national dimension which played a very special role in Polish reception ... [Chopin] was – as we know – definitely opposed to this way of reading his own works.'

76   Jim Samson, 'A Biographical Introduction', in *The Cambridge Companion to Chopin*, p. 6.

77   This reading of Chopin's *ballades* is advanced by Samson in 'Extended Forms: The Ballades, Scherzos and Fantasies', in *The Cambridge Companion to Chopin*, pp. 101–23. See especially p. 111: 'Through their response to literature and also to vocal music Chopin's ballades aligned themselves to a central – almost a defining – preoccupation of an early romantic aesthetic in music, a preoccupation with the expressive and narrative capacities of musical language.'

78   Samson, 'A Biographical Introduction', p. 7.

# Heinrich Bewerunge and the Cecilian Movement in Ireland

1    Emmet Larkin, 'The Devotional Revolution in Ireland, 1850–1875', *American Historical Review*, Vol. 77, No. 3 (June 1972), p. 649.

2    For a useful summary of Fenian thinking in respect of the political complexion of the Catholic Church in Ireland, see R.F. Foster, *Modern Ireland 1600–1972* (Harmondsworth, 1988), pp. 393–5.

3    See Emmet Larkin, *The Making of the Roman Catholic Church in Ireland, 1850–1860* (Chapel Hill, 1980), p. xx and *passim*.

4    Emmet Larkin, *The Making of the Roman Catholic Church*, pp. xxiii–xxiv: '. . . between 1856 and 1860, he [Cullen] proceeded to consolidate his recently won predominance in such a fashion as to leave MacHale [archbishop of Tuam] and his episcopal supporters with little room for manoeuvre anywhere except in their own dioceses. Though Cullen had been partially frustrated, for example, in his more formal efforts to regulate the political conduct of the Irish clergy between 1852 and 1856, he was able by 1860 to limit their worst excesses on the hustings by still being able to secure at Rome the appointment of bishops who thought as he did about the role in politics appropriate to priests . . . Moreover, Cullen had also by 1860 acquired an absolute control over the three great Irish educational establishments – Maynooth, the Irish College at Paris, and the Catholic University.'

5    For a detailed account of Cullen's habitual reliance on the offices of the Propaganda Fide to ratify and support his policy-making in Ireland, see Larkin, *The Making of the Roman Catholic Church*, *passim*, and especially pp. 15–57.

6    See Kieran A. Daly, 'Lyra Ecclesiastica: Bulletin of the Irish Society of St Cecilia' (MA diss., Queens University, Belfast, 1991), Appendix VI (a), p. 460, where these decrees are reproduced.

7    Larkin, *The Making of the Roman Catholic Church*, p. 27.

8    See Decree XV, cap. 73 and cap. 74, reproduced in Daly, 'Lyra Ecclesiastica', Appendix VI (b), p. 461. Chapter 73 explicitly directs that the Regensburg (Ratisbon) edition of the chant was to be used in all Irish seminaries and churches.

9    See *Magister Choralis/A Theoretical and Practical Manual/of Gregorian Chant/for the use of/the clergy, seminarists, organists/choir-masters, choristers etc./by/Rev Francis Xavier Haberl/Cathedral choir-master, Ratisbon/Translated and Enlarged/(from the fourth German Edition)/by Rev N. Donnelly,/Cathedral Church of the Immaculate Conception Dublin* (Ratisbon, New York and Cincinnati, Frederick Pustet, 1877). Also, *Lyra Ecclesiastica/Monthly Bulletin of the Irish Society of St Cecilia/and/List of Catholic Church Music/Volume 1/1879* (Dublin, M.H. Gill and Son). Also, *A Grammar/of Gregorian Music/with/Numerous Exercises and Examples:/a complete Collection of the Liturgical Chants at High Mass,/Vespers, Compline and other functions; Dumont's Masses of the/1st, 2nd and 6th Tones; the Mass De Angelis; etc., etc./by the Very Rev William J. Walsh DD/Canon of the Cathedral Chapter of Dublin;/President, St Patrick's College, Maynooth* (Dublin, M.H. Gill and Son, 1885).

10   Nicholas Donnelly (1837–1920) was born in Dublin, where he was educated by the Vincentian Fathers at Castleknock. He entered the Irish College in Rome

in 1854 and was ordained there in 1860. He returned to Ireland in 1860 and served as a curate in various parishes in Dublin including the pro-cathedral, Marlborough Street, where he remained from 1864 until 1879. He was founding president of the Irish Society of St Cecilia in 1878. Auxiliary bishop of Dublin and bishop of the titular see of Canea from 1883 until his death.

11  The German Society was established in 1868. Irish links to it were in the main established through Donnelly. See Daly, 'Lyra Ecclesiastica', pp. 46–8.

12  Renehan was also sometime president of St Patrick's College, Maynooth.

13  See Donnelly, *Magister Choralis*, 'Preface', p. xi.

14  See Donnelly, *Magister Choralis*, 'Preface', p. i, wherein the Latin citation of this decree is given; Donnelly maintains that the wording of the decree derives from a similar decree published by the English hierarchy at Westminster in 1873. The Irish decree in question is that translated by Daly in 'Lyra Ecclesiastica' (see note 8 above).

15  Donnelly, *Magister Choralis*, 'Preface', p. xi.

16  *Lyra Ecclesiastica*, Vol. 1, No. 1 (1879), p. 1.

17  *Lyra Ecclesiastica*, Vol. 1, No. 1 (1879), p. 2.

18  For a detailed scrutiny of the journal's dependence on material reprinted and/or translated from other journals, see Daly, 'Lyra Ecclesiastica', pp. 76–9, and *passim*.

19  *Lyra Ecclesiastica*, Vol. 1, No. 1 (1879), p. 38.

20  This is not to gainsay the fact that such a 'code of aesthetics' was not necessarily shared by certain members of the lay Catholic community: an observation borne out by objections to the Cecilian movement discussed later in this chapter. It is also useful to observe that the formation of a Dublin Diocesan Committee of the Society of St Cecilia in 1885 weakened the nationwide effectiveness of the movement as a whole. On this point, see Daly, 'Lyra Ecclesiastica', pp. 174ff.

21  See Walsh, *A Grammar of Gregorian Music*, 'Preface', p. vii.

22  Walsh, *A Grammar of Gregorian Music*, 'Preface', pp. iii–iv.

23  See, for example, Karl Gustav Fellerer's article 'Cäcilianismus', in F. Blume (ed.), *Die Musik in Geschichte und Gegenwart* (Basle, 1973), Bd. 2, pp. 624–6, where (p. 625) the establishment of the Cecilian movement in Ireland is attributed to Bewerunge in 1876 (i.e. some twelve years prior to his arrival in the country). Although Fellerer does cite Donnelly as the editor of *Lyra Ecclesiastica* (again, mistakenly giving the year 1876) in the bibliography to his article, the fact remains that Bewerunge is unduly credited here and elsewhere with having originated the movement in Ireland. That he did not do so is amply demonstrated by the sources considered in this chapter.

24  See Daly, 'Lyra Ecclesiastica', pp. 196ff. Membership of the Irish Society of St Cecilia does seem difficult to determine with any exactitude, given that numbers fluctuated from year to year. Additionally, the founding of diocesan and parochial branches of the society complicated its own estimations of membership. Although the vicissitudes in the affairs of the society were considerable throughout its existence (1878–1903), the impact it had upon musical awareness in Ireland was extensive. *Lyra Ecclesiastica* documents its activities in remarkable detail, especially in the years 1879–83 and 1883–91, when the journal was edited by Donnelly and by Joseph Seymour respectively. The con-

cern voiced in early volumes by individual organists and other musicians as to the condition of music education in Ireland, the remarkable range of Cecilian performances and yearly festivals held under the auspices of the society and the development of Cecilian committees in rural Ireland collectively attest to the significance of the Cecilian movement in Irish cultural history during the quarter-century in which it flourished. I am indebted to Kieran Daly's exhaustive scrutiny of that movement (see note 6) which should be consulted for its abundantly detailed reading of *Lyra Ecclesiastica* and its definitive account of Irish Cecilianism prior to Bewerunge's appointment to St Patrick's College, Maynooth.

25   For a survey of the activities of the Cecilian movement in Europe and the United States, see Fellerer, 'Cācilianismus' and Daly, 'Lyra Ecclesiastica', pp. 14–47. Two decrees entitled *motu proprio* were promulgated by Pius X in respect of music on 22 November 1903 and on 24 April 1904. The second of them maintained that the new Vatican edition of the Chant would be based on a comparative study of all authoritative source materials.

26   Fellerer, 'Cācilianismus', p. 626: 'Mit der Uberwindung der Regensburger Choralausg., des Lebenswers FX. Haberls, hat der deutsche Cācilianismus einen schweren Schlag erhalten.'

27   The following account of Bewerunge's life is based on the *Kalendarium* of St Patrick's College, Maynooth for 1923–4. I have also consulted Fellerer, 'Bewerunge, Heinrich', *Die Musik in Geschichte und Gegenwart*, Bd. 15 (1973), pp. 764–5. See also Fellerer's *History of Catholic Church Music*, trans. Francis A. Brunner (Baltimore, 1961; repr. Connecticut, 1979), p. 190: 'Ireland felt the [Cecilian] movement especially through the efforts of Henry Bewerunge, a pupil of Franz Xavier Haberl at Regensburg, who began to teach at St Patrick's, Maynooth, in 1888.' If nothing else, this assessment grossly underestimates the impact of the movement in Ireland prior to Bewerunge's arrival.

28   (Bishop) Donnelly was approached by the trustees of the college for advice and he contacted Haberl, who subsequently advanced Bewerunge for the position. This information is recorded in the *Report of the President for the Years 1887–8 (Maynooth)*, and reproduced in Daly, 'Lyra Ecclesiastica', p. 275. There is some irony in Donnelly's having been responsible for Bewerunge's appointment, given the latter's disruptive impact on the journal which he had established, directly as a result of his studies with Haberl.

29   For a catalogue of Heinrich Bewerunge's arrangements, original compositions and scholarly writings, see Harry White and Nicholas Lawrence, 'Towards a History of the Cecilian Movement in Ireland: An Assessment of the Writings of Heinrich Bewerunge (1862–1923), with a Catalogue of his Publications and Manuscripts', in Gerard Gillen and Harry White (eds.), *Music and the Church (Irish Musical Studies* 2) (Dublin, 1993), pp. 78–107.

30   For the citation of these writings see White and Lawrence, 'Towards a History of the Cecilian Movement', pp. 97–8.

31   Heinrich Bewerunge, 'Graz Report – The Thirteenth General Meeting of the German Society of St Cecilia', *Lyra Ecclesiastica*, September 1891, p. 65.

32   Bewerunge describes the music of E.V. Bauduin in this report as 'disgusting trash'.

33   Bewerunge, 'Graz Report', pp. 67–9.

34   Heinrich Bewerunge, 'Palestrina and Orlando di Lasso', *Irish Ecclesiastical Record*, December 1894, pp. 1088–9.

35   See Bewerunge, 'Palestrina and Orlando di Lasso', p. 1089, for a list of secondary sources consulted by Bewerunge.

36   Bewerunge, 'Palestrina and Orlando di Lasso', pp. 1108–9.

37   Bewerunge, 'Palestrina and Orlando di Lasso', p. 1111.

38   Bewerunge, 'Palestrina and Orlando di Lasso', p. 1112.

39   See, for example, the discussion of precisely this issue with regard to Louis Spohr's *Des Heilands letzte Stunden* in Glenn Stanley's 'Religious Propriety versus Artistic Truth', *Acta Musicologica*, Vol. 61, Fasc. 1 (1989), pp. 66–82.

40   See George O'Neill, 'Musicians in Controversy', *New Ireland Review*, Vol. 12 (1899), pp. 309–313; p. 309; also 'Sacred Music as a Living Art', *New Ireland Review*, Vol. 12 (1899), pp. 331–6.

41   O'Neill, 'Musicians in Controversy', p. 310.

42   Quoted in O'Neill, 'Sacred Music as a Living Art', p. 331.

43   O'Neill, 'Sacred Music as a Living Art', p. 334.

44   See Robert Dwyer, 'Imitations of Palestrina', *New Ireland Review*, Vol. 15 (1900), pp. 155–60 at p. 155.

45   Heinrich Bewerunge, 'Cecilian Music', *New Ireland Review*, Vol. 15 (1900), pp. 73–84 at p. 76.

46   Bewerunge, 'Cecilian Music', p. 84. See also Joseph Ryan, 'Assertions of Distinction: The Modal Debate in Irish Music', in Gillen and White (eds.), *Music and the Church* (Irish Musical Studies 2), pp. 62–77.

47   This point is discussed in 'Cecilian Music', p. 84. See also Heinrich Bewerunge, 'The Teaching of Music in Irish Schools', *Irish Ecclesiastical Record*, December 1897, pp. 437–40.

48   Heinrich Bewerunge, 'The Vatican Edition of Plain Chant', *Irish Ecclesiastical Record*, January 1906, Vol. 19 (fourth series), pp. 44–63 (hereafter, 'The Vatican Edition', Part One); 'The Second Part of the Vatican Edition of Plain Chant', *Irish Ecclesiastical Record*, November 1906, Vol. 20 (fifth series), pp. 414–28 (hereafter, Bewerunge, 'The Vatican Edition', Part Two); 'The Vatican *Kyriale* – a Rejoinder', *Irish Ecclesiastical Record*, May 1906, Vol. 21 (fourth series), pp. 421–45. For further bibliographical details on these and related articles, see the catalogue of Bewerunge's works in White and Lawrence, 'Towards a History of the Cecilian Movement', pp. 97–8.

49   See Bewerunge, 'The Vatican Edition', Part One, pp. 44–6.

50   Bewerunge, 'The Vatican Edition', Part One, pp. 46–8.

51   Bewerunge, 'The Vatican Edition', Part One, p. 61.

52   Bewerunge, 'The Vatican Edition', Part One, p. 62.

53   Bewerunge, 'The Vatican Edition', Part One, p. 63.

54   Bewerunge, 'The Vatican Edition', Part Two, p. 419.

55   See Bewerunge, 'The Vatican *Kyriale* – a Rejoinder'.

56   Willi Apel, in his standard history of *Gregorian Chant* (Indiana, 1958), acknowledges Bewerunge's particular contribution to metrical theory in the chant and an approach to the *cursus* problem which provides 'a much more reliable basis of investigation than Mocquereau's tone terminations' (p. 300). See White and Lawrence, 'Towards a History of the Cecilian Movement', pp. 94–6, for further references to and discussion of Bewerunge's chant scholarship.

57   See note 26 above.
58   For a detailed critique of Bewerunge's editorship of *Lyra Ecclesiastica* see Daly, 'Lyra Ecclesiastica', pp. 280–355. Daly observes that the rapport between the readers of *Lyra* and its editor was so poor that it soon became apparent that 'he enjoyed having the last word in any music debate' (p. 297). Requests for 'Cecilian intelligence', meanwhile, were increasingly greeted with silence.
59   James Joyce, 'The Dead', in *Dubliners* ([1914] Harmondsworth, 1976), p. 192.
60   'The Dead', p. 173. Joyce's fidelity to actual circumstance in his fiction is incidentally borne out by the fact that the organist in St Mary's, Haddington Road, at the turn of the century was one Mary Jane Gormley (see Daly, 'Lyra Ecclesiastica', p. 406). As auxiliary bishop of Dublin, Nicholas Donnelly was pastor of this church from 1904 until his death. He instituted a choir of men and boys there upon his appointment and this 'Guild of Choristers under the protection of St Cecilia' represents his final contribution to church music reform in Ireland.
61   Richard Terry, *Catholic Church Music* (London, 1907), p. 39.
62   This was established by Martyn in 1902. The terms of his endowment specified that the choir should consist of men and boys only and that 'no music could be used in the choir, composed later than the year 1700' (see Daly, 'Lyra Ecclesiastica', pp. 379–80). There is some irony in the fact that these terms did not exclude the appointment of a woman as choral director, given that the Palestrina Choir in recent years has enjoyed renewed success under the direction of Ite O'Donovan and Orla Barry.
63   See Ryan, 'Assertions of Distinction', pp. 63–75, for details of this curious admixture of cultural chauvinism and musicological enquiry.

## Music and the Literary Revival

1   'O.Z.', in *New Ireland Review*, Vol. 11 (1894–5), p. 647 (my italics).
2   Brendan Rogers, 'An Irish School of Music', *New Ireland Review*, Vol. 13 (1900), p. 151.
3   Arnold Bax, 'A Radio Self-Portrait' (1949), in Lewis Foreman (ed.), *Farewell, My Youth and other Writings by Arnold Bax* (Aldershot, 1992), p. 166.
4   It occurs in the poem 'Easter 1916', from the collection *Michael Robartes and the Dancer* (1921).
5   Terence Brown, 'Cultural Nationalism 1880–1930', *The Field Day Anthology of Irish Writing* (Derry, 1991), Vol. 2, p. 519.
6   The phrase occurs in 'The Man and the Echo', from the collection *Last Poems* (1939). Many of the poems in this collection meditate on the continuity which Yeats perceived between the Celtic revival and the acts of rebellion (notably the 1916 Rising) which led to the formation of the Irish Free State.
7   Seamus Deane, 'The Literary Myths of the Revival', in *Celtic Revivals* (London, 1985), p. 28. The reading of Yeats which follows here is largely indebted to Deane.
8   Terence Brown, 'Cultural Nationalism', p. 518.
9   For a useful summary of these endeavours and the distinctive ambitions which preoccupied Hyde and Yeats between 1888 and 1898, see F.S.L. Lyons, *Culture and Anarchy in Ireland 1890–1939* (Oxford, 1979), pp. 37–51.
10   See 'The Battle of Two Civilisations' in D.P. Moran, *The Philosophy of Irish Ireland* (Dublin, n.d. [1905]), pp. 94–114. This essay originally appeared in the *New*

*Ireland Review*, Vol. 13 (1900), pp. 323–36. Denis Patrick Moran (1871–1936) was a journalist whose trenchant repudiation of the revival reads as an extreme formulation of Hyde's programme for 'de-anglicisation'. His critique of Irish cultural regeneration was immensely influential insofar as it reflected the insistence upon complete sociocultural (and political) autonomy which led (among other things) to Sinn Féin. Although Moran did not address the question of music in *The Philosophy of Irish Ireland*, his complete rejection of any kind of cultural cross-fertilisation allows us to infer from his identification of 'two civilisations' an unshakeable hostility towards the European aesthetic: 'Ireland will be nothing until she is a nation, and, as a nation is a civilisation, she will never accomplish anything worthy of herself until she falls back upon her own language and traditions, and recovering there her old pride, self-respect and initiative, develops and marches forward from thence' (*The Philosophy of Irish Ireland*, p. 113).

11   The political background to this period is traced in Roy Foster, *Modern Ireland 1600–1972* (Harmondsworth, 1988), pp. 431–93.

12   Foster, *Modern Ireland*, p. 492.

13   Seamus Deane, 'Yeats and the Idea of Revolution', in *Celtic Revivals*, p. 46: 'Yeats's aesthetic became, then, more and more politicised under the pressure of the crisis which had afflicted his country. It could not but emerge as a conviction that the Irish had a crucial, redemptive role to play in the recovery of European civilisation from barbarism. Easter Week made the Great War look like a mindless, despiritualised carnage. Cuchulain's (and, by extension, Ireland's) cycle of recurrence became finally complete in the sacrifice of Pearse.'

14   It is apparent nevertheless that this wider interpretation of Yeats's poetic escaped the attention of many of his contemporaries, who regarded his endorsement of the Rising in poems such as 'Easter 1916' as an expression of political and cultural nationalism.

15   Arnold Bax observes that Yeats was 'tone-deaf' in the foreword to Aloys Fleischmann (ed.), *Music in Ireland* (Cork and Oxford, 1952), and he remarks that 'there was no talk of music whatever' during his sojourn in Dublin amongst the central figures of the revival. In *W.B. Yeats: A Classified Bibliography of Criticism* (Chicago, 1990), K.P.S. Jochum notes several settings of Yeats's poetry (pp. 943ff.), together with original music by Florence Farr, Sara Allgood and Arthur Darley for various Yeats plays included in the *Collected Works in Verse and Prose* (Stratford-on-Avon, 1908). Edward Elgar's incidental music and funeral march for the Yeats–Moore *Diarmuid and Grania* (op. 42) is also noted, but of the settings of Yeats's verse in general, Jochum remarks: 'Yeats himself was less than happy with these compositions; Robert Frost relates that Yeats once "said that [there was] nothing he hated more than having his poems set to music – it stole the show." ' (p. 943). This remark bears out the pervasive indifference, even hostility, with which Yeats regarded the prospect of music as a rival art to poetry.

That he could accept music as an atmospheric adjunct to his own verse dramas seems beyond doubt; his various experiments (with Florence Farr) on the recitation of verse 'to the psaltery' confirms his limited conception of music as a subservient resource. The passage cited later in this chapter from *Explorations* (1905) exemplifies Yeats's perception of music as an expression of peasant culture. Notwithstanding Yeats's indifference to and ignorance of art music, his abiding interest in aspects of the ethnic repertory and the ballad tradition deserves further research. See Michael Yeats, 'Words and Music', *Yeats Society of Japan*, annual report No. 8 (Tokyo, 1973), pp. 7–18.

16 For further commentary on this relationship between music and literature in Ireland, see the epilogue to this study. The epigraph from the *New Ireland Review* which opens the present chapter (see note 1 above) underlines the conventional association between poetry and music which enjoyed such popularity in the reception of Irish culture at the turn of the century. In this instance, the 'music' of Yeats's verse is deemed to be its outstanding quality. This preoccupation with lyricism excludes any consideration of music as an actual mode of artistic discourse. The tradition of comprehending music as a property of verbal art runs deep in Ireland, and its manifestations in Hardiman, Ferguson, Hyde (*Love Songs of Connacht*) and Yeats are of cultural (as well as literary) significance.

17 See the epigraph from Bax's 'A Radio Self-Portrait' (note 3 above). It was Bax who was to take the vital step from Irish literature to art music independently of the folk tradition, otherwise regarded as indispensable to Irish musical composition.

18 The latter view is taken by Percy Young in *A History of British Music* (London, 1967), where Stanford in particular represents a widespread failure to obviate 'the pull of respectability' in British music of the period 1870–1920.

19 See Denis Gwynn, *Edward Martyn (1859–1924) and the Irish Revival* (London, 1930), which cites Yeats's description of Martyn soon after the latter's withdrawal from the Irish Literary Theatre: 'an unhappy, childless, unfinished laborious man, typical of an Ireland that is passing away' (p. 115).

But Martyn's vision of Ireland did not pass away, however much Yeats disdained it. Gwynn describes the creation of the Irish Literary Theatre as having appeared to Martyn as 'the most significant action of his own life'; Martyn's increased preoccupation with 'Irish Ireland' after 1900 (as in his presidency of Sinn Féin, 1906–8) and his fervent espousal of church music are both expressive of a profoundly authoritarian reading of Ireland's potential as a 'Catholic power' cut off from the wellsprings of her European (Catholic) heritage. Such a reading was self evidently repugnant to Yeats, but of more consequence is the fact that Martyn's patronage of music was part of this envisaged cultural synthesis. Thus music became expressive of an Ireland which Yeats contemptuously dismissed. And Yeats's dismissal did not countenance much opposition.

20 See 'September 1913' (Yeats), from the collection *Responsibilities* (1914).

21 Deane, 'Yeats and the Idea of Revolution', in *Celtic Revivals*, p. 39.

22 Joseph Ryan, 'Nationalism and Music in Ireland', (PhD diss., National University of Ireland, 1991), p. 175. See also Axel Klein, *Die Musik Irlands im 20. Jahrhundert* (Hildesheim, 1996), *passim*, for an incisive survey of music in late nineteenth-century Ireland and for biographical, critical and analytical commentary on all of the composers discussed in the present chapter.

23 Such works include *The Bohemian Girl* (1843), *Maritana* (1845) and *The Lily of Killarney* (1862).

24 Cited in Olinthus J. Vignoles, *Memoir of Sir Robert P. Stewart, Kt., Mus. Doc.* (London, n.d. [1898]), p. 5. It is worth adding that from the resignation of Lord Mornington (appointed in 1764) until the appointment of John Smith in 1845 the chair of music at Trinity College had been vacant.

25 For biographical information on Stewart see Vignoles, *Memoir of Sir Robert P. Stewart*, *passim*; also Ryan, 'Nationalism and Music in Ireland', pp. 223–7. On

the Robinson family see Ryan, 'Nationalism and Music in Ireland', pp. 177–87, and on Culwick, see Ryan, 'Nationalism and Music in Ireland', pp. 228–31. Young, *A History of British Music*, p. 494, records that Joseph Robinson's performance of Mendelssohn's music for *Antigone* in the Antient Concerts was its first hearing outside Germany.

26   As was the case, for example, with John Goss and Frederick Gore Ouseley.

27   A Miss Hamilton, cited in Vignoles, *Memoir of Sir Robert P. Stewart*, p. 89. Further details on *The Eve of St John* are in Ryan, 'Nationalism and Music in Ireland', pp. 226ff.

28   Vignoles, *Memoir of Sir Robert P. Stewart*, p. 194.

29   See Stewart's letter on 'Irish Church Music' in Vignoles, pp. 173–5, which is dismissive of Petrie's technical knowledge of Ireland and which glosses the history of Irish church music. The close of this letter betrays a level of *naïveté* which is significantly high: 'The chief puzzle to me . . . is this: How came it that Ireland sank into that utter state of barbarism after the English invasion? War and murder may do a great deal to make nations wretched, but how are we to believe that the fine arts got wiped out in a land filled with lovely and lively people, male and female?' (p. 175).

In a letter to Arthur Thomas Froggatt dated *c.* 1892 by Vignoles (pp. 188–9), Stewart is candid on the impoverished condition of art music in Ireland: 'And yet Dublin is a little like a capital city, so far as a set of Government, big buildings, handsome environs, railways and tram-cars go. All these, however, cannot get us a good orchestra, and I miss that a great deal. Ireland is not a musical country. The people, of course, will tell you she is.' Despite his political *naïveté*, Stewart was well placed to perceive the discrepancy between common assent and conditions as they actually stood.

30   Stewart passionately defended *The Ring* (1876) in an article addressed to the editor of the *Musical Standard* dated 29 May 1882.

31   For details of this performance, see Vignoles, *Memoir of Sir Robert P. Stewart*, pp. 17–19, which includes an account of the preparations and the participation of some ten musical societies: 'Hibernian Catch Club, Anacreontic, University Choral Society, Orpheus Society, Amateur Harmonic, Amateur Melophonic, Dublin Madrigal, The Society of Antient Concerts, Ladies' Choral Society, Philharmonic Brass Band'. This polonian catalogue indicates the pervasively amateur status of art music in Ireland, *c.* 1850. See Ita Beausang, 'Dublin Musical Societies, 1850–1900', in Patrick F. Devine and Harry White (eds.), *The Maynooth International Musicological Conference 1995: Selected Proceedings, Part Two (Irish Musical Studies 5)* (Dublin, 1996), pp. 169–78.

32   Ryan, 'Nationalism and Music in Ireland', p. 197.

33   *Freeman's Journal*, 8 November 1851, p. 1, cited in Ryan, 'Nationalism and Music in Ireland', p. 197.

34   Ryan, 'Nationalism and Music in Ireland', p. 197.

35   Further research on this matter of replication along religious lines is required, but the examples considered here would suggest that the practice was widespread, if not pervasive.

36   For further on the state of Irish music education in the nineteenth century, see Ryan, 'Nationalism and Music in Ireland', pp. 188–95, on which this account is largely based. See also Marie McCarthy, 'The Transmission of Music and the

Formation of National Identity in Early Twentieth-Century Ireland', in Patrick F. Devine and Harry White (eds.), *The Maynooth International Musicological Conference 1995: Selected Proceedings, Part Two* (Dublin, 1996), pp. 146–59, and the same author's 'Music Education and the Quest for Cultural Identity in Ireland, 1831–1989' (diss., University of Michigan, 1990).

37    It is instructive to contrast the marginal condition of art music in Ireland with the consensus of interest in Britain identified by Percy Young:

> 'During the later nineteenth century in Britain music was insecure, but whatever separatist tendencies there might have been, there could be descried a certain community of interest and understanding. *The basic vocabulary of the popular ballads was that of the oratorio.* The cult of classical music, through the prestigious acquisition of domestic pianos, was widespread. Those of the working classes who aspired towards middle-class values took their culture as seriously as circumstances permitted. *There was, in fact, no segregation of musical tastes.*

'Young, *A History of British Music*, p. 525 (my italics). No more contradictory state of affairs in relation to music in Ireland could realistically be envisaged.

38    Ryan, 'Nationalism and Music in Ireland', p. 203.

39    'Music in Dublin', *Hibernia*, 2 January 1882, p. 7.

40    'Music in Dublin', pp. 6–7.

41    'Music in Dublin', p. 7.

42    See note 23 above and the epilogue below.

43    Cited in Harry Plunket Greene, *Charles Villiers Stanford* (London, 1935), p. 37.

44    Charles Villiers Stanford (1852–1924). Born in Dublin and educated there and in Cambridge, where he later became professor of music (1885). After a period of study in Leipzig and Berlin he achieved initial success as a composer in London. Appointed professor of composition at the Royal College of Music from its foundation (1883) where he remained for over forty years. Knighted in 1902. A full-length study of his life and works by Jeremy Dibble is currently in preparation for Oxford University Press.

45    In Dan H. Laurence (ed.), *Shaw's Music (The Bodley Head Bernard Shaw), The Complete Musical Criticism in Three Volumes* (London, 1981), Vol. 1 (1876–90), p. 515. The original source is an unsigned note in the *Pall Mall Gazette*, dated 15 May 1888 (Laurence).

46    For an example see Shaw's essay on the *Irish Symphony*, 'a record of fearful conflict between the aboriginal Celt and the professor', published in *The World*, 10 May 1893, and reproduced in Laurence, *Shaw's Music*, Vol. 3, pp. 876–83.

47    I follow here Carl Dahlhaus in *Nineteenth Century Music*, trans. J. Bradford Robinson (Berkeley, 1989), p. 38: 'Nationalistic music, it seems, invariably arises as an expression of a politically-motivated need, which tends to appear when national independence is being sought, denied or jeopardised, rather than attained or consolidated . . .' This reading of nationalism in music as it applies to Ireland clearly excludes Stanford as a 'nationalist' composer.

48    Ryan, 'Nationalism and Music in Ireland', p. 258.

49    For a discussion of Stanford's collaboration with Alfred Perceval Graves in the arranging and adaptation of Irish airs, see Greene, *Charles Villiers Stanford*, pp. 160ff. His editions of Moore and Petrie (*The Complete Petrie Collection of Irish Music* [London, 1902–5]) are hampered by his lack of Irish, but nevertheless

testify to his enduring commitment to the preservation of the ethnic repertory. Greene's emphatic conclusion that 'Stanford was not a collector, he was a musician with a genius for the setting of his country's tunes' (p. 182) is underpinned by the (correct) assumption that Stanford's cultural position in relation to the ethnic repertory remained exogamous. See also Stanford, 'Some Thoughts Concerning Folk Song and Nationality', *The Musical Quarterly*, No. 2, Vol. 1 (1915), pp. 232–45.

50 See Ryan, 'Nationalism and Music in Ireland', p. 258.

51 This work, of all Stanford's compositions, perhaps most easily illustrates his untroubled juxtaposition of Brahmsian pastiche and the arrangement of traditional airs.

52 A sensitive appraisal of Stanford which reflects this tendency can be found in Ryan, 'Nationalism and Music in Ireland', pp. 243ff. See also Axel Klein, 'Irish Composers and Foreign Education: A Study of Influences', in Patrick F. Devine and Harry White (eds.), *The Maynooth International Musicological Conference 1995: Selected Proceedings, Part One (Irish Musical Studies* 4) (Dublin, 1996), pp. 271–84.

53 Arnold Bax, *Farewell, My Youth*, in Foreman (ed.), *Farewell, My Youth*, p. 22.

54 Young, *A History of British Music*, p. 517.

55 Shaw, cited in Young, *A History of British Music*, p. 524.

56 See Ryan, 'Nationalism and Music in Ireland', p. 253, for a discussion of the first rhapsody and the fourth (the 'Ulster') which clarifies the extent of Stanford's use of the traditional repertory in these works.

57 Aloys Fleischmann's observations on Stanford in 1935 provide a postscript to this failure: '. . . even English critics have nowadays become aware of Stanford's inability to rid himself of the stage-Irishman's conception of his country, and of the extent to which the folk-song element in his music is ingrafted, and obviously so, rather than an inherent growth' (see 'The Outlook of Music in Ireland', *Studies*, Vol. 24 [March 1935], p. 124).

58 See note 10 above.

59 See note 15 above and Jochum, *A Classified Bibliography, passim*.

60 The Royal Dublin Society, founded in 1731, began to promote recitals of chamber music in 1886. Its objective being 'to aid in the development of an enlightened musical taste', it provided a forum for art music which was remote from the ferment of Irish cultural revival but which was indispensable to what support there was for the European musical aesthetic.

61 See chapter 4 above.

62 Rogers, 'An Irish School of Music', p. 150.

63 Rogers, 'An Irish School of Music', p. 152.

64 The account of the Feis Ceoil given here follows Ryan, 'Nationalism and Music in Ireland', pp. 284ff.

65 Ryan, 'Nationalism and Music in Ireland', p. 291.

66 From the *Freeman's Journal*, 17 May 1897, p. 2.

67 From the *Freeman's Journal*, 18 May 1897, p. 5.

68 In this respect it is interesting to note the list of adjudicators recorded by the *Freeman's Journal* in the year when Hamilton Harty's *Irish Symphony* was entered in the festival's composition category: the adjudicators in that year (1904) included three professors from the Royal Academy of Music (Alberto Randeg-

ger, Luigi Denga, Willy Hess), Franklin Taylor, professor at the Royal College of Music and G.R. Sinclair, organist of Hereford Cathedral. Such names represent the pedagogical *status quo* of the British musical establishment in the early years of the twentieth century.

69    For details of these competitions, which featured works by Carl Hardebeck, Michele Esposito and Hamilton Harty (among others), see Ryan, 'Nationalism and Music in Ireland', pp. 294ff. A full-scale history of the Feis Ceoil would determine the extent to which these composition competitions reflected the influence of the literary revival and contributed to the emancipation of an Irish art music.

70    Michele Esposito (1855–1929), a brilliantly gifted pianist from Naples, studied piano and composition at the conservatory there and later moved to Paris to further his career. According to the testimony of John Larchet, a pupil and later his close colleague, it was on the advice of Saint-Saëns that Esposito came to Ireland to assume a temporary appointment at the Royal Irish Academy of Music. He remained in Ireland until shortly before his death. Throughout his long career he dominated music in Dublin as a pianist, teacher and composer for almost half a century. His enormous impact on standards of keyboard playing at the Academy, his promotion of and participation in annual chamber music concerts at the Royal Dublin Society and his founding of the Dublin Orchestral Society (1899) collectively transformed both the quality and consistency of public music-making in Dublin.

T.W. Rolleston (1857–1920) was a figure of some importance in the literary revival. He was instrumental in the founding of the Irish Literary Society of London (1891) and the National Literary Society in Dublin (1892). In 1885 he founded *The Dublin University Review*.

71    *Deirdre* (Irish Musical Festival Prize Cantata, 1897), words by T.W. Rolleston. Music by M. Esposito. Vocal score (Dublin, n.d. [1897?]) [p. 1].

72    The work is discussed in Ryan, 'Nationalism and Music in Ireland', pp. 301–4.

73    See *Roseen Dhu*, Irish vocal suite, lyrics by Alfred Perceval Graves, adapted from old Irish airs by Michele Esposito, op. 49 (London, n.d. [1901]) [p. iii].

74    Raymond Warren, 'Orchestral Music', in David Greer (ed.), *Hamilton Harty: His Life and Music* (Belfast, 1979), p. 89. Herbert Hamilton Harty (1879–1941) was a student of Esposito before establishing a reputation in Britain as a conductor and arranger. Some of his most important compositions are notably concerned with Irish themes or inspired by Irish mythology.

75    'It was more the certainty of a good performance than the actual prize that appealed to me and to others . . . who competed for these prizes' (Harty, in David Greer [ed.], *Early Memories* [Belfast, 1979], pp. 28–9).

76    Ryan, 'Nationalism and Music in Ireland', p. 316.

77    For an extended appraisal of the genesis, structure and early reception of this work, see David Greer, 'The Composition of *The Children of Lir*', in Gerard Gillen and Harry White (eds.), *Musicology in Ireland* (*Irish Musical Studies* 1) (Dublin, 1990), pp. 74–98.

78    Arnold Bax, 'Ancient Dominions', in Foreman (ed.), *Farewell, my Youth*, p. 138.

79    Lewis Foreman, *Bax: A Composer and His Times* (Aldershot, 1983), p. 27.

80    Lewis Foreman, *Bax: A Composer and His Times*, p. 25.

81    Lewis Foreman, *Bax: A Composer and His Times*, p. 21. My account of Bax's career follows this work.

82   See Foreman, *Bax*, p. 27: 'The songs of the peasant people made an immediate effect on Bax, . . . The, to him, horrific example of Stanford ensured that he would try to absorb the essence of Irish music into his own without merely quoting it . . . Under the influence of Ireland Bax's music immediately found direction.'

83   Lewis Foreman states that 'Although Ireland would fascinate Bax for the rest of his life, *St Patrick's Breastplate* [1923] is his last overt demonstration of emotional involvement with things Irish. He celebrated Ireland's achievement of statehood, and could then relax and divert his energies into other paths' (*Bax*, p. 203).

84   In Foreman (ed.), *Farewell, My Youth*, p. 99.

85   In Foreman (ed.), *Farewell, My Youth*, p. 99.

86   For a richly xenophobic characterisation of 'the Itinerant German Philharmonic Society, facetiously termed "Feis Ceoil"', see the *All Ireland Review*, 30 June 1900, p. 5, cited in Ryan, 'Nationalism and Music in Ireland', pp. 297–8.

87   This argument is taken up in the epilogue to the present study. Lewis Foreman identifies Bax's horn call with that used by Elgar in his incidental music to the Yeats–Moore play *Diarmuid and Grania* (1901). See Foreman, *Bax*, p. 61.

88   In Foreman (ed.), *Farewell, My Youth*, p. 87. For an extended appraisal of Bax's literary career, see Foreman, *Bax*, 'Appendix A: Dermot O'Byrne', pp. 378–82.

89   Cited in Foreman, *Bax*, p. 381. It is perhaps significant that this assessment was deleted from the second edition of Boyd's study, when 'Dermot O'Byrne' had faded from view.

90   Foreman, *Bax*, p. 381.

91   W.B. Yeats, 'Samhain: 1903', in *Explorations* (London, 1905), p. 13.

92   See Foreman (ed.), *Farewell, My Youth*, p. 133: Bax made this remark in the course of his foreword to *Music in Ireland*.

93   Foreman, *Bax*, p. 381.

94   Foreman, *Bax*, p. 139. Foreman quotes a letter from Bax to Tilly Fleischmann in which he remarks that 'Willy Yeats told me in a public drawing-room that "A Dublin Ballad 1916" was a masterpiece, and this has pleased me more than any praise my music has received!' (*Bax*, p. 379).

95   In Foreman (ed.), *Farewell, My Youth*, p. 95.

96   See Foreman, *Bax*, p. 443.

97   See Foreman, *Bax*, p. 111.

98   *Music in Ireland*, p. iii.

# Seán Ó Riada and the Crisis of Modernism in Irish Music

1   Otto Beck in *Langrishe Go Down* by Aidan Higgins (London, 1978). Higgins's novel is set in Ireland in the 1930s; Beck, a German student, refers to the absence of music as an index of Ireland's cultural isolation from Europe.

2   John Larchet, 'A Plea for Music', in W. Fitzgerald (ed.), *The Voice of Ireland* (Dublin and London, n.d. [1923?]), p. 509.

3   Aloys Fleischmann, 'Historical Survey', in Aloys Fleischmann (ed.), *Music in Ireland: A Symposium* (Cork and Oxford, 1952), p. 6.

4   Denis Donoghue, 'The Future of Irish Music', *Studies*, Vol. 44 (Spring 1955), p. 111. Donoghue is here closely paraphrasing Bax's remarks in the foreword to

*Music in Ireland* (as note 3 above). In this article, Donoghue not only repudiates folk music as a direct source of compositional style; he also urges a radical appraisal of music education in Ireland by which the reception of art music would prevail over the instruction of mediocre performers: 'The truth is that while Ireland is full of failed pianists, the number of mature, appreciative listeners is still comparatively small. We can manage without piano-dabblers, but we cannot do without appreciative audiences' (pp. 113–14). It is fair to say that the validity of this assertion has rarely been grasped in Irish music education.

5    Louis Marcus, 'Seán Ó Riada and the Ireland of the Sixties', in Bernard Harris and Grattan Freyer (eds.), *Integrating Tradition: The Achievement of Seán Ó Riada* (Ballina and Pennsylvania, 1982), p. 22. Marcus here undoubtedly overstates the case, given the achievements of Stanford in particular, but the originality and flair of Ó Riada's scoring, and above all else his projection of traditional melodies whole and entire, stand radically apart from the long tradition of orchestral arrangement of Irish music.

6    The fair copy of this work held in the library of the National Symphony Orchestra (formerly the Radio Telefís Éireann Symphony Orchestra) attributes the work to John Reidy. Ó Riada ceased to employ the anglicised form of his name from about 1960. Although the published score of *Hercules* (Dublin. Woodtown Press, 1970) attributes the work to 'Seán Ó Riada', the original inscription aptly symbolises the independence of this work from any material reference to the ethnic tradition.

7    See the passages from Ó Riada, *Our Musical Heritage* (broadcast 1962; published Portlaoise 1982) discussed below. In a major interview between Ó Riada and Charles Acton published in *Éire–Ireland*, Vol. 6, No. 1 (1971), pp. 106–14, Ó Riada's disdain for the European tradition of art music is particularly shrill: 'Beethoven couldn't write a tune to save his life and most of the European composers likewise. And when they did they were but cheap vulgar tunes' (p. 112).

8    Ó Riada wrote six *nomoi* in total, beginning with *Hercules Dux Ferrariae*. He derived the title *nomos* from Paul Henry Lang's usage in *Music in Western Civilisation* (1941) to describe a composition 'strictly following the laws of classical aesthetics'. According to Charles Acton, Ó Riada was attracted to the term because it avoided any connotation of dependence on established genres including the symphony and the concerto. (See Acton, 'Seán Ó Riada: The Next Phase', *Éire–Ireland*, Vol. 2, No. 4 [1967], p. 116.) Acton remarks in this interview that *Nomos no. 2* 'can be considered as a young composer's farewell to the European music of his formal training via a pessimistic text from Sophocles' (p. 121).

9    The work of Ó Riada's contemporaries and immediate predecessors, including Seóirse Bodley, Brian Boydell, John Kinsella, James Wilson, Gerard Victory and perhaps most significantly A.J. Potter, comprises a vital contribution to the history of Irish music to 1970. But this contribution must be distinguished from the *cultural* history of music in Ireland, at least for the purposes of this study. For a detailed survey of the educational background and stylistic development of Ó Riada's contemporaries and immediate predecessors, see Axel Klein, *Die Musik Irlands im 20. Jahrhundert* (Hildesheim, 1996) and 'Irish Composers and Foreign Education: A Study of Influences', in Patrick F. Devine and Harry White (eds.), *The Maynooth International Musicological Conference 1995: Selected Proceedings, Part One (Irish Musical Studies 4)* (Dublin, 1996), 271–84.

10    Terence Brown's reading of 'the prevailing republican creed' of Ireland in the 1930s and 1940s is that 'the ancient Gaelic nation had finally thrown off the thrall of foreign subjugation and that her true destiny lay in cultivating her national distinctiveness as assiduously as possible' (Terence Brown, *Ireland: A Social and Cultural History 1922–79* [London, 1981], p. 146). The cultural enforcement of Irish language revival certainly led to what Brown describes as 'the elevation of Irish traditional music to a position of official esteem, second only to the Irish language' (p. 146), but this narrow regard, like the revival itself, did not reflect the actual condition of music, traditional or otherwise, in Ireland. The Oireachtas continued to attract competitors for its annual festivals and the Irish Folk Song Society continued to produce its journal, but neither body much affected the growth of a musical consciousness that was in any case constricted by the blinkered, platitudinous nationalism of Ireland in the 1930s.

11    Brown, *Ireland: A Social and Cultural History*, p. 158. The contradiction urged by Sean O'Faolain in particular between de Valera's vision of Ireland (which found its most eloquent apologist in Daniel Corkery) and his own can be briefly formulated. It was a contradiction between Catholic, nationalist Ireland and Ireland as a modern, newly emancipated European state. The cultural implications of this contradiction were sharply apparent, especially in music.

12    Sean O'Faolain, 'A Broken World', cited in Brown, *Ireland: A Social and Cultural History* , p. 159.

13    Aloys Fleischmann, 'Ars Nova', *Ireland Today*, Vol. 1 (July 1936), p. 41.

14    Aloys Fleischmann (1910–92), composer, musicologist, conductor. Fleischmann was born in Munich of German parents who had settled in Cork; educated in Ireland and Germany and appointed professor of music at University College, Cork, where he held the chair from 1934 until 1980.

15    John Francis Larchet (1884–1967), composer, music educator and conductor. Larchet was musical director of the Abbey Theatre from 1908 to 1934, professor of music at University College, Dublin, from 1921 until 1958 and senior professor of composition at the Royal Irish Academy of Music from 1920 until 1955 (in succession to Michele Esposito).

16    Frederick May (1911–85), composer and pianist. A student of Larchet; educated subsequently in London and Vienna. He succeeded Larchet for a time as musical director at the Abbey Theatre and was a founder member of the Music(al) Association of Ireland in 1939.

17    Eamonn Ó Gallochobair (1906–82), composer, broadcaster, conductor, critic. Educated in Dublin, musical director at the Abbey Theatre in succession to May. Subsequently assistant music director, Radio Éireann.

18    Brian Patrick Boydell (1917–), composer, teacher, music historian. Educated in Dublin and London; on the staff of the Royal Irish Academy of Music from the late 1940s; held the chair of music at Trinity College, Dublin, from 1962 until 1982.

19    Larchet, 'A Plea for Music', p. 508.

20    Larchet, 'A Plea for Music', p. 508. For further information on Larchet and an assessment of his career and compositions, see Joseph Ryan, 'Nationalism and Music in Ireland' (PhD diss., National University of Ireland, 1991), pp. 350–73. Larchet has not yet received the detailed consideration which his influence as an educator and teacher of composition demands.

21   This preoccupation found its most significant outlet in Larchet's activities as a teacher of composition.

22   Ryan, 'Nationalism and Music in Ireland', p. 371.

23   Larchet's authority as a teacher allowed him to distinguish between musical instruction and music education: a distinction barely recognised in Ireland during his lifetime. His conviction that 'One hour's lecture a week to the whole school will do more to create a real love of music in our children than any other form of study' was a rarely articulated commitment to the importance of musical awareness (as against the attainment of technical proficiency): 'When every child on leaving school will have an understanding of music and a knowledge of how to listen to it intelligently, then the future of Ireland as a musical nation will be secure.' (See John Larchet, 'Music in the Secondary Schools', in Fleischmann [ed.], Music in Ireland, p. 36.) The failure to grasp this distinction between education and instruction is perhaps the major deficiency in Irish music education of the twentieth century.

24   Aloys Fleischmann, 'Composition and the Folk Idiom', Ireland Today, Vol. 1 (November 1936), p. 42; cited in Ryan, 'Nationalism and Music in Ireland', p. 419. Fleischmann's satirical indictment of 'the traditional outlook' compellingly prefigures the attenuation of Ó Riada's compositional technique: 'The advocates of the traditional outlook relieve their devotees of all hard labour, of prolonged dealings with contrapuntal and fugal intricacies, of the study of the musical literature of the past, not to mention that of contemporary movements. A few folk tunes, as much knowledge of composition as may be gained in an elementary harmony class, and for their purposes the equipment of the youthful prodigy is complete. He can be sent out to missionarise, as an authority and a composer, while, but for his outlook, the technique of composition awaits his beck and call, for him to acquire if he had the brains and the will' (p. 44). Of course Fleischmann's attack is directed against the cult of folksong arrangement, especially given its status in the Ireland of the 1930s, but his remarks speak also to Ó Riada's disavowal of Europe a generation afterwards. The occasionally tiresome but rarely ephemeral debate on the nature and development of Irish music conducted throughout this period in journals such as The Bell, Studies, Ireland Today and The Dublin Magazine plainly attests to a degree of awareness which deserves to be better researched today.

25   Frederick May, 'Music and the Nation', The Dublin Magazine, Vol. 11 (July–September 1936), p. 51.

26   I follow here Ryan and Brown respectively in their accounts of the Dublin Philharmonic Society and the cultural significance of Radio Éireann. See Brown, Ireland: A Social and Cultural History, pp. 208–9, and Ryan, 'Nationalism and Music in Ireland', pp. 379–95. The fundamental importance to music in Ireland of Radio Éireann demands a full-scale study which has yet to be undertaken.

27   The Bell, nevertheless, occasionally aired discussion of the ideology of Irish music, as in an exchange between John Beckett and Aloys Fleischmann published in Vol. 17 of the journal (1951–2) which centred upon Beckett's impatient rejection of Harty and Moeran as composers who refused to countenance 'the disintegration of the tradition of their art', and Fleischmann's exasperated rejoinder: 'If membership of the twelve note school is the important criterion in assessing composition, one may assume that in dealing with the English scene

the work of Britten and Rawsthorne would be classed as "redundant", while Elizabeth Lutyens would rank as a harbinger to the new millennium.' One may note in passing that the tendentious prestige of serialism which is debated in this exchange undermined the *a priori* dispute between the ideologies of 'folk' and 'art' music. This development was to prove significant in Seán Ó Riada's struggle with modernism and its potential address upon Irish music. See John Beckett, 'Music', *The Bell*, Vol 17, No. 2 (1951), pp. 56–9, and A. Fleischmann, 'Letters to the Editor [Music]', *The Bell*, Vol 17, No. 2 (1951), pp. 53–5.

28   Brian Boydell, 'The Future of Music in Ireland', *The Bell*, Vol. 16, No. 4 (1951), p. 21.

29   Boydell, 'The Future of Music', p. 23: 'This development of the top layer of musical activity at the expense of more general encouragement has also a great deal to do with its cretinous growth, for since the public have never been introduced to music in their school days, the small percentage that discover it by chance can only form an audience for its support in the largest towns.'

30   Boydell, 'The Future of Music', p. 25.

31   Boydell, 'The Future of Music', pp. 26–8.

32   See notes 3 and 4 above.

33   Fleischmann, *Music in Ireland*, p. 9.

34   Fleischmann, *Music in Ireland*, p. 84.

35   The contributors to *Music in Ireland* include Larchet, Boydell, Frederick May and Eamonn Ó Gallochobair. But the book also gains strength from other contributors directly engaged with the music profession in Ireland, including the concert pianist Charles Lynch, whose beguiling tact (reminiscent of Larchet in particular) does not eclipse a record of poor performance conditions throughout most of the country (together with the familiar plea for an adequate concert hall in the capital city).

36   For a cogent summary of May's position see his contribution to *Music in Ireland*, 'The Composer in Ireland', pp. 164–77. May's comparisons between postwar Vienna and Dublin strikingly endorse the general picture of impoverished musical infrastructures in Ireland; they also focus upon the lack of financial support for Irish composers as against their contemporaries in Finland and Sweden: 'A composer who tried to make a living by composition in Ireland would be inviting death by slow, or perhaps not so slow, starvation' (p. 168).

37   For a particularly sensitive appraisal of this work and of May's compositional development as a whole, see Ryan, 'Nationalism and Music in Ireland', pp. 404–11 and 425–30.

38   See the article by Fleischmann cited in note 27 above for a bleak account of the reception afforded to contemporary styles and techniques of composition in Ireland up to and including the early 1950s. The string quartet remained unpublished until it was issued by the Contemporary Music Centre (Dublin) in 1986.

39   See May, 'The Composer in Ireland', p. 169: 'one of the most destructive and useless types of criticism is that which starts out from an unwarrantable premise, such that all good music must be demonstrably national in feeling, and then proceeds to chain down the unfortunate composer on this ready-made bed of Procrustes'. Given that May's circumstances constrained him to arrange Irish melodies rather than pursue the modernism of the string quartet, it is not hard to understand his sustained polemic (much of it conducted in *The Bell*)

against the blinkered reliance on the ethnic tradition as a yardstick of compositional relevance.

40  *Music in Ireland*, pp. 210–17.

41  *Music in Ireland*, p. 212.

42  Eamonn Ó Gallochobair, 'Atavism', *Ireland Today*, Vol. 1 (September 1936), p. 57, quoted in Ryan, 'Nationalism and Music in Ireland', p. 420.

43  See Ryan, 'Nationalism and Music in Ireland', p. 448.

44  Ryan, 'Nationalism and Music in Ireland', p. 422. One might want to add that it is difficult to arrive at any comprehensive assessment of Ó Gallochobair's work, given how little of it has received even the smallest scrutiny.

45  Ó Riada, *Our Musical Heritage*, p. 21.

46  Ó Riada, *Our Musical Heritage*, p. 2.

47  Acton, 'Seán Ó Riada: The Next Phase', p. 115.

48  Acton, 'Seán Ó Riada: The Next Phase', p. 119.

49  Acton, 'Seán Ó Riada: The Next Phase', p. 115.

50  See Aloys Fleischmann, 'Seán Ó Riada', *Counterpoint* (November 1971), p. 13: '. . .there is little connection between his music in traditional vein and his original compositions. In the orchestral work *Seoladh na nGamhan* [1959], this cleavage comes to a head, in so far as the first and last sections are almost wholly traditional while the middle section is strictly serial, and though each section is effective in itself, the contrasting elements remain irreconcilable. In his perceptive obituary tribute Mr Gerard Victory suggested that the pessimism of *Nomos II* was due to the composer's sense of frustration at the impasse which he was facing to-day, and though the pessimism of this work emanates from the Sophocles text itself, it is true that Seán Ó Riada in the last few years produced a diminishing amount of original music, and devoted all his time and energy to traditionally-based work. With twenty or thirty years of achievement ahead of him he might well have bridged the gap. The loss with his passing is unimaginable.' I quote this obituary at length because I judge it to be characteristically perceptive as to both Ó Riada's potential and the actuality of his accomplishment.

51  In Acton, 'Interview with Seán Ó Riada', p. 111.

52  See Harris and Freyer (eds.), *Integrating Tradition*, p. 134 (interview between Grattan Freyer and Paddy Moloney).

53  The possibilities of development attached not only to Ó Riada's ensemble, but famously to The Chieftains, whose players (under Paddy Moloney) effectively comprised a regrouping of Ceoltóirí Cualann after the latter's dissolution.

54  No reliable or complete catalogue of Ó Riada's works has yet been published: incomplete listings are available in Harris and Freyer (eds.), *Integrating Tradition*, and in Tomás Ó Canáinn and Gearóid Mac an Bhua, *Seán Ó Riada: A Shaol agus a Shaothar* (Baile Átha Cliath, 1993).

55  Gearóid Mac an Bhua (Gerard Victory) notes in *Seán Ó Riada: A Shaol agus a Shaothar*, p. 171, that apart from the chamber piece *Nomos no. 6*, commissioned by the Belfast Music Festival in 1966, Ó Riada wrote no further music in the European tradition beyond 1963 (the year in which *Nomos no. 2* was completed). This does not of course include the two mass settings (1968 and 1970), which must rank as original compositions, but not in the European sense of that term.

56    Ó Riada, *Our Musical Heritage*, p. 20.

57    The 'coda' to Ó Riada's lectures (he seems to have been unaware of the irony implicit in this usage) is a particularly disagreeable address, bombastically given to a crassly worded politicisation of the ethnic repertory.

58    Brown, *Ireland: A Social and Cultural History*, p. 314.

59    See note 5 above.

60    Marcus, 'Seán Ó Riada and the Ireland of the Sixties', p. 16ff. (my italics).

61    See Marcus, 'Seán Ó Riada and the Ireland of the Sixties', p. 20.

62    Isolation did not entail neglect in Ó Riada's case. The issue rather is the extent to which Ó Riada's increasingly exclusive preoccupation with traditional melodies influenced the perception of art music in Ireland.

63    Gráinne Yeats comments on a notable change of style and approach to Carolan in Ó Riada's final recording (*Ó Riada's Farewell*) in which his solo harpsichord renditions are a good deal less extrovert and more introspective than those featured in his performances with Ceoltóirí Cualann. See Harris and Freyer (eds.), *Integrating Tradition*, pp. 85–6.

64    Marcus, 'Seán Ó Riada and the Ireland of the Sixties', pp. 19–20. It is quite clear from Ó Riada's contemporaries – Marcus, Seán Mac Réamoinn, Seán Lucy, Tomás Mac Anna, George Morrison – that his reputation rested in the main on the spectacular success of the film scores and the recordings and performances associated with Ceoltóirí Cualann. It was this music which endowed Ó Riada with the prestige usually reserved in Ireland for writers, whereas his original compositions – and his increasing lack thereof – engaged far less attention. The dismay registered by a very few commentators (such as Charles Acton) when the success of Ó Riada's performances more and more certainly entailed the failure of his original voice was a matter of irrelevance as far as Ó Riada's general standing was concerned. This is what makes the assessments of Marcus and Acton so significant. (See also my reading of Seamus Heaney's poem 'In Memoriam Sean O'Riada' in the epilogue to this study.)

65    Seán Ó Riada, 'An Open Letter to Charles Acton' (1971), in Harris and Freyer (eds.), *Integrating Tradition*, p. 151.

66    Charles Acton, 'A Reply to Seán Ó Riada' (1971), in Harris and Freyer (eds.), *Integrating Tradition*, p. 158.

67    These remarks are based on the score lodged in the National Symphony Orchestra library (National Concert Hall, Dublin) and the (tape) recording of the first performance (1965) held in the gramophone library of Radio Telefís Éireann. I have been unable to trace a second performance of the work: an index, perhaps, of the reception afforded to Ó Riada's achievement as an original composer in the European tradition, despite his acclaim in other spheres.

68    *Nomos no. 4*, which is in effect a piano concerto, is foremost in importance among these works.

69    See Acton, 'Seán Ó Riada: The Next Phase', p. 121.

70    In his account of the cultural significance of Gael Linn in the revival movement of the 1950s and 1960s, Terence Brown singles out the first two of these films and Ó Riada's music in particular as 'immensely popular' manifestations of cultural nationalism. See Brown, *Ireland: A Social and Cultural History,* pp. 230–1.

71    *Mise Éire* was the first feature-length film made in the Irish language. In *Cinema and Ireland*, by Kevin Rockett, Luke Gibbons and John Hill (New York, 1988), Ó

Riada's music is briefly acknowledged as contributing to the emotional depiction of high nationalism which the film celebrates (p. 86). Given that *Cinema and Ireland* advertises itself as the 'first comprehensive study of the cinema in Ireland and of representations of Ireland on the cinema screen', it is scarcely surprising that Ó Riada's music for cinema and television has enjoyed little scrutiny to date.

72    Ó Riada's use of the horn is particularly striking in both scores: its prominence as a solo instrument which carries the weight of romantic projection is exactly similar in each case.

73    Quoted in Marcus, 'Seán Ó Riada and the Ireland of the Sixties', p. 21.

74    Marcus, 'Seán Ó Riada and the Ireland of the Sixties', p. 21.

75    This is the description of *Ó Riada's Farewell*, the composer's final recording, given in Harris and Freyer (eds.), *Integrating Tradition*, pp. 204–5.

76    This review and the correspondence which ensued is reproduced in Harris and Freyer (eds.), *Integrating Tradition*, pp. 145–60.

77    In a calmer exchange between Acton and the composer published in *Éire–Ireland* in 1967 (see note 7 above), Ó Riada remarked that although his work with Ceoltóirí Cualann was finished, 'the European tradition can struggle along with me for the time being' (p. 113).

78    See Charles Acton, 'Seán Ó Riada: Changed Sound of Irish Traditional Music' (slightly revised obituary notice from *The Irish Times*, 4 October 1971), in Harris and Freyer (eds.), *Integrating Tradition*, p. 163.

79    The tributes by Seán Mac Réamoinn and Seán Lucy included in Harris and Freyer (eds.), *Integrating Tradition*, pp. 8–14, typify the tone and style of such assessments.

80    It is vital to my argument to emphasise a distinction between the inherent achievement of Ó Riada's contemporaries in composition and the *reception* of that achievement in Ireland. It is the latter, of course, which is of particular account in cultural history.

## Epilogue: Music and the Irish Literary Imagination

1    An earlier version of this epilogue appears in Gerard Gillen and Harry White (eds.), *Music and Irish Cultural History* (Irish Musical Studies 3) (Dublin, 1993), pp. 212–27.

2    Seamus Deane, 'Poetry and Song 1800–1890', *The Field Day Anthology of Irish Writing* (Derry, 1991), Vol. 2, pp. 4–5.

3    See the discussion of Moore's writings and the excerpt from *Intolerance* cited in chapter 2 of this study.

4    Cited in Ann Saddlemyer, 'Synge's Soundscape', *Irish University Review*, Vol. 22, No. 1 (1992), p. 62.

5    Cited in Saddlemyer, 'Synge's Soundscape', p. 62.

6    See especially the reading of *Riders to the Sea* offered in 'Synge's Soundscape', pp. 63–5. A new study of Synge's *The Aran Islands* (1907) hypothesises that the book is organised according to the principles of sonata-allegro form. See William E. Hart, *Synge's First Symphony: The Aran Islands* (Connecticut, 1993).

7    See Katharine Worth, *The Irish Drama of Europe from Yeats to Beckett* (London, 1978), pp. 125ff.

8   For a useful introduction to this topic see Matthew Hodgart and Mabel Worthington, *Song in the Works of James Joyce* (New York, 1959).

9   Joyce's exploitation of the associative powers of music to summon emotion and feeling is particularly intense in 'The Dead'. The story depends on music as a code of deeply felt remembrance, particularly in regard to Greta Conroy's love for Michael Furey and the distance which this (long past) relationship interposes between Greta and her husband, Gabriel. The singing of *The Lass of Aughrim* vividly reanimates the significance of this relationship and dominates the long internal monologue (narrative voice) with which the story ends. The impact of the ballad is all the greater because of the gradual force of recollection which gathers through the story by means of successive musical elements, songs and anecdotes.

10   A detailed discussion of the sheer presence of music in *Ulysses* obviously lies beyond the scope of this epilogue. But it is relevant to the central argument of this book to indicate that Joyce's reliance on music is not confined to the referential impact of musical allusion: Bloom's deliberations during Mass in All Hallows College in the 'Lotuseaters' episode, for example, affords a rare instance of European musical sensibility in Irish fiction. Bloom casually thinks of sacred music (Mercadante, Mozart, Palestrina) as an exact correlative of the kind of pictorial art and statuary which flourished under papal patronage.

11   The Chopin–Joyce comparison sustained in chapter 3 of this study speaks to this argument. In either case, the artist depended on pre-existent musical material. In Ireland, the condition of music was such that it produced an original *literature* of international significance. Given the developments examined in this book, no such achievement in music was possible.

12   Douglas Dunn, 'Real Presences', *The Irish Times*, 1 June 1991, Weekend Supplement, p. 9.

13   Seamus Heaney, 'In Memoriam Sean O'Riada', *Field Work* (London, 1979), p. 30. All subsequent quotations are from this edition.

14   This is particularly true of postwar Irish drama. See Harry White, 'Brian Friel, Thomas Murphy and the Use of Music in Contemporary Irish Drama', *Modern Drama*, Vol. 33 (1990), pp. 553–62. The function of music in Samuel Beckett is another important instance which deserves scrutiny. See Mary Bryden (ed.), *Samuel Beckett and Music* (Oxford, 1998), including Harry White, ' "Something is Taking its Course": Dramatic Exactitude and Paradigm of Serialism in Samuel Beckett', pp. 159–71.

# BIBLIOGRAPHY

Acton, Charles, 'Seán Ó Riada: The Next Phase', Éire–Ireland, Vol. 2, No. 4
(1967), pp. 113–22.

—— 'Interview with Seán Ó Riada', Éire–Ireland, Vol. 6, No. 1 (1971), pp.
106–14.

—— 'A Reply to Seán Ó Riada', in Harris and Freyer (eds.), Integrating Tradition: The Achievement of Seán Ó Riada, pp. 153–60.

—— 'Seán Ó Riada: Changed Sound of Irish Traditional Music', in Harris and
Freyer (eds.), Integrating Tradition: The Achievement of Seán Ó Riada, pp.
161–64.

Anon, 'Music in Dublin', Hibernia, 2 January 1882, pp. 6–7.

Apel, Willi, Gregorian Chant (Indiana, 1958).

Ball, F.E. (ed.), The Correspondence of Jonathan Swift, DD (London,
1910–14).

Barrington, (Sir) Jonah, Personal Sketches of His Own Times (London,
1827–32).

Barry, Kevin, Language, Music and the Sign (Cambridge, 1987).

—— 'James Usher (1720–72) and the Irish Enlightenment', Eighteenth-Century
Ireland, Vol. 3 (1988), pp. 115–22.

Bax, Arnold, 'A Radio Self-Portrait' (1949), in Foreman (ed.), Farewell, My
Youth and other Writings by Arnold Bax, pp. 164–7.

—— 'Foreword', in Fleischmann (ed.), Music in Ireland.

Beausang, Ita, 'Dublin Musical Societies, 1850–1900', in Devine and White
(eds.), The Maynooth International Musicological Conference 1995: Selected
Proceedings, Part Two (Irish Musical Studies 5), pp. 169–78.

Beckett, John, 'Music', The Bell, Vol. 17, No. 2 (1951), pp. 56–9.

Berman, David, 'The Culmination and Causation of Irish Philosophy', Archiv
für Geschichte der Philosophie (1982), pp. 257–79.

Bewerunge, Heinrich, 'Graz Report – The Thirteenth General Meeting of the
German Society of St Cecilia', Lyra Ecclesiastica, September 1891, pp.
65–70.

—— 'Palestrina and Orlando di Lasso', Irish Ecclesiastical Record, December
1894, pp. 1088–113.

—— 'The Teaching of Music in Irish Schools', Irish Ecclesiastical Record,
December 1897, pp. 437–40.

—— 'Cecilian Music', New Ireland Review, Vol. 15 (1900), pp. 73–84

—— 'The Vatican Edition of Plain Chant', Irish Ecclesiastical Record, Vol. 19
(January 1906), pp. 44–63.

—— 'The Vatican Kyriale – A Rejoinder', Irish Ecclesiastical Record, Vol. 19 (May
1906), pp. 421–45.

—— 'The Second Part of the Vatican Edition of Plain Chant', *Irish Ecclesiastical Record*, Vol. 20 (November 1906), pp. 414–28.

Blacking, John, 'Some Problems of Theory and Method in the Study of Musical Change', *Yearbook of the International Folk Music Council*, Vol. 9 (1977), pp. 1–26.

Boyd, Ernest, *Ireland's Literary Renaissance*, 1st edn (London, 1916).

Boydell, Brian, 'The Future of Music in Ireland', *The Bell*, Vol. 16, No. 4 (1951), pp. 21–9; also replies from Aloys Fleischmann, Vol. 16, No. 5, pp. 5–10; P.J. Malone, Vol. 16, No. 5, pp. 10–13; Joseph O'Neill, Vol. 16, No. 5, pp. 13–18.

—— 'The Dublin Musical Scene 1749–50 and its Background', *Proceedings of the Royal Musical Association*, Vol. 105 (1979), pp. 77–89.

—— 'Music, 1700–1850', in Moody and Vaughan (eds.), *A New History of Ireland IV: Eighteenth-Century Ireland 1691–1800* (Oxford, 1986), pp. 568–629.

—— *A Dublin Musical Calendar* (Dublin, 1988).

—— *Rotunda Music in Eighteenth-Century Dublin* (Dublin, 1992).

Brady, Ciaran (ed.), *Interpreting Irish History: The Debate on Historical Revisionism 1938–1994* (Dublin, 1994).

Brown, Terence, *Ireland: A Social and Cultural History 1922–79* (London, 1981).

—— 'Cultural Nationalism 1880–1930', in Deane (ed.), *The Field Day Anthology of Irish Writing*, Vol. 2, 516–59.

Bumpus, John S., *Sir John Stevenson: A Biographical Sketch* (London, 1893).

Bunting, Edward, *A General Collection of the Ancient Irish Music . . .* (Dublin and London, 1797).

—— *A General Collection of the Ancient Irish Music...* (London, 1809).

—— *The Ancient Music of Ireland, arranged for the Pianoforte . . .* (Dublin, 1840).

Burke, Edmund, *A Philosophical Inquiry into the Origin of Our Ideas of the Sublime and the Beautiful* (London, 1757), ed. J.T. Boulton (London, 1958).

—— *The Works of the Right Honourable Edmund Burke* (London, 1877).

Burney, Charles, *An Account of the Musical Performances . . . in Commemoration of Handel* (London, 1785; repr. 1979).

—— Review of *Historical Memoirs of the Irish Bards* [Joseph Cooper Walker], *The Monthly Review*, Vol. 57 (December 1787), pp. 425–39.

—— *A General History of Music* (London, 1789; modern edition, 1957).

Burrows, Donald, 'Handel's Dublin Performances', in Devine and White (eds.), *The Maynooth International Musicological Conference 1995: Selected Proceedings, Part One* (Irish Musical Studies 4), pp. 46–70.

Cairns, David and Richards, Shaun, *Writing Ireland: Colonialism, Nationalism and Culture* (Manchester, 1988).

Cambrensis, Giraldus, *Topographia Hiberniae* (c. 1187), trans. John. J. O'Meara, in Deane (ed.), *The Field Day Anthology of Irish Writing*, Vol. 1, pp. 239–40.

Campbell, Thomas, *A Philosophical Survey of the South of Ireland, in a Series of Letters to John Watkinson, MD* (Dublin, 1778).

Canny, Nicholas, 'The Formation of the Irish Mind: Religion, Politics and Gaelic Irish Literature 1550–1750', *Past and Present*, Vol. 95 (1982), pp. 91–116.

Carpenter, Andrew and Deane, Seamus, 'The Shifting Perspective (1690–1830)', in Deane (ed.), *The Field Day Anthology of Irish Writing*, Vol. 1, pp. 962–1007.

Chechlínska, Zofia, 'Chopin Reception in Nineteenth-Century Poland', in Samson (ed.), *The Cambridge Companion to Chopin*, pp. 206–21.

Conran, Michael, *The National Music of Ireland* (Dublin, 1850).

Cooper, Barry, *Beethoven's Folksong Settings: Chronology, Sources, Style* (Oxford, 1994).

—— 'Beethoven's Folksong Settings as Sources of Irish Folk Music', in Devine and White (eds.), *The Maynooth International Musicological Conference 1995: Selected Proceedings, Part Two* (Irish Musical Studies 5), pp. 65–81.

Corkery, Daniel, *The Hidden Ireland* (Dublin, 1924).

Cullen, Louis, 'Catholics under the Penal Laws', *Eighteenth-Century Ireland*, Vol. 1 (1986), pp. 23–36.

Dahlhaus, Carl, *Nineteenth-Century Music*, trans. J. Bradford Robinson (Berkeley, 1989).

Daly, Kieran, '*Lyra Ecclesiastica*: Bulletin of the Irish Society of St Cecilia' (MA diss., Queen's University, Belfast, 1991).

—— *Catholic Church Music in Ireland 1878–1903* (Dublin, 1995).

Davies, N., *God's Playground: A History of Poland* (Oxford, 1981).

Davis, Thomas, *et al.* (eds.), *The Spirit of the Nation* (Dublin, 1845).

Deale, Edgar, *A Catalogue of Contemporary Irish Composers* (Dublin, 1968; 2nd edn, 1973).

Dean, Winton and Hicks, Anthony, *The New Grove Handel* (London, 1982).

Deane, Raymond, 'The Honour of Non-Existence: Classical Composers in Irish Society', in Gillen and White (eds.), *Music and Irish Cultural History* (Irish Musical Studies 3), pp. 199–211.

Deane, Seamus, *Civilians and Barbarians*, Field Day Pamphlet No. 3 (Derry, 1983).

—— *Celtic Revivals* (London, 1985).

—— 'Arnold, Burke and the Celts', in Deane, *Celtic Revivals*, pp. 17–27.

—— 'Pearse: Writing and Chivalry', in Deane, *Celtic Revivals*, pp. 63–74.

—— 'The Literary Myths of the Revival', in Deane, *Celtic Revivals*, 28–38.

—— 'Yeats and the Idea of Revolution', in Deane, *Celtic Revivals*, pp. 38–51.

—— 'Swift and the Anglo-Irish Intellect', *Eighteenth-Century Ireland*, Vol. 1 (1986), pp. 9–22.

Deane, Seamus (ed.), *The Field Day Anthology of Irish Writing*, 3 vols. (Derry, 1991).

—— Editorial Introduction to Robert Emmet's 'Speech from the Dock' (1803), in Deane (ed.), *The Field Day Anthology of Irish Writing*, Vol. 1, pp. 933–5.

—— 'Thomas Moore', in Deane (ed.), *The Field Day Anthology of Irish Writing*, Vol. 1, pp. 1053–6.

—— 'Poetry and Song 1800–1900', in Deane (ed.), *The Field Day Anthology of Irish Writing*, Vol. 2, pp. 1–8, 9–111.

Deasy, Marian, 'New Edition of the Airs and Dance Tunes From the Music Manuscripts of George Petrie LL.D., and a Survey of His Work as a Collector of Irish Folk Music' (PhD diss., National University of Ireland, 1982).

Denman, Peter, *Samuel Ferguson: The Literary Achievement* (Bucks., 1990).

Deutsch, O.E., *Handel: A Documentary Biography* (London, 1955).

Devine, Patrick F. and White, Harry (eds.), *The Maynooth International Musicological Conference 1995: Selected Proceedings, Part One and Part Two* (*Irish Musical Studies* 4 and 5) (Dublin, 1996).

Dibble, Jeremy, *Charles Villiers Stanford* (Oxford, in preparation).

Dolan, Eileen, 'The Musical Contributions and Historical Significance of Edward Bunting (1773–1843), a Pioneer in the Preservation of the Heritage of Irish Music' (diss., Catholic University of America, 1977).

Donnelly, (Rev) Nicholas (trans. and ed.), F.X. Haberl, *Magister Choralis* (Ratisbon, New York and Cincinnati, 1877).

Donoghue, Denis, 'The Future of Irish Music', *Studies*, Vol. 44 (Spring 1955), pp. 109–14.

Dowden, Wilfrid S. (ed.), *The Letters of Thomas Moore* (Oxford, 1964).

Duffy, Charles Gavan, 'Thomas Moore' (1842), in Deane (ed.), *The Field Day Anthology of Irish Writing*, Vol. 1, pp. 1250–4.

—— *Thomas Davis: The Memoirs of an Irish Patriot 1840–46* (London, 1890).

—— *Short Life of Thomas Davis* (London, 1896).

Dunn, Douglas, 'Real Presences', *The Irish Times*, 1 June 1991, Weekend Supplement, p. 9.

Dunne, Tom, 'The Gaelic Response to the Conquest: The Evidence of the Poetry', *Studia Hibernica*, Vol. 20 (1980), pp. 7–30.

Dwyer, Robert, 'Imitations of Palestrina', *New Ireland Review*, Vol. 15 (1900), pp. 155–60.

Eddy, W.H. (ed.), *Satires and Personal Writings by Jonathan Swift* (London, 1967).

Ellis, Steven G., 'Writing Irish History: Revisionism, Colonialism, and the British Isles', *The Irish Review*, No. 19 (1996), pp. 1–21.

Fadlu-Deen, Kitty, 'Contemporary Music in Ireland' (diss., National University of Ireland [University College, Dublin], 1968).

Fellerer, Karl Gustav, 'Cäcilianismus', in F. Blume (ed.), *Die Musik in Geschichte und Gegenwart*, Bd. 2 (Basel, 1973), pp. 624–6.

—— 'Bewerunge, Heinrich', *Die Musik in Geschichte und Gegenwart*, Bd. 15 (Basel, 1973), pp. 764–5.

—— *History of Catholic Church Music*, trans. Francis A. Brunner (Baltimore, 1961; repr. Connecticut, 1979).

Ferguson, Samuel, 'A Dialogue between the Heart and Head of an Irish Protestant', *The Dublin University Magazine* (1833), repr. in Deane, *The Field Day Anthology of Irish Writing*, Vol. 1, pp. 1177–84.

—— Review of James Hardiman, *Irish Minstrelsy; or, Bardic Remains of Ireland, with English Poetical Translations* (1831), in *The Dublin University Magazine* (April, August, October and November 1834).

Fleischmann, Aloys G., 'The Outlook of Music in Ireland', *Studies*, Vol. 24 (March 1935), pp. 121–30.

—— 'Ars Nova', *Ireland Today*, Vol. 1 (July 1936), pp. 41–8.

—— 'Composition and the Folk Idiom', *Ireland Today*, Vol. 1 (November 1936), pp. 37–44.

—— 'Music' (Letters to the Editor), *The Bell*, Vol. 17, No. 4 (1951), pp. 53–5.

Fleischmann, Aloys G. (ed.), *Music in Ireland: A Symposium* (Cork and Oxford, 1952).

—— 'Historical Survey', in Fleischmann (ed.), *Music in Ireland*, pp. 1–9.

—— 'Seán Ó Riada', *Counterpoint* (November, 1971), pp. 12–14.

—— 'Seán Ó Riada's *Nomos II*', *Éire–Ireland*, Vol. 7 (1972), pp. 108–15.

—— 'Aspects of George Petrie: IV. Petrie's Contribution to Irish Music', *Proceedings of the Royal Irish Academy*, Vol. 72, Section C, No. 9, pp. 195–218.

—— *The Sources of Irish Traditional Music, 1583–1855* (New York, 1997).

Flood, W.H. Grattan, *A History of Irish Music* (Dublin, 1905; repr. Shannon, 1970).

Foreman, Lewis, *Bax: A Composer and His Times*, 2nd edn (Aldershot, 1983).

Foreman, Lewis (ed.), *Farewell, My Youth and other Writings by Arnold Bax* (Aldershot, 1992).

Foster, Roy, 'We Are All Revisionists Now', *The Irish Review* (1986), repr. in Deane (ed.), *The Field Day Anthology of Irish Writing*, Vol. 3, pp. 583–6.

—— *Modern Ireland 1600–1972* (Harmondsworth, 1988).

Fox, Charlotte Milligan, *Annals of the Irish Harpers* (London, 1911).

Gibbons, Luke (ed.), 'Challenging the Canon: Revisionsim and Cultural Criticism', in Deane (ed.), *The Field Day Anthology of Irish Writing*, Vol. 3, pp. 561ff. (incl. essays and excerpts by Conor Cruise O'Brien, Seamus Deane, Terence Brown, Richard Kearney, Declan Kiberd, Denis Donoghue and Edna Longley).

Gillen, Gerard and White, Harry (eds.), *Musicology in Ireland* (*Irish Musical Studies* 1) (Dublin, 1990).

—— *Music and the Church* (*Irish Musical Studies* 2) (Dublin, 1993).

—— *Music and Irish Cultural History* (*Irish Musical Studies* 3) (Dublin, 1995).

Goldsmith, Oliver, 'Carolan: The Last Irish Bard', *The British Magazine* (July 1760), repr. in Deane (ed.), *The Field Day Anthology of Irish Writing*, Vol. 1, pp. 667–8.

Grant, Kerry S., *Dr Burney as Critic and Historian of Music* (Ann Arbor, 1983).

Graves, Alfred Perceval, *Irish Literary and Musical Studies* (London, 1914; repr. New York, 1967).

Greene, Harry Plunket, *Charles Villiers Stanford* (London, 1935).

Greene, John, 'The Repertory of Dublin Theatres, 1720–45', *Eighteenth-Century Ireland*, Vol. 2 (1987), pp. 133–48.

Greer, David (ed.), *Early Memories* (Belfast, 1979).

—— *Hamilton Harty: His Life and Music* (Belfast, 1979).

—— 'The Composition of The Children of Lir', in Gillen and White (eds.), *Musicology in Ireland*, pp. 74–98.

Griffith, Arthur (ed.), *Thomas Davis: The Thinker and the Teacher* (Dublin, 1916).

Grindle, W.H., *Irish Cathedral Music* (Belfast, 1989).

Gwynn, Denis, *Edward Martyn (1859–1924) and the Irish Revival* (London, 1930).

Harbison, Janet, 'The Belfast Harper's Meeting, 1792: The Legacy', *Ulster Folklife*, Vol. 35 (1989), pp. 113–28.

Harris, Bernard and Freyer, Grattan (eds.), *Integrating Tradition: The Achievement of Seán Ó Riada* (Ballina and Pennsylvania, 1982).

Harrison, Frank L., 'Music, Poetry and Polity in the Age of Swift', *Eighteenth-Century Ireland*, Vol. 1 (1986), pp. 37–64.

Hart, William E., *Synge's First Symphony: The Aran Islands* (Connecticut, 1993).

Heaney, Seamus, 'At the Water's Edge' (Tryptych), from *Field Work* (London, 1979), p. 14.

—— 'In Memoriam Sean O'Riada', from *Field Work* (London, 1979), p. 30.

Henebry, Richard, *Irish Music* (Dublin, n.d. [1903?]).

—— *Handbook of Irish Music* (Cork, 1928).

Higgins, Aidan, *Langrishe Go Down* (London, 1978).

Hodgart, Matthew and Worthington, Mabel, *Song in the Works of James Joyce* (New York, 1959).

Hogan, Ita M., *Anglo-Irish Music 1780–1830* (Cork, 1966).

Hyde, Douglas, 'The Necessity for De-Anglicising Ireland' (1892), in Breandán Ó Conaire (ed.), *Douglas Hyde: Language, Lore and Lyrics* (Dublin, 1986), pp. 153–70 (orig. publ. in *The Revival of Irish Literature* [London, 1894]).

Jochum, K.P.S., *W.B. Yeats: A Classified Bibliography of Criticism* (Chicago, 1990).

Jordan, Hoover H., *Bolt Upright: The Life of Thomas Moore* (Salzburg, 1975).

Joyce, James, 'The Dead', in *Dubliners* (1914) (Penguin Classics Edition, Middlesex, 1976).

Joyce, Patrick Weston, *Ancient Irish Music* (Dublin, 1873).

Kearney, Richard (ed.), *The Irish Mind: Exploring Intellectual Traditions* (Dublin, 1985).

Kearney, Richard, 'The Transitional Crisis of Modern Irish Culture', in *Irishness in a Changing Society*, ed. Princess Grace Irish Library (Gerrards Cross, 1988), pp. 78–94.

—— *Transitions: Narratives in Modern Irish Culture* (Dublin, 1988).

Kelly, James, 'Eighteenth-Century Ascendancy: A Commentary', *Eighteenth-Century Ireland*, Vol. 5 (1990), pp. 173–88.

Kennedy, Brian, *Dreams and Responsibilities* (Dublin, n.d.).

Klein, Axel, *Die Musik Irlands im 20. Jahrhundert* (Hildesheim, 1996).

—— 'Irish Composers and Foreign Education: A Study of Influences', in Devine and White (eds.), *The Maynooth International Musicological Conference 1995: Selected Proceedings, Part One (Irish Musical Studies* 4), pp. 271–84.

Larchet, John, 'A Plea For Music', in W. Fitzgerald (ed.), *The Voice of Ireland* (Dublin and London, n.d. [1923?]), repr. in T. Maher, *The Harp's a Wonder* (Mullingar, 1991), pp. 121–6.

—— 'Music in the Secondary Schools', in Fleischmann (ed.), *Music in Ireland*, pp. 32–6.

Larkin, Emmet, 'The Devotional Revolution in Ireland, 1850–1875', *American Historical Review*, Vol. 77, No. 3 (June 1972), pp. 625–52.

—— *The Making of the Roman Catholic Church in Ireland, 1850–1860* (Chapel Hill, 1980).

Laurence, Dan H. (ed.), [The Bodley Head Bernard Shaw] *The Complete Musical Criticism in Three Volumes* (London, 1981).

Lee, John, *A Favourite Collection of the So Much Admired Old Irish Tunes, the Original and Genuine Compositions of Carolan, the Celebrated Irish Bard. . .* (Dublin, 1780).

Leerssen, J.Th., 'How *The Wild Irish Girl* [1806] Made Ireland Romantic', in C.C. Barfoot and Theo D'haen (eds.), *The Clash of Ireland: Literary Contrasts and Connections* (Amsterdam and Atlanta, Ga., 1989), pp. 98–117.

Lyons, F.S.L., 'The Burden of Our History' (1978), in Deane (ed.), *The Field Day Anthology of Irish Writing*, Vol. 3, pp. 580–2.

—— *Culture and Anarchy in Ireland 1890–1939* (Oxford, 1979).

McCarthy, Marie, 'Music Education and the Quest for Cultural Identity in Ireland, 1831–1989' (diss., University of Michigan, 1990).

—— 'The Transmission of Music and the Formation of National Identity in Early Twentieth-Century Ireland', in Devine and White (eds.), *The Maynooth International Musicological Conference 1995: Selected Proceedings, Part Two (Irish Musical Studies* 5), pp. 146–59.

McCormack, W.J., *Ascendancy and Tradition in Anglo-Irish Literary History from 1789 to 1939* (Oxford, 1985).

—— 'Vision and Revision in the Study of Eighteenth-Century Irish Parliamentary Rhetoric', *Eighteenth-Century Ireland*, Vol. 2 (1987), pp. 7–36.

—— 'The Intellectual Revival', in Deane (ed.), *The Field Day Anthology of Irish Writing*, Vol. 1, pp. 1173–6.

MacDonagh, Oliver, *Ireland: The Union and its Aftermath* (London, 1977; 2nd impression, 1979).

MacWhite, Eoin, 'Thomas Moore and Poland', *Proceedings of the Royal Irish Academy*, Vol. 72, Section C, pp. 49–62.

Marcus, Louis, 'Seán Ó Riada and the Ireland of the Sixties', in Harris and Freyer (eds.), *Integrating Tradition: The Achievement of Seán Ó Riada*, pp. 16–27.

May, Frederick, 'Music and the Nation', *The Dublin Magazine*, Vol. 11 (July–September 1936), pp. 50–6.

—— 'The Composer in Ireland', in Fleischmann (ed.), *Music in Ireland*, pp. 164–77.

Maynooth College, *Report of the President for the Years 1887–8* (Maynooth, 1878).

Moody, T.W., Martin, F.X., Byrne, F.J., and Vaughan, W.E. (eds.), *A New History of Ireland* (Oxford, 1978–).

Moore, Thomas, *Intolerance: A Satire* (London, 1808).

——'Letter on Music' (1810), cited in Deane (ed.), *The Field Day Anthology of Irish Writing*, Vol. 1, pp. 1054–5.

—— 'Mr Moore's Supressed Preface to the IRISH MELODIES', *The Dublin Examiner*, June 1816, pp. 107–9.

—— *Memoirs of Captain Rock: The Celebrated Irish Chieftain, with Some Account of his Ancestors* (London, 1824).

—— *The Life and Death of Lord Edward Fitzgerald* (London, 1831).

—— *Irish Melodies [with] Symphonies and Accompaniments by Sir John Stevenson, Mus. Doc., and Sir Henry Bishop* (Dublin, 1879; repr. 1963).

Moran, D.P., 'The Battle of Two Civilisations', in *The Philosophy of Irish Ireland* (Dublin, n.d. [1905]), pp. 94–114.

Myers, R.M., *Handel's Messiah: A Touchstone of Taste* (New York, 1948).

Nangle, B.C., *The Monthly Review, First Series, 1749–1789, Indexes of Contributors and Articles* (Oxford, 1934).

Neal, John and William, *A Collection of the Most Celebrated Irish Tunes* (Dublin, 1724), facsimile edition, the Folk Music Society of Ireland, with Introduction by Nicholas Carolan (Dublin, 1986).

Ní Chinnéide, Veronica, 'The Sources of Moore's Melodies', *Journal of the Royal Society of Antiquaries in Ireland*, Vol. 89, Part 2 (1959), pp. 109–34.

O'Brien, Gerard, 'Illusion and Reality in Late Eighteenth-Century Politics', *Eighteenth-Century Ireland*, Vol. 3 (1988), pp. 149–56.

Ó Buachalla, Breandán, 'Poetry and Politics in Early Modern Ireland', *Eighteenth-Century Ireland*, Vol. 7 (1992), pp. 149–75.

Ó Canainn, Tomás and Mac An Bhua, Gearóid, *Seán Ó Riada: A Shaol agus a Shaothar* (Baile Átha Cliath, 1993).

Ó Casaide, Seamus, 'Bibliography of Bunting's Printed Collections', *Journal of the Irish Folk Song Society*, Vol. 5 (orig. vols. 22–5) 1927 (repr. London, 1967), pp. xxxv–xxxvii.

O'Donoghue, D.J. (ed.), *Essays Literary and Historical by Thomas Davis* (Dundalk, 1914).

Ó Gallochobair, Eamonn, 'Atavism', *Ireland Today*, Vol. 1 (1936), pp. 56–8.

O'Grady, Standish, *History of Ireland: Heroic Period* (London, 1878–80).

O'Neill, George, 'Musicians in Controversy', *New Ireland Review*, Vol. 12 (1899), pp. 309–13.

—— 'Sacred Music as a Living Art', *New Ireland Review*, Vol. 12 (1899), pp. 331–6.

Ó Riada, Seán, *Our Musical Heritage* (Portlaoise, 1982).

—— 'An Open Letter to Charles Acton', in Harris and Freyer (eds.), *Integrating Tradition: The Achievement of Seán Ó Riada*, pp. 147–52.

O'Sullivan, Donal, 'A Short Account of Bunting as a Collector', *Journal of the Irish Folk Song Society*, Vol. 5 (orig. vols. 22–5) 1927 (repr. London, 1967), pp. xiii–xvi.

—— *Carolan: The Life, Times and Music of an Irish Harper* (London, 1958).

—— *Songs of the Irish* (Dublin, 1960).

'O.Z.', 'From a Modern Portrait Gallery. V – W.B. Yeats', *New Ireland Review*, Vol. 2 (1894–5), pp. 647–59.

'P' (George Petrie), 'Our Portrait Gallery, No. 41. Edward Bunting', *The Dublin University Magazine*, Vol. 29 (January 1847), pp. 64–73.

—— Review essay on Moore, Bunting, Beethoven, Holden, Fitzsimons and Smith in *The Dublin Examiner*, August 1816, pp. 241–53.

—— *The Ancient Music of Ireland* (Dublin, 1855).

Pilkington, Matthew, *The Progress of Music in Ireland* (1725), ed. Bryan Coleborne in Deane (ed.), *The Field Day Anthology of Irish Writing*, Vol. 1, pp. 409–12.

Renehan, (Rev) L.J., *Grammar of Gregorian and Modern Music* (Dublin, 1858; rev. and ed. Rev R. Hackett, 1865).

Rimmer, Joan, 'Patronage, Style and Structure in the Music Attributed to Turlough Carolan', *Early Music*, Vol. 15 (1987), pp. 164–74.

Rockett, Kevin, Gibbons, Luke and Hill, John, *Cinema and Ireland* (New York, 1988).

Rogers, Brendan, 'An Irish School of Music', *New Ireland Review*, Vol. 13 (1900), pp. 149–59.

Ryan, Joseph J., 'Nationalism and Music in Ireland' (PhD diss., National University of Ireland, 1991).

—— 'Assertions of Distinction: The Modal Debate in Irish Music', in Gillen and White (eds.), *Music and the Church* (Irish Musical Studies 2), pp. 62–77.

—— 'Nationalism and Irish Music', in Gillen and White (eds.), *Music and Irish Cultural History* (Irish Musical Studies 3), pp. 101–15.

Saddlemyer, Ann, 'Synge's Soundscape', *Irish University Review*, Vol. 22, No. 1 (1992), pp. 55–68.

St Patrick's College Maynooth, *Kaldendarium in exeuntem annum MCMXXIII et proximum MCMXXIV* (Dublin, 1923).

Samson, Jim (ed.), *The Cambridge Companion to Chopin* (Cambridge, 1992).

—— 'Myth and Reality: A Biographical Introduction', in Samson (ed.), *The Cambridge Companion to Chopin*, pp. 1–8.

—— 'Extended Forms: The Ballades, Scherzos and Fantasies', in Samson (ed.), The Cambridge Companion to Chopin, pp. 101–23.

Samuel, Harold, 'John Sigismund Cousser in London and Dublin', Music and Letters, Vol. 61 (1980), pp. 158–71.

Stanford, Charles Villiers (ed.), The Complete Petrie Collection of Irish Music (London, 1902–5).

—— 'Some Thoughts Concerning Folk Song and Nationality', The Musical Quarterly, Vol. 1, No. 2 (1915), pp. 232–45.

Stanley, Glenn, 'Religious Propriety versus Artistic Truth', Acta Musicologica, Vol. 61 (1989), Fasc. I, pp. 66–82.

Steiner, George, In Bluebeard's Castle (London, 1971).

Stokes, William, The Life of George Petrie (London, 1868).

Terry, Richard, Catholic Church Music (London, 1907).

Tessier, Thérèse, La Poésie Lyrique de Thomas Moore (1779–1852) (Paris, 1976).

Thuente, Mary Helen, The Harp Re-strung: The United Irishmen and the Rise of Literary Nationalism (Syracuse, 1994).

Townsend, Horatio, An Account of the Visit of Handel to Dublin (Dublin, 1852).

Uí Ógáin, Ríonach, 'Traditional Music and Irish Cultural History', in Gillen and White (eds.), Music and Irish Cultural History (Irish Musical Studies 3), pp. 77–100.

Usher, James, Clio: or, a Discourse on Taste (London, 1769; facsimile reprint, New York, 1970).

Vignoles, Olinthus J., Memoirs of Sir Robert P. Stewart, Kt., Mus. Doc. (London, n.d. [1898]).

Walker, Joseph Cooper, Historical Memoirs of the Irish Bards (Dublin, 1786; facsimile reprint, New York, 1971).

Walsh, T.J., Opera in Dublin 1705–1797 (Dublin, 1973).

—— Opera in Dublin 1798–1820 (Oxford, 1993).

Walsh, (Very Rev) William J., DD, A Grammar of Gregorian Music (Dublin, 1885).

Ward, Catherine Coogan, Ward, Robert E., and Wrynn, John F., SJ, (eds.), Letters of Charles O'Conor of Belnagare: A Catholic Voice in Eighteenth-Century Ireland (Washington, D.C., 1988).

Warren, Raymond, 'Orchestral Music', in David Greer (ed.), Hamilton Harty: His Life and Music (Belfast, 1979).

White, Harry, 'The Need for a Sociology of Irish Folk Music', International Review of the Aesthetics and Sociology of Music, Vol. 15, No. 1 (June 1984), pp. 3–13.

—— 'Handel in Dublin: A Note', Eighteenth-Century Ireland, Vol. 2 (1987), pp. 182–6.

—— 'Musicology in Ireland', Acta Musicologica, Vol. 60 (1988), Fasc. III, pp. 290–305.

—— 'Carolan and the Dislocation of Music in Ireland', Eighteenth-Century Ireland, Vol. 4 (1989), pp. 55–64.

—— 'Music and the Perception of Music in Ireland', *Studies*, Vol. 79, No. 313 (1990), pp. 38–44.

—— 'Musicology, Positivism and the Case for an Encyclopedia of Music in Ireland', in Gillen and White (eds.), *Musicology in Ireland* (*Irish Musical Studies*, 1), pp. 295–300.

—— 'Brian Friel, Thomas Murphy and the Use of Music in Contemporary Irish Drama', *Modern Drama*, Vol. 33 (1990), pp. 553–62.

—— 'Church Music and Musicology in Ireland', in Gillen and White (eds.), *Music and the Church* (*Irish Musical Studies* 2), pp. 333–9.

—— 'Music and the Irish Literary Imagination', in Gillen and White (eds.), *Music and Irish Cultural History* (*Irish Musical Studies* 3) pp. 212–27.

—— 'The Preservation of Music and Irish Cultural History', *International Review of the Aesthetics and Sociology of Music*, Vol. 27 (1996), pp. 123–38.

—— ' "Something is Taking its Course": Dramatic Exactitude and the Paradigm of Serialism in Samuel Beckett', in Mary Bryden (ed.), *Samuel Beckett and Music*, (Oxford, 1998), pp. 159–71.

—— 'Ireland: Art Music', in Stanley Sadie (ed.), *The New Grove Dictionary of Music and Musicians*, 7th edn (London, in preparation).

White, Harry and Lawrence, Nicholas, 'Towards a History of the Cecilian Movement in Ireland: An Assessment of the Writings of Heinrich Bewerunge (1862–1923), with a Catalogue of His Publications and Manuscripts', in Gillen and White (eds.), *Music and the Church* (*Irish Musical Studies* 2), pp. 70–107.

Whyte, Lawrence, *Dissertation on Italian and Irish Musick, with Some Panegyrick on Carrallan our late Irish Orpheus in Poems on Various Subjects, Serious and Diverting* (Dublin, 1740), edited by Bryan Coleborne in *The Field Day Anthology of Irish Writing*, Vol. 1, pp. 412–15.

Williams, Harold (ed.), *The Poems of Jonathan Swift* (Oxford, 1937).

Worth, Katharine, *The Irish Drama of Europe from Yeats to Beckett* (London, 1978).

Yeats, Gráinne, 'Carolan, Turlough', in Stanley Sadie (ed.), *The New Grove Dictionary of Music and Musicians* (London, 1980), pp. 3, 813.

—— *The Harp of Ireland, the Belfast Harpers' Festival 1792, and the Saving of Ireland's Harp Music by Edward Bunting* (Belfast, 1992).

Yeats, Michael, 'Words and Music', *Yeats Society of Japan*, annual report No. 8 (Tokyo, 1973), pp. 7–18.

Yeats, W.B., *Collected Poems* (London, 1961).

Young, Percy, *A History of British Music* (London, 1967).

Zimmerman, Georges-Denis, *Songs of Irish Rebellion: Political Street Ballads and Rebel Songs 1780–1900* (Dublin, 1967).

# Newspapers and Periodicals

*All Ireland Review*
*The Belfast Newsletter*
*The Bell*
*Chambers' Edinburgh Journal*
*The Dublin Examiner*
*The Dublin Magazine*
*Dublin Review*
*The Dublin University Magazine*
*The Dublin University Review*
*Faulkner's Dublin Journal*
*Freeman's Journal*
*Hibernia*
*Ireland Today*
*Irish Ecclesiastical Record*
*The Irish Review*
*The Monthly Review*
*Journal of the Folk Song Society*
*Lyra Ecclesiastica*
*The Nation*
*New Ireland Review*
*Studies*
*Young Ireland*

# INDEX

219

Ulster, 96
ultramontanism, 11, 75, 79
*Ulysses* (Joyce), 5, 157
Unionism, 96, 97
United Irishmen, 8, 42, 45, 51, 54
University College, Cork, 130, 138, 139
University College, Dublin, 81, 123, 130, 131
University of Dublin Choral Society, 102
Usher, James, 25
*Utrecht Te Deum and Jubilate* (Handel), 32

Vallancey, Colonel, 23, 24
*Vereinfachte Harmonielehre* (Riemann), 82
Victory, 143
*View of the Present State of Ireland, A* (Spenser), 3, 21, 24
Vignoles, O.J., 99
Vinci, 27
Vivaldi, A , 15, 27

Wagner, Peter, 81
Wagner, R., 101, 130
Wales, 112
Walker, Joseph Cooper, 7–8, 14–15, 20–4, 37, 40, 49, 57
  on Ascendancy music, 33–4
  on Carolan, 35
  on Handel, 31
  review by Burney, 23–5
Wallace, William Vincent, 105, 152
Walsh, Edward, 153

Walsh, T.J., 32
Walsh, William, 77, 79–80, 90, 92
*Wanderings of Oisin, The* (Yeats), 118, 123
Warren, Raymond, 116
Weare, William, 38
Wellesz, Egon, 135
White, Harold, 132
Whyte, Laurence, 15, 17–18, 19, 31
Wicklow, County, 155
*Wild Irish Girl, The* (Morgan), 49
Williams, Vaughan, 116, 135, 156
*With the Wild Geese* (Harty), 116–17
Wolfe Tone, Theobald, 54, 57
Wood, Henry, 120
Worth, Katharine, 156

Yeats, Gráinne, 15
Yeats, W.B., 5, 7, 63, 106, 114, 131, 149, 158
  and Bax, 118, 119–20, 122
  Celtic vision of, 94–6
  on folk music, 121–2
  literary revival, 65, 66, 92–3, 109
  and music, 10, 97, 98, 116, 124, 152, 154–5, 155, 159
  and nationalism, 4, 96–7
Young, Percy, 105, 107–8
Young Ireland movement, 3, 8, 51, 53 60, 62, 65, 69–70, 71, 98, 113, 132, 134

Zimmerman, Georges-Denis, 69–70